Don't Stop .

By

Charlie Green

Copyright © Charlie Green 2023

Forward by Sarah Stevenson Jennings MBE

I felt perfectly at home while reading Charlie's autobiography. So full of humour, warmth and real-life battles.

I connected with Charlie's story through our Yorkshire roots and, of course, our love and dedication to martial arts. But, more importantly, Charlie's inspiring battle of survival and resilience against all odds.

An incredibly human tale, I hope you enjoy reading Don't Stop Believing every bit as much as I did. Brilliantly written, it was everything I expected and more.

Go, Charlie - what an amazing story of strength and fortitude. I am so proud to know you and be able to call you my friend.

Sarah Stevenson Jennings MBE

For Beccs & her amazing dad, Geoff; thanks for everything x

1. Beginnings

On Wednesday, 22nd November, 1972, a new born baby was bequeathed the gift of life in the maternity ward of Jessop Hospital, a sprawling, red-brick structure, close to Sheffield city centre. It was raining heavily when the child's mother entered labour, but stopped abruptly the instant the baby had its bum smacked. The clouds parted and the sun reappeared, first time in days, beating down with reckless abandon upon the carpet of glistening, grey slate rooftops, decorating the surrounding area. It was almost as if the weather was in celebratory mood, heralding the arrival of someone really special. Only time would tell with that one; but the omens were certainly good. The bouncing baby boy weighed an impressive 6lb 8oz and the nurses said he was a real bobby dazzler with his curly, dark hair, piercing blue eyes and developing cheeky grin. A baby brother for sister, Beverley, and brothers, Nicholas and Robert, aged eight, five and two respectively, I'm reliably informed the child's parents, Anne and Russ, took an instant shine to their new son, a big relief really, seeing as it was little old me.

Delivered into a stout Roman Catholic background, I was subsequently baptised Charles Richard Green. Even though I'd been born in Sheffield, I would be brought up in the industrial town of Barnsley, a dozen or so miles to the north; Hoyland to be precise, a pit village bordering junction 36 of the M1 motorway, surrounded by endless acres of beautiful, lush, green countryside, which would become my childhood playground in the years ahead. With a population of 11,852 in the last census, Hoyland was always more of a small town than a village. It had a shopping centre, marketplace, secondary school, leisure centre and library; but village was how it had always been portrayed, so I'll leave it at that if it's alright with you. The community was typically working class, serving up generations of industrial cannon fodder, feeding the abundance of factories, coal mines and steelworks which populated the local area. Salt-of-the-earth is a much-flaunted term; but people hailing from my home-town were exactly that; honest, decent, reliable folk that you could trust with your life. As a consequence, I experienced very little trouble growing up; or at least nothing to get excited about. The council estates and rows of terraced houses which dominated the town were invariably self-policing. Any hint of bother was very firmly nipped in the bud, courtesy of a clip round the ear by intervening residents or strict, no-nonsense, judge and jury policemen, administering on-the-spot punishment. Respect was everything. It was a trait instilled into nippers from an early age, a quality I heartily embraced and have carried with me throughout my life. My home was 13 Shaftesbury Drive, located on the edge of the sprawling Cloughfields council estate. Nowadays, the property would be classed as a trendy town-house, but we always looked upon it as a glorified terrace, three or four interconnected houses, flanked by snickets, narrow alleyways providing short-cuts to houses and roads behind. The houses were cramped affairs, especially for a family of six; a living room, dining room and kitchen downstairs, with three-bedrooms and a bathroom upstairs. As you'd expect, my parents snaffled the master bedroom, with me and my two brothers cramped into the back bedroom and my sister in the tiny box-room at the front. I'd hang around in postage stamp sized front and back gardens, playing cars and toy soldiers and bang-bang war games. More often than not, though, I could be found on extensive playing fields a stone's throw from the house. A gang of us would gather, all roughly the same age, playing games of football, cricket and golf. Daz Kilner was usually on the scene. So, too, was Kev Shipp, Les Hannighan, a cracking lad called Craig Stewart and big Phil Rudd, all of whom I'm still in contact with today. Phil was a complete nutcase, calling everyone he met, *Jack*. I can still hear him now, in fact: morning, *Jack*. How's it going, *Jack*? Three bags full *Jack*. Daft bastard. He towered over me from day one and continued to grow at a phenomenal rate to the point where he stands six-feet-eight-inches nowadays. Every time I see him, I instinctively think of the scene in

Full Metal Jacket, where Gunnery Sergeant Hartman screams: I didn't know they stacked shit that high! Only joking, Phil. I love you really, mate. Not sexually, obviously. I mean, I don't want you getting any ideas now, do I, big fella…?

I loved our games and never wanted to go in, dreading my mum, appearing from out of nowhere to shout my name, usually when it started to get dark or when there was school in the morning. I attended St Helens Catholic School, an institution run by nuns, who always taught in full regalia: bandeau, veil, guimpe, crucifix and pleated habit. They may have looked like extras from the *Sound of Music*, but mess around or misbehave at your peril. A rap across the knuckles with a ruler, or six of the best with the slipper or cane, very quickly restored order. It hurt like crazy, throbbing and stinging for hours afterwards. Not that I should grumble. It was an integral part of my upbringing, teaching me the difference between right and wrong, instilling lifelong attributes of honesty, decency and thoughtfulness, essential commodities for the path I eventually chose. Thinking back, I can see mum now, standing there like Hilda Ogden, curlers and fag-end, floral pinnie wrapped round her waist, unbuttoned cardie, flapping freely in the wind.

"Charles," she'd bellow, cupping hands around her mouth. "Come on now, son. How many times do you need telling? It's bath night, remember." Honestly, I swear she shouted so loud one night, I saw birds taking off from adjacent rooftops and an old chap turning his hearing aid down, thinking it was malfunctioning. Either way, off I'd trudge, curly mop blowing in the breeze, hands and face as black as coal, looking like I'd just come off afternoons at Elsecar Main pit. All I was missing was a hard hat, orange overalls and knee pads. There would be the customary tear in my jeans and my new plimsols or trainers would have a sole hanging off, earning me a quick skelp round the head on the walk past. "Look at the state of you again, our Charles. And what have you done to your shoes? What do you think we are, lad? Made of money…?"

Casting disgruntled glances at my mates, I'd be frogmarched inside and sent straight upstairs for a date with a tub full of Matey and a tablet of coal tar soap. Or at least that was the intention; little did mum know that, more often than not, I had other ideas. I may have lost round one, but was determined to come out on top. Bypassing the bathroom, I'd throw open the bedroom window and clamber out, using the window ledge to swing like a monkey, landing with a thump atop next door's car port. A quick scramble down the drainpipe and I was trotting triumphantly back down the snicket, sticking two fingers up at mum, peering out incredulously from the living room window. I was greeted like a returning hero by my pals, throwing arms around me and ruffling my hair amidst a volley of jubilant cheers. Unfortunately, the celebrations were always short lived. Gulping like Shaggy off *Scooby Doo*, I'd suddenly spot my dad, standing silhouetted in the doorway, doing a pretty good impression of Michael Myers, terrorising the neighbourhood in a Cloughfields version of *Halloween*. There was no knife, though; his only weapons were a big, bearded scowl and raised index finger, pointing at me like Lord Kitchener in the infamous World War One recruiting poster, warning me what to expect if I didn't do as I was told. I may have been daft, but I certainly wasn't stupid. Realising the game was up, I'd disappear back inside as fast as my legs would carry me, sparing myself the ignominy of a slapped arse in front of the gang.

As the years progressed and we were all allowed to stay out a little bit later, the streets became our playground, endless games of tigs, hiddie, kick-can and British bulldogs beneath the orange glow of street lamps. It wasn't all fun and laughter, though. Around eight years old, I was diagnosed with Von Willebrand disease after being referred to the hospital with frequent bruising and excessive bleeding. A disorder in which the blood doesn't clot properly, I was told I'd never be able to take part in competitive sport and would need to tread extra carefully the rest of my life. As soon as the words left the consultant's lips, my mum knew there wasn't a cat in hell's chance of that happening. I was a free spirit and would live my life as I saw fit. And so it came to pass: my formative years continued uninterrupted and at full throttle. We'd roam the town, exploring competing council estates, occasionally getting chased by rival gangs for daring to venture on to their turf. I never liked running, but *did* enjoy the thrill of it, the adrenalin rush of wondering might transpire if we were caught. Not that we ever were. We were way too nimble on our feet, disappearing like greased lightning down snickets and ginnels, hopping over walls and shortcutting through back gardens, not stopping until we made it back to the safety of Cloughfields, a bit like *The Warriors* on the film of the same name, making it back to their revered Coney Island. Sometimes, I'd go with a couple of mates to the neighbouring village of Elsecar, lending a hand in stone-throwing raids against lads from Jump, the next settlement along. Elsecar was known as Scotch village to the Jumpers, a reference to the large number of Scottish people who settled there to work in the pits. Prior to the raids, the Jumpers would line up on a hill and unleash their battle cry:

"Scotties, have only got one ball…Hoylanders, have got two but small!"

The Hoyland reference wound me up more and more each time I heard it. If I'd have been able to get my hands on the perpetrators, I swear I'd have hit them with that many lefts they would have begged for a right. Not that it would have ever got that far. The raids were pretty tame affairs really and I'm glad as well, because many of my best friends in later life were Jumpers, brilliant lads one and all, who could always be relied upon in any number of situations. Sometimes, we'd hang around the shopping centre, which wasn't much to shout about to be fair. Centrepiece was the Co-op supermarket and a council-operated library. Directly opposite was Yorkshire Bank with a selection of other shops nearby; a wallpaper shop; a couple of newsagents and beer-offs; a DIY store and several hairdressers and takeaways. We'd window shop a while, then stop off for chips and scraps at our favourite chippie, located on Princess Street. Served on greaseproof paper in sheets of last week's Barnsley Chronicle, it was just what the doctor ordered, perfectly complemented by lashings of salt and vinegar. We'd eat them with our fingers, making mischief as we walked. Nothing serious, though, because we knew we wouldn't half cop it if we got caught, either at home or next day at school. On rainy nights, we'd stay in and watch telly with the family, all scrunched up on the three-piece suite, drinking tea and dunking biscuits. We'd tune into programmes such as *Dallas*, desperate to discover who shot JR. *Coronation Street* was a big favourite, proper characters and realistic storylines, unlike the ridiculous twaddle served up nowadays. I adored *Only Fools and Horses*; but then again, *who* didn't? *Minder* was also brilliant, especially the rough and tumble fisticuffs scenes. That stated, nothing compared to repeats of seventies classic, *Kung Fu*, depicting the adventures of Kwai Chang Caine, a Shaolin monk, travelling through the old American west, armed only with spiritual training and his skill in martial arts. Starring David Carradine, the fight scenes were immense, a mix of normal speed and slow motion, vividly displaying the incredible pace, synchronisation and coordination which was an intrinsic part of the ancient Chinese discipline. Most of all, though, I liked it best when there was a good film on, especially something with a bit of action in it. Arnie was my favourite by far: *Predator*, *The Terminator* and *Commando* were right up my street, full on action films, which guaranteed my attention from start to finish. *Star Wars* was another. I wasn't really into science fiction, but the second I read the intro, a long time ago in a galaxy far, far away, I was instantly converted. Sylvester Stallone's *First Blood* ticked all the boxes and I absolutely loved the *Rocky* series. Adrian! Adrian! Dad would often rent VHS films from the video shop round the corner and we'd watch them over and over, making sure we got our money's worth before they needed to go back. One day, he came home with a film he assured me I'd love. He didn't tell me why. He just put it on and let me work it out for myself. About ten minutes into it, I had it sussed.

"I can't believe it. All the people on here…they talk just like us!"

They did as well, lots of *thee's* and *tha's,* enunciated in a perfect Barnsley accent, practically unintelligible to people residing outside the immediate local area. The film was *Kes*, the big screen version of famous Hoyland author Barry Hines' classic tale, *A Kestrel for a Knave*, the story of Billy Casper, a tormented, working-class boy, battling abuse both at home and at school. Son of a single mother, Billy's existence was bleak at best, until he developed an interest in falconry and began training a kestrel. As the film progressed, I realised it wasn't just the accent I recognised: I was familiar with lots of locations as well. The fields where Billy flew his hawk and the grim, industrial landscape, where he perched on a grassy hillside, reading *Desperate Dan* before heading off to school. The Princess Street chippie, which I frequently visited and where Billy treated himself to fish and chips, using bullying, domineering brother Jud's bet money. And Tankersley Old Hall, the setting for the farm, where he climbed a dilapidated wall, stealing a chick from a nest. I couldn't believe it: Hoyland was famous and I liked it. Liked it a lot, in fact, wishing I could be famous one day, albeit with little or no idea how I was going to get there. A clue lay within another film dad fetched from the video shop; a whole series of them, in fact, starring Bruce Lee, the legendary Hong Kongese and American fighter turned film star, the father of modern martial arts. Films like *Enter the Dragon, Fist of Fury* and *The Big Boss* captured my imagination like nothing before or since. Morning, noon and night, I'd sit glued to the telly, watching videos over and over, mesmerised by Lee's speed and style and mouth-watering, magnificently choreographed fight scenes. My mum, dad, brothers and sisters would literally have to drag me off the carpet to get me to bed. As I was being manhandled away, I'd picture each of them as gangsters and villains, practising make believe moves in my mind's eye, demolishing one after another with vicious flying, back and spinning kicks, fists, knees and elbows. One by one they'd go down, collapsing at my feet, overcome by my incredible skill and power; or at least in my dreams. In reality, I was extra careful to avoid any kind of physical contact, lest my dreams suddenly came tumbling down. Hoyland's answer to Bruce Lee, maybe; but the last thing I wanted was a clout or a good hiding for the privilege.

2. Football Crazy

By the time I entered my teens, I was becoming increasingly infatuated with martial arts. I continued to watch the films and would dig out snippets of information from newspapers and magazines, gathering all the latest developments on a growing UK circuit, while keeping a close watch upon news from across the pond, where the sport was already firmly established and continuing to grow exponentially. I'd rehearse moves in the bedroom mirror, putting these into practise on the field, pretend fighting with Phil, Daz and others, dreaming that one day we'd be able to put our developing skills to proper use in a ring somewhere. It was always possible. It just seemed extremely unlikely, that's all. Where could we go to practice for a start? Where could we go and learn? Without proper guidance, our dreams were dead in the water. There were rumours of a martial arts gym on the south side of Sheffield somewhere, but nobody knew where exactly. We're talking mid-eighties, remember. I mean, we could hardly Google it, could we? The good news was I'd left the nuns behind and moved to Kirk Balk School, commencing secondary education. All things considered it wasn't a bad school. No worse than any other in the area, anyway. The teachers were mostly alright, plus which, Hoyland Leisure Centre was situated adjacent, complete with gym, squash courts and swimming pool, a magnet for sports fanatics like myself.

With martial arts participation out of the question, I kept my focus very much on football. Selected for the local under-16s at age eleven, I was now a prolific goalscorer for the school team. Playing wing or inside forward, with the ability to turn on a sixpence and an explosive burst of pace, I was eventually scouted by my beloved Barnsley FC and invited for trials. Unfortunately, I received the notification a week late and so never got selected to play, despite turning up for training. It was a big blow at the time, but I refused to let it get me down. A hardy creature, I would never give up on my dreams of making it as a professional. All the setback did was make me more determined; to never, ever stop believing. I'd buy all the magazines, *Shoot*, *Match* and *Football Monthly*, cutting out my favourite players, decorating the bedroom wall and door. On TV, *Match of the Day* and *The Big Match* were compulsory viewing, a chance to study skills and tactics. I'd even sit through the football match scene in *Kes* whenever I could, screaming with laughter at the antics of the beleaguered players, suffering under the jurisdiction of the infamous, infuriating and indefatigable, Mr Sugden. Sugden was played by legendary Barnsley actor, Brian Glover, who also starred in classic films, *Alien 3* and *An American Werewolf in London*. He was also the voice behind the Tetley Tea adverts, a big no-no in our house, I might add, where good old Yorkshire Tea ruled the roost; splash of milk last with a chocolate digestive on the side. A former professional wrestler, who performed under the name of Leon Arras the man from Paris, you'd have been a brave man to tackle him. He would certainly have ruffled a few feathers in martial arts, that's for sure. Built like the proverbial brick-shithouse, he suited the Sugden role perfectly, a big, brussen, bullying games master, who made life hell for Billy, forcing him to wear oversized shorts and play in goal, before punishing him for his performance with a humiliating cold shower in front of his mates. I had to feel sorry for Billy. If I'd met him in real life, I'm certain we would have been pals, even though we didn't have much in common. Other than birds, I suppose, though it might be worth mentioning at this point that mine definitely weren't of the feathered variety. Alright, alright, calm down: this is supposed to be a book about my martial arts prowess, remember. If you want to read about my love life, then I'm afraid you're going to have to wait for the X-rated version, due next year. And, if you believe that, there goes Phil Rudd, look, on his way for an audition for the part of Grumpy in this year's Christmas panto, *Snow White and the Seven Dwarfs*. Seriously, though, I couldn't help thinking Billy needed to grow a pair. For those who have watched the film, it was clear he already had, dangling between his legs as he hoisted himself bollock-naked over the shower wall. What I meant was he should have resisted Sugden's insufferable bullying with every ounce of his being. Fought back verbally and even physically if need be. I know I would have. It was always my way. Even from a very young age. I didn't allow anyone to push me around. It was my life. I made my own choices and wasn't going to bow down to anybody, no matter how big and ugly they were. Any bully who risked messing with me would only do so once and that came with a cast iron guarantee. On the other side of the coin, I found it impossible not to harbour a deep admiration for at least a small part of Sugden's make-up. Alright, so he was a bully. I've already made my opinions on such behaviour crystal-clear. Anyone who uses intimidatory behaviour or physical violence to harm or coerce someone in pursuit of a desired outcome is scum in my eyes and needs treating as such. But I can't deny there was a couple of things Sugden and I had in common. First and foremost, we both liked to win. Not just occasionally. Not just every now and then. I'm talking all the time. When Sugden lost the on-screen football match, his reaction to the defeat was palpable, with Billy bearing the brunt of it. I'm not saying I'd have reacted the same; obviously I wouldn't. It would have gone against everything I've ever stood for. But I *would* have been disappointed, because the desire to succeed is something I was born with. Something inherent. Something I've always carried round with me. For as long as I can remember, I've had an insatiable and indelible desire to come out on top in everything I do. It's been my blessing; but it's also been my curse. Blessing in so much as it provided the spark, drive and determination to propel me to the very top of my sport; but curse because it produced a mindset which would never let me off the hook, pushing me to the limits in pursuit of excellence. When everyone else was out having fun, I'd be stuck in a gym somewhere, pounding a bag or punishing myself on a running machine. The other thing Sugden and I had in common was a love of football. Bruce Lee and martial arts and all that kind of stuff was great; but the sad truth was it remained a minority sport and I always assumed it would lead nowhere. Football remained my calling. It was my only hope of making something of my life, escaping forty odd years of blood, sweat, toil and tears in the melting shop of a steelworks or the deepest, darkest depths of the nearest coal mine.

All my mates were the same: football mad. With a catholic background, I developed a strong leaning towards Glasgow Celtic, an allegiance born in the eighties but which still burns strong today. I could often be seen walking around the village in a green and white hooped top, singing Scottish football songs. If it wasn't Celtic colours I was wearing, it was the red shirt of Barnsley FC. Most of my mates were also big Barnsley fans and together we'd catch a bus from Hoyland into town on alternate Saturdays to watch the Reds play. We'd also pick up midweek games and travel to away matches as often as possible. I'm talking early eighties now and, trust me, we had a right side down at Oakwell. Players such as Ronnie Glavin, Ian Banks, Mick McCarthy and Derek Parker are as much my heroes today as they were back then, skilful, flamboyant individuals, capable of performing at the highest level. We played in the old Second Division, nowadays the Championship, and could beat anyone on our day. Chelsea, Crystal Palace, Newcastle United, Brighton & Hove Albion and Manchester City; all fell prey to the mighty Reds in league and cup. I distinctly recall making a perilously long trip over the Pennines on the foggiest of foggy nights, watching us draw nil apiece at Anfield in the quarter final of the League Cup. Thousands of like-minded supporters made the trip, comfortably out-singing the Kop in a match only a flurry of missed chances prevented us from winning. Unfortunately, we lost the replay 3-1, despite taking an early lead. The legend that was Kenny Dalglish scored twice, with Graham Souness getting the other. It mattered on the night, but meant nothing in the fullness of time. We'd put in a brilliant performance and could rightly hold our heads high. A big positive that came from the defeat, however, was it reinforced my long-standing desire to become a professional footballer. Everywhere I went, I had a football glued my foot, dribbling it down the pavement en route to meet my mates. If there was nobody out, I'd spend hours thumping the ball against a wall, chasing down the rebound and fetching it under control before going again. There was a garage block near our house and I'd use the doors as pretend goals, taking pot shots and then running around in celebration, punching the air as if I'd just scored the winning goal at Wembley. The only problem was the doors were made out of tin. Each time the ball hit, they shook and rattled, making a noise like rolling thunder, ensuring I was repeatedly being told off by irate car owners, appearing from nearby houses, gesticulating like one of those look-our-way, inflatable dancing gimmicks, sited outside car washes and the like.

During winter, tennis courts in the local park became redundant, allowing us to enjoy a game of tennis football. Serves were drop-kicked and the ball had to land within the lines to count. More than one bounce and the point was won. Receivers were permitted to ball juggle and play keepy-uppy in advance of returning. Knees, head and chest were also permitted, making it a brilliant game for practising and enhancing ball skills. We'd also partake in a round of football golf. Using coats or jumpers as markers, positioned several hundred yards away, we'd take turns kicking separate balls to see who could reach the mark in the least number of shots. Kids from across town would converge to take part in twenty a side matches on the field. Coats or jumpers were positioned at opposite ends, acting as goalposts. When no one was looking, goalkeepers would craftily kick and drag garments inwards a few inches; not enough to cause an argument but sufficient to make the job between the sticks that little bit easier. Games would take place in all weathers. Postponements were only sanctioned in the most extreme circumstances, typically weather events of Biblical proportions: a foot of snow or a proper deluge. Same as *Kes*, players wore football shirts pertaining to local football league teams; Barnsley, Sheffield

Wednesday or Sheffield United. There was no Barcelona or Real Madrid attire back then; but Celtic, Manchester United or West Ham shirts weren't uncommon alongside a myriad of multi-coloured jumpers and T-shirts. The pace was fast and furious. Slide tackles would be going in thick and fast and players of both sides were soon be covered in mud, plenty with case-ball imprints tattooed across foreheads. As for the pitch, well…there was countless divots and a bit of litter blowing about, but the main concern was freshly laid piles of dog shit, coiled up python-like across the playing area. A communal shit patrol before the game got rid of most. Inevitably, though, some got missed and usually finished up smeared down the length of trousers or jeans, causing an explosion of anger and exasperation; kids' touching the mess then having a good finger sniff to be sure.

"Look at this bleeding lot…my mother will go spare when I get in!"

Games were self-refereeing. Goal! No, it wasn't! Yes, it was! No, it wasn't…it flicked the post and went wide! Lots of arguments and protestations. But no real conflict. Disputes were usually settled amicably and the game continued unabated. After one side scored ten, ends would be swapped. There was no half-time rest period. How could there be? *A-Team* was on at five with a bite to eat and bath time to follow in advance of school in the morning. Goals would be going in thick and fast with the score continually mounting, generating a full-time score of around 20-18, a close fought, full blooded encounter played over two, sometimes three hours. Sometimes, if there wasn't many out, we'd kick into one goal against the same keeper, again using jumpers as goalposts. These could be three a side encounters, or sometimes games of knock-out-Wembley, where everyone played for themselves against the rest. Score a goal and you were though to the next round. Fail to score and you were out. Round two would commence with five players instead of six. Round four was four players and so on until the final pairing contested a best of three goals final. As usual, I had to win and generally did. It was just the way I was and nothing but nothing was going to alter me.

Then, one Monday evening, everything changed. I was on my way out with the ball as usual when I bumped into Daz Kilner, approaching at pace from the opposite direction. I enquired where he was going and he treated me to a big, toothy grin as he gleefully revealed the news: a martial arts gym had opened in a spare room above the catholic club. Hoyland Taekwondo, it was called. And, even better, it was open now and they were signing up new members. For the first time in my life, you could have knocked me down with a feather. I hoofed the ball straight back over the garden fence and went with him. My love of football would never diminish. From this moment forward, though, my priorities changed. Dreams of a professional football career vanished for good. From here on in, I wanted to be a martial artist. I think it's fair to say we couldn't get to the catholic club fast enough.

3. Hoyland Taekwondo

We weaved a path through the village to the catholic club. A simple, prefabricated, two-story affair, it was an establishment I knew intimately well. Just round the corner from St Helens Catholic School, I'd been sneaked inside on more than a few occasions, sitting quiet as a mouse, sipping on a glass of lemonade, watching it all go off. With strong Irish roots, my family didn't half know how to enjoy themselves. As a young boy, I couldn't believe adults could behave in such an outlandish manner, pouring ale down their throats like it was going out of fashion, while screaming with laughter at the inanest of things. I vividly recall grandma Loui, dominating proceedings, standing on a chair with a microphone, singing Irish favourites such as *Molly Malone*, *The Irish Rover* and *Danny Boy*. There was no denying it: she was absolutely brilliant, bringing the house down with her exuberant performances, a million miles removed from the rubbish shown on TV nowadays. I loved my grandma and grandpa; on both sides. They were always there for me during my formative years. Nothing was too much trouble and what I'd give to be able to spend a few more precious hours in their company.

As we headed across the car park, we realised the door was locked. Not to the club, but a separate entrance, leading upstairs to the room above. A handwritten note, sellotaped to the glass announced: Hoyland Taekwondo. Training sessions, Monday and Wednesday. 6.30 till 9. New members welcome. Closed Bank Holidays. The date was 26th August, Bank Holiday Monday: the last full week of summer holiday freedom before a return to school in a week's time. I looked at Daz and he looked at me. He was absolutely crestfallen at the news, shaking the handle as if the door would magically open and we'd enter a roomful kids, kicking shit out of one another. I slung an arm round him, telling him not to worry. I mean, it was hardly his fault, was it? We'd been mates all our lives, so weren't going to fall out about it, plus which, it would be back open in a couple of days, anyway. We trudged back to mine and got the ball out, heading for the field for a kickabout, which unsurprisingly didn't last long. Head filled with martial arts, we soon called it a day. Daz sulked off home and I went inside, watching cricket on telly, before disappearing upstairs to practise a few preparatory moves.

It didn't half drag to Wednesday, but at least we made the best of it. Too hot for footie, we got the pellet rifles out and headed for nearby woodlands for a few fun and games. Phil was there, as was Daz and Kev, plus a few other mates, army mad Chris Oldfield and the Johnson and Footitt brothers, Chris and Simon and Lee and Paul. Our weapons were mostly 177 in calibre, though Chris Oldfield had a 22 and the Johnsons turned up looking like Butch Cassidy and the Sundance Kid, toting hand-held Gat-guns, stuck down the back of their pants. Imagine nine or ten kids nowadays, armed to the teeth, ambling through the village, taking pot-shots at pigeons, sparrows, street lamps and the like. Firearms would be all over them like a rash. It's a good job it wasn't like that back then; knowing our lot, we probably wouldn't have given up without a fight. Arriving at the woods, I instinctively gave a wide berth to the big tree where I fell off a Tarzan swing a few years previous, landing on my head. As my mates collapsed in heaps of laughter, I literally crawled off home, traversing fields and streets on all fours, suffering with excruciating back pain. Luckily for me, a good night's sleep worked wonders and next morning I was good to go again, albeit a tad sore. We found a few tin cans, lining them up on low hanging branches as target practise. It was alright, like; but we soon got bored and decided to up the ante a bit, taking aim at one other on the strict proviso no one fired above shoulder height. Frequent rifle cracks ripped through the trees, immediately followed by sharp cries of pain as kids were hit. Ouch! *Ouch*! I remember laughing my socks off at Phil, dancing a jig with a hand clasped over his buttock, cursing and swearing like a Tourette sufferer on speed. Elvis mad, he resembled a gangling, wayward version of The King himself, rehearsing frequent pelvis gyrations ahead of a forthcoming stage show. Not that he was the only one. I got nicked on the arm and poor old Kev took one in the nether regions, leaving him hobbling around like he'd just shit himself.

The day after, we were back at the club and big Phil had decided to join us, sore arse and all. I doubted he'd stick it to be fair; a game of football was usually too much effort for the long streak of piss, so how was he going to contend with the discipline, strength and fortitude required to make his mark in martial arts? Little did I know, but I couldn't have been more wrong. It was another red-hot day. The sun had been cracking the flags since early morning and the door was tied open with a piece of string, permitting a welcome influx of fresh air. Unable to restrain ourselves, we charged up the staircase like a herd of rampaging elephants, barging unceremoniously into the room. A man in a white suit with a black V-neck collar raised a hand, curtailing our exuberance. A rough-looking bugger, we knew the black V-neck signified black belt and so immediately zipped it, waiting quietly in a corner until summoned. It was a medium-sized, rectangular room, no bigger than a penalty area in size, with a small changing room at one end. Windows stretched the length of east and west facing walls. With no curtains up, the sun was shining in unimpeded, penetrating the room like freshly cast gold ingots. It smelled fusty in the heat, oily almost, a bit like plasticine, a sickly-sweet aroma which permeated the nostrils, permanently stamping itself upon the subconscious of all who experienced it. I'd expected a floor covered with mats, soft, durable EVA foam rubber. No such luck. It was exclusively carpet, interspersed with areas of hard tiles, which I could only surmise must hurt if anyone took a tumble. Fifteen or twenty kids were enjoying a warm up session, bending, stretching and jumping; rolling shoulders and rotating necks to such an extent I swear I could hear bones cracking. I say kids, but the age range of students was anywhere between ten and twenty plus, with a mishmash of fluctuating heights to boot, further amplified by the arrival of Phil, who was easily tallest in the room. Everyone was wearing a dobok taekwondo uniform, comprising white, V-neck jacket and pants, worn for both training and competition. Standing waiting in jeans and T-shirt, I felt instantly envious and I know the others did, too, desperate to enrol and put on the white suit. After the warm up, we were approached by the instructor, who introduced himself as Carradine, namesake of the actor who played Kwai Chang Caine in *Kung Fu*. I wanted to make a joke of it but didn't dare. He looked like Caine as well; tall, lean and muscular, with short, dark hair, sun-tanned complexion and thick, black eyebrows, resembling furry caterpillars, traversing his brow. Unfortunately, that's where the resemblance finished. While the on-screen Carradine was gentle, softly spoken and peaceful, the instructor was stern, aggressive and possessed a voice like a foghorn. Apparently, he was an ex-squaddie, fresh out of the army, even though he was only about nineteen or twenty. He asked what he could do for us. When we said we wanted to become members, he gave us forms to fill in; name; address, date of birth; reasons for joining. We signed our names at the bottom, paying our quid a week subs and that was it: we were in. Happy as Larry, I said:

"When can I fight?"

"Show us what you've got first," he replied, eyeing me with a mix of humour and disdain. His reaction left me seething, determined that he'd soon be smiling on the other side of his face. It was the moment I'd been waiting ages for and there was no way I was going to let myself down now. I immediately set myself, planting my feet on the ground, fists clenched at waist height, left foot and arm pointing forward. Then I set off at a sprint. Five or six yards in, I jumped. Both feet in the air, I pirouetted one hundred-and-eighty degrees, landing a flying kick at head height, albeit at an imaginary target. Carradine's reaction was encompassed in a single word: wow! He threw an arm round my shoulder, whispering gently into my ear. I punched the air with delight as words parted his lips: I had my fight and, even better, it would be in the next half hour. He pointed out who I would be fighting, a kid about my age, similar height and weight. He informed my opponent next and we spent the next twenty, thirty minutes eyeing one another up. I could tell he wasn't scared. So what? Neither was I. I couldn't wait to get going, in fact. He might look the business in his dobok; but it didn't mean he was any better than me, did it? Right on time, we were summoned to the floor and instructed upon the rules. Competition fights normally consisted of three two-minute rounds. As this was classed as sparring, however, it would be limited to one round only. We grimaced in unison at the news. We'd eyeballed each other so much in the run-up, it was obvious we both wanted a full-blown slugfest. Unfortunately, it wasn't to be. Kicks to the head and body were permitted, while punches were restricted to body only. Any punch to the head would result in instant disqualification. There was no head protector or gumshield, but we were both made to wear chest guards, more commonly known as hogu, protecting the most common taekwondo scoring area, avoiding injury from fists and kicks. Before the fight commenced, we were made to show each other complete respect. Standing to attention, feet together and hands at our side, we bowed simultaneously from the waist. And that was it: Carradine checked his watch, clapping hands to get things started. There was no dancing around, sussing each other out. We both went straight on the offensive, moving up close, trading fast moving kicks and punches. It was all very hectic and we both landed some pretty decent connections. I can't say he hurt me. And I couldn't say I hurt him, either. If I did, credit to him, because he did a pretty good job of concealing it. To the outsider, it would appear we were evenly matched; but it was only an illusion. Close up, I could tell he was a year or so older than I was and had obviously been training a while. Even so, by the final few seconds, I felt I had the measure of him and could easily have finished it had the contest been allowed to continue. As it was, Carradine declared the session a draw. I was disappointed but elated at the same time. Disappointed because I felt

I'd done enough to win, but elated because I knew for certain I'd found my calling in life. We bowed again and shook hands. The animosity was gone and we got along great from there on in. Moreover, all three of us, myself, Phil and Daz, were welcomed into the fold with open arms, determining there and then to make the best of the opportunity which had presented itself.

As mentioned, classes were twice weekly and I don't think we missed a single one thereafter. I say *we*, but can only really speak for myself. The others may well have cried off once or twice; I genuinely can't remember. But I know I didn't. It was the highlight of the week, even relegating *Match of the Day* or a visit to watch the mighty Reds into a very poor second. I lived and breathed every session. Utterly besotted, I'd watch, work, listen and learn, applying myself a hundred per cent, straining every sinew to be the best I could possibly be. I convinced myself at a very early stage that one day I'd be British champion. It may have seemed a million miles off. And to say it wouldn't be easy was the understatement of the century. But I wouldn't allow *anything* to get in my way. Like *The Terminator*, I was out there. I couldn't be bargained with. I couldn't be reasoned with. I couldn't feel pity. Or remorse. Or fear. And I absolutely *would not stop*, ever, until I had my hands on the title. It was all about belief, a commodity I seemingly had in excess. Endlessly, I'd tell myself: *don't stop believing*. I'd say it before I went to bed and again when I woke up. It became my mantra and is as relevant to everything I'm about today as it was all those years ago.

At the conclusion of each session, I'd obsessively analyse, assimilating what I could have done better and how I could improve various aspects of performance. I'd rehearse techniques in the bedroom mirror, the same as I'd always done. Blocks. Strikes. Kicks. Punches. Repetition was key. Practise most definitely made perfect, the same as it did in any other activity or walk of life. That stated, I was repeatedly reminded by Carradine there was another vital element in the make-up of a successful martial artist: natural ability. And I invariably puffed my chest out with pride whenever he took time to tell me this was something I possessed in abundance. In between, I'd go to school and continue to play and watch football and trawl the village with my mates; but my heart and soul belonged to taekwondo. Summer transcended into autumn, by which time the club membership had drastically altered. Lots of old faces disappeared, with a multitude of new ones stepping in to take their place. Wastage was a natural consequence of the demands of the sport. Some lost interest. Others simply couldn't hack it and a few unsuitables were *made* to leave by the ever-watchful Carradine, making sure people weren't using combat training for inappropriate reasons. It didn't mean there was anything wrong with those who fell by the wayside. It was probably the other way round, in fact. Those of us who persevered, becoming more addicted with every session; *we* were the ones who needed looking at, students like myself and Phil. I make no bones about it: training was rock hard, but the benefits were immense, physically as well as mentally. All the little things which caused me so much pain and anguish prior to enrolment suddenly paled into insignificance and didn't matter anymore. When the alarm went off, I'd leap out of bed. If I was asked to nip down the shop, mow the grass, or take the bin to the gate, I'd just get on with it, because I was happy and content in myself. That doesn't mean I wasn't happy and content before. Course I was. I couldn't have asked for better family or friends and always strove to make the best of every day. It was just that now I felt part of something, blessed with an unquenchable sense of direction in life. Confidence had never been a problem; but now it was sky high. Nothing phased me. And I mean, *nothing*. I felt I could achieve anything, constantly setting myself training linked improvement goals, be it perfecting a new technique or working that little bit harder to improve fitness levels already through the roof. Self-discipline and self-esteem were also massively on the rise. I was more mentally aware than ever and had a heightened sense of physical and mental well-being. I started to feel invincible. Not in an aggressive sense. No way. What I meant was I felt totally safe in every aspect of life, whether it was going to the footie or simply walking the streets at night. Taekwondo was a mix of attacking and defensive techniques and, if someone randomly decided to have a go, I was more than capable of defending myself and with vigour if necessary. I clearly had talent, ambition and determination. The only question was: how far could I go? As Christmas approached, it was decreed the time had arrived for my first grading, a test of a student's knowledge of basic techniques; poomsae, self-defence and sparring skills. Perhaps that would go a way to providing the answer…?

4. First Fight

Originating in Korea after World War Two, taekwondo is a traditional martial art, characterised by punching and kicking techniques, with emphasis upon head-height kicks, spinning jump kicks and fast kicking moves; a form of martial art in which participants attack or defend using hands and feet. Students traditionally progress at their own pace through a martial arts syllabus, moving through a belt ranking system of white, yellow, green, blue and red, with intermediate coloured stripe grades along the way. It takes an average of three years to reach black belt, otherwise known as dan standard. Ranked martial artists can progress to second dan status after a minimum waiting period of twelve months upon satisfactorily refining and improving skill sets and expertise. Additional dan status is also attainable, stretching all the way through to ninth dan, which denotes Grand Master, an achievement which can literally take decades to achieve.

As for little old me, for all my rapid progress at Hoyland Taekwondo, I was still a white belt, staring down a very long journey indeed if I was to successfully progress through the belts system, due to commence with a trip to nearby Mexborough for my first grading. The biggest problem I had was getting a lift to the venue. A suburb of Doncaster, it was nigh on impossible to get to by bus, meaning a car journey of nine or ten miles. Dad was working that evening and it looked like I might actually miss my big moment. I was in a right old mood as a consequence, stomping about like big Phil when he first discovered Superman was a bloke dressed up. Fortunately, I had a silver tongue to fall back upon, a persuasive eloquence which had carried me through countless tricky situations in the past and would continue to do so throughout my life. I eventually persuaded grandpa William to take me in his dodgy yellow Ford Escort, which, worryingly, seemed to spend more time broken down than on the road. I just hoped it made it or I could be looking at months before a fresh opportunity was scheduled.

The big day arrived in a hurry. I'd been instructed to arrive at six, so we set off ninety minutes early, just in case. It was a good job. The journey was a nightmare from start to finish. We must have been driving fifteen minutes, when I brought the flat of my hand down on the dash in realisation grandpa was heading in totally the wrong direction. I asked where the hell he was going and his response made me want to throw up.

"Kexborough, he replied, flicking an indicator, swinging a left, persevering with the imagined route in his head. "That's what you said, isn't it?"

"Kexborough!" I screamed, almost passing out at his stupidity. In my mind's eye, he became tonight's sparring opponent. I hit him with a flying head kick, knocking him spark out, as if I ever would, because I loved every bone in the stupid old bugger's body really. "I said *Mexborough*, dimwit! Kexborough is the other side of Barnsley!"

Back on route, I hurriedly resumed mental preparations, refocusing on the task ahead, replaying various techniques in my head. We were back where we started now, passing through Hoyland, heading down towards the sprawling metropolis of Wombwell, Barnsley's second town. Confidence was growing we'd still make it on time. Then he stopped abruptly, clambering out and disappearing into a corner shop, emerging several minutes later with a packet of Woodbines and a carrier bag filled with crisps, chocolate bars and coca cola. He opened the bag, offering me a lucky dip. I told him to bugger off. Pop, crisps and mars bars were the *last* thing I needed in advance of such an important event. We got held up in roadworks next, mis-timing temporary traffic lights at Brampton Bierlow, creating a right old snarl up. I can't say I was surprised when a burning smell suddenly infiltrated the interior. Cool as a cucumber, he told me not to worry. It often happened, he explained, especially when idling in traffic. A glance at the temperature gauge showed it creeping up towards the danger zone. Much more and it would overheat for sure. And grandpa knew it just as well as I did, diverting into a layby, switching the engine off, giving it chance to cool down a bit. I was getting really nervous now and was constantly checking the time. The event didn't bother me one bit; not now. I had my head sorted and was convinced I'd smash it when the time arrived. It was a foregone conclusion, in fact. I just couldn't bear the thought of having to explain myself to all and sundry if we didn't make it. Little did I know, but worse was to come. A few minutes later, we set off again; or would have done if the engine had started. Each turn of the key fetched a depressing clunk accompanied by a sad, soul-destroying whirr. He looked at me and I stared him down, demanding answers. I could tell he didn't know what to say. He mumbled something about alternators and starter motors, but may as well have been speaking Swahili for what sense he made. I was a footballer turned martial artist. Not a bloody motor mechanic. I'd all but given up hope when, miraculously, it started. I couldn't believe my luck as the engine burst into life, purring like a cat as we sped off down the road. As a Welcome to Mexborough signpost illuminated in the headlamps, I whooped then punched the air with delight. A quick stop to ask directions and we finally arrived, pulling up outside the church hall where the event was being held.

"There you go, our Charles," grandpa enthused, pulling on the handbrake. "I told you I'd get you here on time, didn't I…?"

We quickly made our way inside. It was an old building, dating back a century or more, with an arch-construction ceiling, supported by a lattice-work of withered oak beams. Noticeboards were awash with information relating to various meeting groups; parent and toddler, book clubs and church assemblies. It was cold outside but warm in, courtesy of big, cast-iron radiators, relentlessly pumping out heat. As soon as I'd registered, I was packed off to get changed into my dobok. There were dozens of other students present, a few from Barnsley and Rotherham, but mainly Doncaster. I spoke to a couple while I was getting ready and they seemed good lads. It didn't matter I was an outsider, because we were all in it together, all pursuing the same dream: to continually improve and progress as far as we could in the ultra-competitive world of martial arts. I joined a group of students, warming up, performing exactly the same routine I practised weekly back home, bending, stretching and jumping; neck and shoulder rotations. At the top end of the room was an elongated table with a white cloth draped over it, peppered with cups and saucers and bottled water. A quartet of men in suits were seated adjacent and I didn't need to be Sherlock Holmes to deduce this was the grading panel, responsible for gauging performances and awarding the appropriate belt. Someone I'd never met before pointed out a chap left of centre. A tall, lean, good looking fellow, with glasses and greying hair, it was Grandmaster Tony Quigley, who studied taekwondo in the sixties, while serving in Korea with the RAF. When he returned to the UK, he was the first person to do so with a taekwondo black belt, which he immediately put to use, teaching the art in clubs throughout Doncaster. Incredibly, I discovered he was also jointly responsible for starting the British Taekwondo Association, news which could easily have put my head in a spin, adversely impacting my performance. Far from it. Not on your nellie, in fact. If anything, it invigorated me, making me more determined than ever to put in the scintillating performance I knew I was capable of.

Gradings were constantly taking place, students of all ages being put through their paces. One or two seemed very nervous, though most approached the task with extreme confidence, mirroring a key trait instilled by prolonged participation in the art. I didn't have long to wait before it was my turn, engaging in pre-arranged poomsae, a mix of non-contact defensive and attacking movements. Very deliberately and with precision timing, I methodically progressed through my repertoire, displaying proficiency in blocks, strikes, kicks and punches. I was given a fitness test next, a tough work-out which involved press ups, sit ups, lunges and mountain climber exercises. Finally, I was tested upon my ability to break an inch thick wooden board, held aloft by an instructor. I'd practised endlessly for this particular section and approached the task with customary vigour and venom, psyching myself up in advance, before attacking the object with a powerful and immaculately timed kick. The wood broke first time, splintering down the middle. Perfectly executed, I sucked in a deep breath, bowing respectfully to the panel, before making way for the next student in line.

The final part of my grading involved competitive sparring. I was pitted against a student named Scott Whitehead, a highly rated red belt from Doncaster, who eventually went on to play professional football with Chesterfield. One of the best young prospects in the country, he was a couple of years older than I was and hot favourite to come out on top in the contest. Oozing confidence, he came at me like a raging bull, but a flurry of kicks and punches sent him reeling in retreat. He assaulted again, spawning identical results. Then again. And, this time, I dropped him with a perfectly timed spinning head kick. He bounced back like he'd landed on a rubber floor. No doubt about it, Scott was as game as they came. But everyone watching knew he'd been beaten by the better man, or should I say boy, because that's all I was at the time. Time was up and I'd overcome my challenge with ease, albeit sustaining a bad back in the process. As a consequence, I was propelled from white to yellow belt with green stripe, leapfrogging a brace of inferior belts in one fell swoop. I thought that was it; but there was more to come. Trophies were awarded for the top performing students and I walked away with the prize for best overall. I also learned Quigley had stated I was the best young prospect he'd ever seen. Commendation indeed, I was bursting with pride as I made a present of the trophy to grandpa William in appreciation of his help. All I wanted now was for his car to start and get us home without any trouble. Lo and behold, it did: the inauspicious start to the evening had clearly been a red herring. Things couldn't have gone better. Not in my wildest dreams. Not even if I'd been allowed to pen the outcome myself.

A few weeks later, I was handed the opportunity to rubber-stamp my progress by fighting in an open championship in Fleetwood, Lancashire. A few other students from Hoyland were also invited, sufficient to warrant the hiring of a 52-seater, enabling family and friends to offer vocal support on the night. It was a long trip up, a hundred miles or more, made to seem triple the distance on account I was seated next to Phil. Squashed against the window, it reminded me of the scene in *Commando*, where Arnie, forced aboard a flight against his will, elbowed his escort in the face, then snapped his neck, before placing a pillow behind his head and wrapping him up in a blanket. I remember thinking if Phil carried on nagging and taking the piss, he'd get the same treatment. It never happened, of course. He was too big for a start, plus which, though it pains me to say it, he was my best pal. Still is, in fact, but don't tell him that, will you? Oops, I nearly forgot. He's probably reading this right now, thinking he's some kind of superstar. Yeah, right. In his dreams, maybe. I'm sad to report the onslaught continued; uphill and down dale, I'd never heard such complete bollocks in my life. By the time we reached the coast, my ears were hurting. And it wasn't over yet. As we passed a cemetery, he leaned into me, cackling like the wicked witch of the west.

"See that, Greenie? That's where you'll end up, because *I* know who you're fighting and he'll bloody well kill you. You're going to die, Greenie. Do you hear me? You're going to *die*…"

It was such a relief to reach the venue, a red-brick working men's club within spitting distance of the sea, just down the coast from Blackpool and its myriad of tourist attractions. Not that the famous Golden Mile was of any interest. It was the wrong time of year for a start, freezing cold and hardly the weather for an extended stroll along the seafront. We entered through the tap room. It was filled with men, smoking and drinking, playing darts, cards and dominoes. A snooker room was positioned adjacent and the sound of colliding balls made a noise like fisticuffs, reminding me of the barroom brawl segment of my favourite western, *Shane*. It smelled of stale ale and the air was filled with smoke, permeating the room like a blood curdling curse of ancient Egypt. A sign on the wall said: *Strippers, Sunday, 12 till 2*. I pillocked Phil *Strippers* was a Motown tribute band and he swallowed it hook, line and sinker. Honestly, if brains were dynamite, I doubt he'd have enough to blow his cap off. The championship was being staged in a concert room at the rear. Mats were laid out beneath the stage with a horseshoe of chairs, several rows deep, overlooking the centrepiece, with standing room only behind. On stage was the judging panel, four people seated at a table in front of a maroon velvet curtain. Changing rooms were at the rear and I was taken aback when I saw how many entrants the competition had attracted; scores of wannabes, changing and limbering up, dreaming of a big win to set them on the road to stardom. Entered into the 48-52kg category, I'd trained hard to ensure I stayed within the weight parameters, constantly leaping on and off scales in the run-up. I got changed, joining the queue for the weigh-in, secure in the knowledge I'd weighed exactly 50kg just twenty-four hours previous. Imagine my shock then when the scales tipped 70kg, a mammoth forty per cent weight increase from the night before. I stamped and kicked like a petulant child, throwing accusations left, right and centre. There must have been some kind of mistake, I screamed; either that or the scales hadn't been calibrated correctly. I jumped straight back on and the needle rocketed round the dial once more, hitting the 70kg marker a second time. *What*? How could this be happening? I didn't understand any of it; couldn't get my head round what was going on. Not for the life of me, I couldn't. Sick of waiting, another entrant in my weight class climbed on and the needle moved again, stopping on 51kg. I looked the lad up and down and could tell I didn't weigh an ounce more than he did. Growing increasingly frustrated, I tried a third time and the scales registered 70kg once more. It was then I felt a clip round the head, twinned by the annoying sound of Phil's raucous laughter, assaulting my eardrums.

"You daft bleeder, Jack. You *do* know you've got your changing bag over your shoulder, don't you…?"

Red-faced, I was finally permitted to enter the cauldron of the competition area, proud as punch in my dobok and new yellow belt with a green stripe. A couple of fights were already in progress, at differing stages of three two-minute rounds, students desperate to progress, giving it their all, kicking seven bells out of one another. The room was filled with the jeers and cheers of an audience several hundred strong, displaying allegiance by shouting down or cheering on various contestants. Soon it was my turn. The Hoyland mob went crazy as I took to the floor, screaming and shouting encouragement as I marched around like I'd already won the damned thing. My opponent was a lad about the same age who everybody called Hodgy. First impressions indicated he was a bit on the tubby side, unfit looking almost, and my confidence, already sky high, experienced another boost as a consequence. If I beat him, which I obviously would, I'd progress to round two and then three and so on, hopefully making it all the way to the final. We bowed to the judges and each other then got stuck straight in. Fifteen seconds in, he caught me with a painful leg kick, following up his success with a perfectly timed head shot. Blood up, I went straight on the offensive but struggled to gain any momentum. My legs felt like I was fighting in diving boots and I was becoming more and more lethargic with every step. I lost the round easily, but recovered impressively in the second, even though I was still way below my best. A big performance in the third and I'd be through for sure. It sounded simple enough, but I still wasn't firing on all cylinders and a hard-fought round left me sweating on what was obviously going to be a close points decision. As the judges deliberated the result, I did the only thing I could think of, parading jubilantly in front of the Hoyland contingent, arms raised in victory, blowing kisses and posing for photos. It turned out to be the worst thing I could have done. I probably did just enough to nick it, but the judges weren't impressed by my showboating and total lack of respect and promptly gave the decision the other way. Totally crestfallen, I was made to feel even worse when I discovered one of the judges was none other than Tony Quigley. What he must have thought was anyone's guess; but it couldn't have been good and it hurt me to think my reputation may have been indelibly tarnished.

Dejected maybe, but I learned a very valuable lesson that bitterly cold night in Fleetwood. Never take anything for granted and always have respect for opponents. The bus was deathly quiet on the way back, but at least I got my own back on Phil. Fast asleep by my side, I borrowed a permanent marker off a bloke up front and scribbled a big, handlebar moustache on his top lip. He went crackers when he found out, but at least it came off eventually. Not long after, he grew a real one, so must have been quite taken by it deep down. Moreover, he still sports a moustache to this day and it really suits him to be honest. Except when he's got soup residue in it, or remnants of a Greggs steak bake. Bloody Neanderthal, he is one…

5. Big Jack

The training continued. It was hard. It was fast. It was comprehensive. Before I knew it, I was a green belt, working towards the next phase of my development: green with an intermediate blue stripe. In between training sessions, I still partook in all the usual teenage stuff with Phil, Daz, Kev and the gang. The football continued uninterrupted. Every Sunday, we'd have a traditional twenty per side mega-match and would watch Barnsley play home and away at every opportunity. Away matches were best by far. Football hooliganism was rife and some of the backs-to-the-wall scrapes we found ourselves in really needed to be seen to be believed, though the less said about that the better. We'd roam the village, having a laugh and generally making a nuisance of ourselves, while chatting up the local talent, though rarely getting anywhere. Seriously, it makes me wonder how I ever accrued my burgeoning Charlie Green sex machine nickname; once again, though, the less said about that the better. Back on the taekwondo front, I wasn't the only one making headway. Phil was also making great strides and, as a way of increasing our fitness, we'd take each other on at various athletic challenges, predominantly sprints and long-distance running. I always won, of course; what else would you expect? Lining up against Phil was like lining up against Herman Munster. In all seriousness, I think Morticia would have stood more chance of beating me than old bollock chops. Joking apart, I was a very capable athlete, even if I say so myself. When I was a bit younger, I totally annihilated a cousin of mine in a cross-country challenge; a cousin who had a growing reputation as a middle and long-distance runner. Little did I know that this cousin would go on to represent Great Britain in the 1500m at the Atalanta, Sydney and Athens Olympic Games. Pride of Barnsley Athletics Club, his name was John Maycock. Another cousin was goalkeeper Mark Crossley, who represented England at U21 level and went on to make almost five hundred first team appearances for a multitude of professional clubs, principally

Nottingham Forest under Brian Clough. All I can say is, it's a good job he never came up against old Charlie boy; the only way he'd have stopped me scoring was by boarding the goals up.

One day, I was hanging around outside our house when I caught sight of Kev, pounding the pavement, heading straight for me. I hadn't seen him for a few days as he'd been labouring for his dad, who owned a local building firm. Arriving breathless and perspiring, I beat him to it.

"If you've come to tell me we're going to get mugged, Kev, here…there's that fiver I owe you."

At least I thought it was funny; I surmised he never heard a word.

"Guess…guess who's house I've been working at?"

Devout catholic, I had a ready-made answer.

"Pope John Paul the second?"

"No, mate, it's somebody more famous than him. It's only big Jack Charlton's, isn't it?"

Wow! It really *was* someone more famous than the Pope; or at least in a football fan's eyes, anyway. Jack Charlton was a former Sheffield Wednesday manager. He was a World Cup winner with England and played more than six hundred games for Leeds United, a footballing legend of the highest order. Instantly jealous, I wanted my own piece of the big man. I'd always known Jack lived locally, but where was a well-guarded secret. I asked the question and Kev couldn't get his words out quick enough: down a big hill and across a field near Worsborough Res, a couple of miles away at most. Without hesitation, I proposed we had a walk over and knock on his door. Kev agreed in a flash and off we trotted, skirting the reservoir, climbing a wall and then traversing an overgrown field towards a big stone house in the distance. Arriving on the doorstep, I reached out and rang the bell. What seemed like an eternity passed without activity. Then the door swung open and a tall man with wispy, thinning hair appeared, peering down his hooter at us. It knew instantly it was big Jack. Luckily for us, he was in a good mood, greeting us with a smile, ruffling Kev's hair in recognition.

"Hello again, son. What's the matter? Couldn't you stay away?"

He invited us inside and made a cup of tea. It was a bit milky for my liking, but I wasn't complaining. I was in the presence of football royalty and was too enthralled soaking up every last second of it. We talked football a bit. He could tell we knew our stuff and so ushered us into a sitting room, jam-packed full with display cabinets, containing trophies and mementos pertaining to his illustrious playing career. Signed match balls. League and cup winning medals. Shirts and programmes. In a separate cabinet was memorabilia relating to his England career, predominantly caps and shirts. On the middle shelf, however, was something really special: Jack's winners' medal from the World Cup Final versus West Germany. We were totally gobsmacked. Not half as much as we were when he unlocked the door, though, allowing us to take turns, trying the medal on. I couldn't believe it: little old Charlie Green from Cloughfields, wearing a gold-embossed medal, inscribed: *FIFA. World Championship Winners. Jules Rimet Cup. Jack Charlton. In England, 1966.* It made me want to be a footballer again, a flying winger, tearing through the opposition defence and scoring the winner for my beloved Barnsley. The change of heart didn't last long, though. Football was obviously brilliant; but my focus remained the same. I desperately wanted to be a martial artist. And nothing but nothing would deter me. Jack made a promise to come and watch us play and legend has it he turned up one afternoon, unfortunately arriving early and departing before kick-off. Sounds about right. If he'd witnessed me playing up front, teasing and tormenting the opposition with my sublime skills, I'd probably be sitting in my rooftop apartment in Dubai now, soaking up the sun with a couple of cold ones, enjoying unfettered views across the Persian Gulf. Time to leave, Jack showed us out. Pausing on the doorstep, I about turned and glared at him, a mischievous gleam forming in my eye.

"Hey up, Jack, what's this I've heard on the radio? Something about burglars, breaking into Sheffield Wednesday's ground?"

"I don't know, son," he replied, thoughtfully fingering his chin. "It's news to me. What did it say, like?"

"That they emptied the trophy room and police are on the look-out for someone with a rolled up blue and white carpet." The big man erupted with laughter, but I hadn't finished with him yet. "They nicked all the cups as well. By all accounts, the canteen lady is livid…"

Back at school, striding the illustrious tiled corridors of Kirk Balk, it seemed I was already becoming something of a celebrity. Everywhere I went, I'd hear kids saying: Hey up, Charlie. How's it going, pal? Hey up, mate. Hey up. Hey up, hey up, hey up. On and on and on. Day after day after day. I'm talking kids aged eleven to sixteen here. Even the sixth-formers started showing me respect and it was obvious why. Even if I say so myself, I'd always been popular. I always went out of my way to help and consequently made friends easily. That stated, my growing reputation on the local taekwondo scene had clearly impacted positively upon my persona. And for all the right reasons, I might add. Not once had I utilised the skills I'd acquired to intimidate, tease or torment. It wasn't my style and never would be. Soon, even the teachers were at it, albeit with a slightly more sophisticated approach. Morning, Charlie. Good afternoon, Charlie. Three bags full, Charlie. I hope you're well? Anything you need, just let me know. It wasn't all sweetness and light, though. I had a few scraps as you'd expect, usually with kids bigger than me, trying to make a name for themselves by kicking shit out of the taekwondo kid. I never once started any trouble, Invariably, though, I'd have little trouble finishing it. Same as competition opponents were finding out to their cost, I was too fast; too nimble and too strong, absolutely battering anyone who dared to have a go. An interesting outlet for my athletic prowess arrived with the formation of a school rugby league team. Those in the know will tell you that rugby league isn't huge in South Yorkshire, where football is definitely king. As such, we didn't even know the rules when signing up to play and were literally making it up as we went along, suffering a series of thumping defeats. Under the stewardship of legendary teacher, Steve Creek, however, we soon got it together, turning the tables on teams physically bigger and with infinitely more experience than us. Hoyland Vikings, we were called, and were soon beating sides from rugby league's northern heartlands; places like Leeds, Bradford, Huddersfield and Halifax. Same as in football, I was a forward, scoring numerous tries as our fledgling reputation gathered pace, most especially when it came to enthusiastically defending ourselves in frequent on-field brawls. We played in a tournament at Blackpool. We'd come a long way in a short space of time and were now going up against the big boys, formidable teams from Castleford and Featherstone. Steve promised us fish and chips and beer if we won. And win we did, with yours truly being named man of the match. He was as good as his word. He knew he had to be or, pardon the pun, he'd have been up the creek without a paddle. It must have cost him a fortune, but he didn't seem to mind and it finished off a fantastic couple of days on the perfect note.

Not long after, I was Austria bound on a school skiing holiday. I'd never been on a plane before and was really looking forward to flying. Unfortunately, it wasn't to be. As more and more kids signed up for the trip, it was decided to take a more cost-effective overland route, a cross-channel ferry, preceding a laborious coach trip through France and Germany. It was nice seeing new countries, but I can't say I enjoyed it, especially France, which I was shocked to find was full of French people. Arriving in Innsbruck like a hurricane, we had a whale of a time. We did very little skiing. In actual fact, we didn't do any. There didn't seem to be much snow about for a start. Not that anyone cared. Not in our gang, anyway. We were more than content exploring the surrounding area, chatting up a few fräuleins. Mainly, though, it was about alcohol. The teachers were constantly in the boozer and so were we, under age or not, tucked away in a corner, so as not to draw attention to ourselves. Arriving back late one night, we crept into our dormitory on tiptoes only to be immediately confronted by an over scrupulous teacher called Mr Turner, who we comically referred to as upside-down-head on account he was bald as a coot, while sporting a big-bearded chin. He didn't half tear a strip off us, confining us to barracks, before disappearing with a right huff on, locking the door behind him. Red rag to a bull, I was straight out of the window and down the drainpipe, returning post haste to the ale-house. Lo and behold, who should walk in ten minutes later but upside-down-head, who wasted no time frogmarching me back to the digs and a midnight phone call to the motherland to have it out with my dad.

"Mister Green," he said, sternly, fingering his beard, face like a bulldog, chewing a wasp. "I think it's only right I inform you that Charles has spent almost the entire holiday in the pub, drinking beer. Can you have a word, please?"

He put me straight on to him and he asked how many I'd had. I belched and hiccupped in the same breath.

"Only about six, Dad,"

"Right. Well, just have one more, then get yourself off to bed, do you hear…?"

In between time, training continued unabashed. Twice weekly, I'd attend the club, working on fitness and refining my skills, aiming for another belt progression as soon as possible. It galls me to say it, but Phil was also improving rapidly, having progressed through series of gradings to yellow belt status. He was also filling out at an incredible rate of knots. He was almost as wide as he was tall by this stage, easily making the 82-86kg category, which was heavyweight by any standards. If he hit anyone they would stay hit and was someone you wouldn't want to cross under any circumstances. With taekwondo predominantly a kicking art, we became more and more conscious that we needed to improve our hand-work as a means of complementing existing skills. One weekend afternoon, fuelled by a few pints, we took the decision to head for a training session at a Thai boxing club, a discipline commonly as muay Thai, a combat sport employing stand-up striking techniques, characterised by the combined use of fists, elbows, knees and shins. The club was located on Sheffield's Wicker, a rough, tough, multi-cultural quarter, close to the city centre, a half-hour bus ride from Hoyland. We found it in no time. With flaking, whitewashed walls, smothered with grime and graffiti, it looked like the kind of establishment where the rats wore rats wore overalls and you'd wipe your feet on the way out. Not that we cared. The club had an excellent reputation for breeding top class fighters and that was all that mattered at the end of the day. We were greeted by the owner, who showed us where to get changed. He was an Asian lad who came across hard as nails, so much so it was all we could do to look him in the eye. We didn't take our dobok, wearing vests, short and trainers instead, mingling in perfectly with other attendees; apart from Phil, that is, who towered above everybody else, looking like Roy Neary in the closing scene of *Close Encounters of the Third Kind*, being escorted inside the mothership by a gaggle of diminutive aliens. After explaining what we wanted to gain from the session, we were led straight to the ring for assessment. Phil was immediately pitted against an Asian boxer, who clearly had all the moves, dancing around the canvas like a moonwalking Michael Jackson, cautiously sussing the big man out. Phil allowed him a few seconds then just went for it, catching him with a vicious leg kick, knocking him clean out, much to the dismay of an array of shocked onlookers. Up next, I found myself facing a similar style opponent. It wasn't quite as quick a victory as Phil's, but the bout was still over in under a minute, a solid right leaving my challenger spark out on the canvass, looking like an Apache brave, listening for trains. That part complete, we were escorted from the danger zone to commence a bit of bag work. With Phil being so big, he was naturally put to work on the heavy bag. Suspended up high by metal chains, he pounded it so fast and so hard that the bracket gave way, collapsing an entire section of ceiling. Covered in dust and filth, the irate owner packed us straight off home for the day. Not only had we sparked his two best fighters, but we'd demolished half his club at the same time. The moral of the story? Don't mess with the Cloughfields boys when they've been out on the piss...

6. British Champion

My schooldays were gone in the blink of an eye. It didn't seem five minutes since I was enduring daily beatings from the nuns at St Helens Catholic School; now I was marching out of the gates of Kirk Balk for the final time in preparation to make my own way in the big bad world. In days of yore, I would have headed straight down the pit, same as countless generations before me. There was very little negotiation about it: that was just the way it was. Fathers would enrol sons at the same colliery years in advance, meaning kids would exit school Friday and enter adult life forty-eight hours later, a seismic shock to the system if ever there was one, commencement of fifty years blood, sweat and tears underground. A back-breaking, energy sapping, soul destroying, devil of an existence for many, it was the perfect working environment for plenty more, a handsomely paid job for life, augmented by lifelong friends, who would never, ever let you down. Unfortunately, that was then: the year-long miners' strike put paid to any ambitions I may have had of working for the NCB. Most of the pits had already closed. Local collieries Elsecar Main and Barrow had gone, as had Cortonwood, located two, three miles away between Wombwell and Brampton Bierlow, the site where the year-long strike originated. One or two far flung collieries remained open, but obviously weren't setting on. And besides, even if they had been, there would have been little point signing up for a career which would be over before it started. Fortunately, it was without too much trouble I landed a job at Cowan & Barrett, a plumbing and heating merchants in Sheffield. A hectic little number, working behind a busy trade counter, dealing with visiting tradespeople, it was just the ticket in my eyes. I got on well with everyone and soon settled into a weekly routine. As an added bonus, every Friday a nice young man from the wages department would pop round and give me a cellophane envelope, filled with money. Seriously, what more could I possibly want?

When Hoyland Taekwondo sadly called it a day, I attempted to fill the void by teaching taekwondo in a room at Cloughfields Community Centre. In true Arthur Daley style, I secured the space free of charge for six months and then a meagre couple of quid per hour thereafter. Just as good, it was only a stone's throw from my newly installed local pub, The Potter's Wheel. Phil wanted to rent the room for identical purposes and I allowed myself a wry smile when I discovered I'd beat him to it, long awaited retribution for him grassing me up several years previous, landing me with a hundred lines for drawing a cartoon version of English teacher, Mrs Orme. I'd intended keeping classes low key, but such was the popularity, I was soon experiencing a nightly invasion of attendees, hoping to enrol. I weeded out as many as I could, but was soon running at full capacity, a situation exacerbated by the arrival of several rising stars from the locally famous Mexborough team. A few months later and on the back of a string of impressive competition victories, I received the news I'd been dreaming of since Bruce Lee inadvertently gate-crashed my life all those years ago. All the hard work and tireless devotion had finally paid off. I was officially informed that I had been selected for a shot at the British Title, competing in the 48-52kg weight category in a competition to be held in Barrow-in-Furness a couple of months later. By the time the event came round, I'd worked out I would be just 17 years and 239 days old, an incredible achievement by any standards. Not that I was surprised. I was fully aware of my capabilities and never stopped believing that one day it would happen. I was just taken aback how quickly it came about, that's all. I was big and I was strong; but I was entering a real man's world now. And it naturally begged the question: would I be good enough? Would I be able to handle myself when the going got tough? Too right I would. No danger on that one. None whatsoever, in fact. I hadn't a clue who I'd be fighting. What they were called. What they looked like. How good they were and how far they had progressed in the sport. And the premise clearly applied in reverse. Anyone who was going to mix it with me had better get ready. Because I would be heading to Cumbria fully prepared and in prime physical condition. And a bigger handful didn't exist anywhere on the planet. I told everyone I could think of my news; family, friends and workmates. Word spread through the village like wildfire. I was already a well-known face and for plenty more reasons than my prowess in taekwondo. But this was different. I became an overnight celebrity. Everywhere I went, people would stop me and say hello. Some I knew. Some I didn't. Some I hadn't seen for years. Some I'd bumped into only last week, but completely ignored me. And I took great pleasure in reminding them of the fact before getting on my way. I couldn't deny I was liking it. Liking it a lot, in fact. Needless to say, I was utterly determined to make the best of the opportunity and bring home the bacon. It was written in the stars and I wouldn't allow anything to get in my way.

Training commenced immediately. Other than the occasional dodgy back, I was already incredibly fit. Elevating myself to fresh peaks was like topping up a brand-new Ferrari, just because you could. I ran for miles in the local countryside. Hill-work was essential for building stamina and there was no lack of inclines in the vicinity, many of which were former colliery slag-heaps, monstrous mounds of dirt, coal and shale, residue from a period of industry sadly consigned to history. I'd pound the muddy banks of nearby canals and circumnavigate the voluminous water feature which was Elsecar Reservoir. In the gym, morning, afternoon and evening, I religiously pumped weights to the point where mum said if my arm and leg muscles became any bigger, I'd float off into the atmosphere. I also made good use of my classes, tapping into the experience and expertise of the Mexborough lads. I'd coached each of them in turn for months now, paying meticulous attention to execution of the art; blocks, strikes, kicks and punches. Now it was my turn. Alan Riley, Sean O'Neil and father and son duo, Tom and Mick Bracken, were just a few of the lads I'd become really friendly with and I couldn't have asked for more by way of support. All the input and attention I'd given was very generously reciprocated, and some! It was tough going, physically as well as mentally, but ideal preparation for the rigours of what lay ahead, with specific focus upon secret weapon practise, a stunning taekwondo move capable of transforming the course of any contest.

Before I knew it, the training period was over and the time to put my body on the line had arrived. The competition was open to fighters in various weight categories, featherweight right through to heavyweight. Fights would be arranged by category with bout winners progressing to the next round until only two remained, who would then contest the final, with the winner being crowned British champion. Eight or nine local fighters were involved and we travelled up together by mini-bus the night before. Located in the extreme north-west of country, bordering the lakes, Barrow-in-Furness was a right old hike from South Yorkshire, constantly battling traffic and stop-starting at various services along the way. As you'd expect, it was a journey filled with piss-taking banter, sometimes crude, occasionally cruel, eternally funny. Everybody partook. It was confidence and character building at the same time and not a single person on board would have had it any other way. We stayed in digs somewhere on the edge of town. Don't ask me where, because I haven't a clue. All I know is it was pretty basic to say the least, shared rooms with dirty cracks all over the walls. I wouldn't have minded, but I'd already heard most of them. I was sharing with my designated coach for the event, Sean O'Neill. A good ten years or so older, Sean was a black belt 1st dan and incredibly experienced in every aspect of martial arts. Additionally, he was the biggest, hardest, roughest, toughest, son of a bitch you were ever likely to come across. Six-foot-five, if he said jump, you'd instinctively ask how high. Don't get me wrong. He was a genuinely nice bloke, incredibly popular and embarrassingly generous. Well, perhaps not generous, like. He was so tight, he squeaked when he walked. He could peel an orange in his pocket and when the kids came along, he had double-glazing fitted so they couldn't hear the ice-cream van. Only kidding, mate. I take it all back. And, if you believe that, there goes a flying pig, look! Seriously, though, Sean was the best man in the world to have in my corner. Knowing I had a wealth of knowledge, guile and know-how to draw upon was the biggest fillip and confidence booster I could have hoped for with what was to come.

The competition was held in huge sports hall, which made the Kirk Balk equivalent look like a spare room on mum's favourite TV show, *Little House on the Prairie*. Elevated seating, of the type you would see at US college basketball games, was erected around the edge of the fighting arena, supporting hundreds of spectators. With so many bouts to get through over so many weights, it had been decreed that two sets of mats would be used during the preliminary rounds, mimicking the format employed at Sheffield's Crucible Theatre during world championship snooker. Once down to semi-final and final bouts, one set would be removed, leaving all eyes concentrated upon a single event, watched over by the judges table at the top. It was well lit and airy inside. The perfect venue, I was determined to make the best of it, fully focused from the moment I set foot in the changing room, purposefully donning my dobok and hogu and carefully positioning my groin guard. It didn't matter that everyone in every single weight category was older than I was. Some had big handlebar moustaches or Hagrid-style beards I couldn't grow in a month of Sundays; not at my tender years, anyway. Some were patently more physically developed than I was, while others strutted around with an air of confidence and self-assuredness that created an irrepressible sense of invincibility, inevitably bequeathing fellow competitors raging inferiority complexes. No matter. They could have been tooled up for all I cared, because I *knew* this was my time. I'd believed it all my life. I believed it on the way up the motorway. And I believed it now. All I needed to do was have the courage of my convictions.

The atmosphere was electric as I stepped out to meet a suave looking Asian green belt, who I recall going by the name of Asif. Early bouts were two rounds of three minutes and I think it's fair to say that, for all my confidence and self-belief, I didn't do myself justice. Don't get me wrong; I knew I'd comfortably done enough to win, but was disappointed I hadn't completely demolished an opponent who clearly presented such an inferior skill set. The bout went to points and the result wasn't long coming: a unanimous decision in favour of the blue corner, Charlie Green. My second bout wasn't much better, another scrappy points win. Not that I had time to dwell on things. A short while later, I was back on the mats for my semi-final bout. We were down to one set of mats now and I knew I would need to improve my game if I was to progress to the final. My opponent was none other than Scott Whitehead, the Doncaster red belt, now black, who I'd sparred during my first grading. With an age and height advantage, he was clear favourite and he knew it just as well as I did. He stared at me unflinchingly during the build-up and I stared back, refusing to look away in case it was misinterpreted as a sign of weakness. Not that there was any animosity between us. Far from it, in fact. We'd met loads of times down the years, enjoying lengthy chats over all manner of martial arts related topics at various events and gradings we'd attended. Time to go, we met face to face, first showing our respect to the judges and then one another, bowing once with hands pressed together in prayer simulation. A quick word from the referee and we were off, two heavily contested rounds of three minutes ahead for a much-vaunted place in the final. I was first on the attack, but Scott repulsed my efforts, employing defensive blocks before going on the offensive with a series of punishing leg kicks. I fought back and fought back hard, sending him reeling with a flurry of powerful chest punches. He came again, then once more, edging ahead, until a burst of retaliatory activity right at the end ensured the round finished all square. Sean ushered me over, mopping my brow and calming me down as only he could. Leaning into me, he whispered into my ear, taking extra care to ensure no one lip read his advice.

"It's now or never, Greenie lad. Look at Whitehead. He's absolutely full of it. He knows the first round was close. But he's convinced he's got you now. It's written all over his face, look. Well, here's what we'll do. We'll let him think it even more. Sucker him in, Greenie. Go out there, puffing and blowing. Pretend you're knackered. Back off and show him just how tired you are. I guarantee it, he'll come for you and try and finish it. That's when you use your secret weapon. You remember your secret weapon, don't you, Greenie? The one we trained long and hard to perfect back in the motherland…?"

My mind flashed back to gruelling training sessions with the Mexborough crew and I immediately gave Sean a knowing wink, rehearsing the aforementioned technique over and over in my mind's eye. Locked and loaded, I bounced up and down on the spot, confident, enthused and invigorated, eager to get going once more. The audience roared and Sean gave me a mighty bear hug, slapping me so hard on the back, the resulting crack resonated through the hall like a snapping bullwhip. I hopped, skipped and jumped back into the fray, meeting Whitehead in the middle, gazing straight into his self-assured, penetrating glare. Sean was right. My opponent was good. Real good. And he was definitely sensing victory. Remembering my instructions, I puffed and blowed, purposely backing off as round two got underway, dancing circles around the mat, giving the distinct impression a battle for survival was my sole tactic. As predicted, Whitehead went straight on the attack, determined to finish it, catching me with several well-placed leg kicks. I allowed him one more for luck, then took an almighty stride backwards. In one swift movement, I brought my knee up high, extending my bottom leg to two o'clock, before bringing the ball of my foot down on my opponent's nose in a perfectly executed axe kick. He was unconscious before he hit the mat; or at least ought to have been. Displaying remarkable strength and courage, he scrambled to his feet, doing a newly born giraffe impression across the mat. The referee placed a hand upon his shoulder, steadying him, while he counted him down, reaching eight before deeming he was fit to continue. In what little time remained, I absolutely battered him with endless flurries of heavy kicks and punches. He defended bravely and somehow managed to ride it out. It was to no avail, though; he was roundly beaten and I had my place in the final.

My challenger in the final was a local black belt called Ganguli. He came with a fearsome reputation, after returning unbeaten from six weeks of event training in Korea under the watchful gaze of supreme, indigenous Grandmasters. I'd caught a glimpse of one of Ganguli's qualifying bouts and was shocked how easily he overcame a well-versed opponent, totally annihilating him in a few short seconds at the back end of round one. It would be easy to pretend I wasn't remotely phased by the contest ahead. In reality, though, I was absolutely shitting myself. Don't misunderstand me: the belief was burning as strong as ever and, somehow, I knew I'd find a way to prevail. I just didn't have a clue how, that's all. Sean did his absolute best, working on my confidence, telling me how good I was and that I'd nothing to be worried about, while advising me to go straight on the attack. It seemed sound advice; or at least until it was time to go, three rounds of three minutes with the competition's hot favourite. As we took our bows, a sudden attack of butterflies felt more like a plague of rampaging locusts, vacating my stomach and pouring into my diaphragm as if trying to effectuate a mass escape. As the audience roared with approval, I followed Sean's instructions and went straight on the offensive. Big mistake. What had been my secret weapon in the previous bout was suddenly my undoing, albeit temporarily. Ganguli's vicious axe kick sent me tumbling to the mat. Stunned, dazed and confused, I jumped back up again, re-engaging like I was connected to my opponent by a length of fishing elastic. He hit me again, same technique, a sledgehammer of a blow which sent me reeling. The referee should have counted me down to be fair, but for some reason let it go. Back at it, we circled and exchanged a couple of kicks. And, while we did, the cogs in my head continued to whirr, rapidly assimilating the situation, considering how best to combat my early setbacks. The good news was I realised he couldn't hurt me. Twice now he'd given me his best shot. Granted, it had left me dazed, but I was confident I could soak up his punishment all day if need be. Belief restored, I returned to the offensive, a display of sheer, raw aggression which brought the audience to its feet. Employing lightning speed, I attacked Ganguli head on, catching him painful leg kicks and a crunching blow to the collar bone. He didn't like it. Not a bit. His eyes became filled with fear and he backed off as far as possible. The way he was performing, I'm sure he would have retreated all the way to the gents' toilet if the referee had allowed it. I knew I had him now. And so it came to pass: round two was a complete walkover. Seriously, I think I could have beaten him blindfolded. And, if we'd been competing in a ring, he would definitely have been on the ropes, because all he did was defend, blocking kicks and punches as if his life depended on it. In layman's terms, I absolutely kicked the shit out of him.

By the time the final round arrived, I was so far ahead he needed snookers. I could easily have boxed clever, coasting to an easy points-win. Not a chance. My attitude, outlook and persona simply wouldn't allow it. Instead, I battered him again, beating the living daylights out of him from start to finish, so much so that the referee didn't bother waiting for the official result, instantaneously raising my arm aloft to the rumbustious and heartfelt cheers of a fully appreciative, enthused audience. Ganguli's corner were less than happy, vociferously contesting the result. Until Sean got involved, that is, putting them right on a few issues. They soon shut up then. But who wouldn't with that big bugger threatening all sorts? As for yours truly, I'd done it, just like I always knew I would. Who'd have thought it, eh? Charlie Green, a raggy lad from Hoyland's Cloughfields estate, British champion? Bit of a result, or what? I'd say so: one nil to the lad!

7. International Debut

I arrived home from Barrow with my face fixed in a permanent grin, anticipating a tickertape reception, fanfare of trumpets and key to the village as an absolute minimum. After all, it wasn't every day of the week Hoyland got the opportunity to greet a new British champion, was it? And what did I get? Jack bloody shit, that's what! The town was alive with people going about their daily business, but not a soul cast a glance in my direction as the mini-bus weaved a path through a series of avenues and thoroughfares en route to my beloved Cloughfields. I was dropped off at the door. Pegging the washing out, mum about turned and waved when she heard the door slam, smiling as I marched towards her, kit bag slung triumphantly over my shoulder. She wasn't smiling a few seconds later, though, turning away in disgust as a few of the lads stuck their big, hairy arses up against the window, to the background of a boisterous, disjointed chorus of: *"By the light of the silvery moon..."*

A couple of weeks later, I was ready to embark upon the next stage of my journey after being invited to participate in Team Great Britain international trials in the sports hall of Dearneside Comprehensive School in nearby Goldthorpe. On the back of my big win, I'd been briefed in advance that all I had to do was turn up and selection would be guaranteed. Nevertheless, I still wanted to make the best possible impression, giving everything during a punishing fitness test which preceded sparring; seemingly endless round of sprints, star jumps, knee jumps, kick-backs and burpees. All in all, it was the toughest work-out I'd ever endured, especially when combined with an hour of strenuous pad-work straight after. The sparring was equally brutal, full-on contact performed at a frenetic pace, with every last fighter giving his all, desperate to stand out from the crowd. As anticipated, I received positive news, returning home with spring in my step, announcing I would be fighting internationally in a challenge competition versus Ireland to be held in Doncaster in a month's time. Proud as punch, dad immediately volunteered to take me, another big fillip at the end of a perfect few weeks and made to feel even better when our Bev bought everyone a chippie tea, a celebratory treat before her long-anticipated wedding, just around the corner now.

The venue was Hatfield Country Club. Surrounded by beautiful countryside and boasting a stunning, immaculately kept eighteen-hole golf course, it was the poshest place I'd visited in my life. People got married there, taking advantage of incredible five-star accommodation and facilities, including the best restaurants for miles around. We were competing in a large function room to the rear, dominated by plush, Axminster carpets and twin bars, force-feeding alcohol like there was no tomorrow. Competition mats were laid out in the middle, with hundreds of chairs arranged around the outside and a judges table at one end. Our head coach was the celebrated Tony Quigley, who spent one-on-one time with team members, discussing and formulating plans, tactics and aspirations. As per usual, I was fighting in the 48-52kg section and couldn't wait to get cracking, eagerly seeking out my opponent, clarifying what I was up against. One of the Irish lads pointed him out and I would have quaked in my boots if I'd been wearing any. Don't stop believing temporarily became *stop believing*, because I seriously didn't think I stood a chance. He was good ten years my senior and absolutely towered over me. A real pretty boy with a thick, black moustache and a Kevin Keegan style perm, he was walking around topless, strutting his stuff, practising strikes and blocks in the company of a gaggle of giggling female groupies, avariciously admiring his suntanned torso and rippling six-pack. Someone conveniently mentioned he was a black belt 3rd dan. Worse still, embroidered upon his dobok were the words: Seamus O'Callaghan, Instructor. Heart in mouth, I raced to find dad, discovering him out front, sipping on a cup of tea. I explained the situation and pleaded with him to leave, unable to bear the thought of him seeing me having the crap beaten out of me. He refused outright, insisting he was staying put; win, lose or draw, he was determined to see me perform. In days of yore, I may have folded. Not now, though; I was a grown up and made of much sterner stuff, stubbornly standing my ground. I told him if he didn't go home, *I* would, meaning he wouldn't get to see me fight either way. It did the trick. Finishing his tea, he reluctantly turned for the exit; but not before pausing to give me an impromptu pep talk.

"Don't worry, our Charles," he enthused, giving me an enormous bear hug. "You're Barnsley bred, remember. Thick in the head. You were born hard. Don't be scared. Don't be intimidated. Just go out there and do the business. Knock him for bloody six…"

That sorted, I commenced the process of getting my head together, fully aware it would be a long and probably painful night ahead if I didn't. It was easier than I thought. Dad departing relieved the pressure enormously, enabling me to boost sapped confidence levels and refocus upon core strengths and achievements. I reminded myself I was a fighter. And a bloody good one as well. A red belt now, I was the current British champion. Soon I'd be a black belt. Fit as a butcher's dog, I wasn't just physically strong, I was also extremely mentally adept. Nothing phased me or ever would. Which begged the question: what the fuck was I getting all wound up about? Alright, so my opponent might look the part. But was he any better than I was? Somehow, I didn't think so. I'd yet to meet anyone who could match my talent, exuberance and determination to succeed. And I seriously doubted I ever would; certainly not this night, anyway. Thinking about it, Seamus wasn't much of a looker, either. And all it took was a glance in the mirror to confirm the assertion. Now *that's* what a pretty boy looks like, I grinned, seductively fingering my chin. The female groupies filed by and I spotted them eyeing me in my freshly pressed dobok, providing final corroboration if I needed it. I winked in return and a blonde in a short skirt and low-cut top winked back, waggling her fingers at me. I smiled: stop believing suddenly became *don't stop believing* again. The confidence had returned and I couldn't have been happier if I tried.

The room was draped in Union Jacks and Irish tricolours. A healthy number of Irish supporters had made the trip over and were already three sheets to the wind, engaging in raucous football style chants with their British cousins. It was only banter, though; both sets of fans remained respectful for the national anthems and swiftly settled down when the competition got started. The overwhelming majority of observers were martial artists of differing degrees of experience. Instinctively polite, dignified and humble, there wasn't a hint of trouble underneath the unruly, boisterous façade. With ten bouts in total, I was informed I was up fourth. While I waited, I warmed up and engaged in a spot of pad-work in the dressing room. Phil and Sean had travelled over to lend their support and were a massive help alongside Quigley, talking tactics and helping me warm up. We lost the first bout on points, bitterly disappointing as it had been one of our bankers. Things didn't get any better. The second bout went exactly the same way and we were soon three down when our contestant was knocked spark out in the first twenty seconds. With the odds stacked firmly against us, Quigley took me to one side for quick team talk. Placing a hand on each shoulder, he curved his lips into a smile then stared deep into my eyes.

"It's on you, Greenie lad. I said when I first saw you that you were one of the best young prospects I'd ever seen. And you haven't proven me wrong. On the contrary, you've surpassed all expectations to progress as far as you have at such a tender age. British champion, lad. Let's say that again, shall we? *British champion*, and now you're representing your country at international level. Remember how you demolished Ganguli? Well, I want you to go out there and do the same to Seamus. Don't get me wrong, he's a decent lad. But let me tell you this much…he can't lace your fucking boots. So, get out there and do a job on him, do you hear? Show us just how good you really are…"

Doting upon Tony's words, I met Seamus head-on. From the very first contact, I was able to relax, because I realised that I had the measure of him. For all his experience and physical superiority, he was totally devoid of answers and found me impossible to handle. I was too strong in every department. I was too quick, for one; too skilled as a martial artist; too resolute, focused and determined, with an insatiable desire to win. His head must have been a spin as I battered him from start to finish of every single round, leaving the judges with the simplest decision of the night. As the referee raised my arm in victory, the British supporters went absolutely wild, thrilled to finally have a win on the board. To the tune of the oh pretty baby chorus from Frank Valli classic, *Can't Take My Eyes Off You*, they collectively began to sing: *"Oh, Charlie Green, you are the love of my life. Oh, Charlie Green, I'd let you shag my wife. Oh, Charlie Green, I want curly hair too…"*

With the score now 1-3, we were at least in with a sniff. I was on such a high after my win, I went straight to the payphone in reception, calling my dad to give him the news, drawing curious glances from passers-by; hotel staff, guests and groups of people, arriving for a meal. It wasn't difficult to understand why. Still wearing my dobok, I must have looked like a Jedi Knight, dialling 999 to report a missing light sabre. The phone answered first ring and it was the big man himself who answered. In typical Barnsley fashion, he didn't say much when I broke the news, responding with a pig-like grunt and a very abrupt I told you so. Then he was gone, disappearing to watch the end of *Crocodile Dundee*. *This is a knife*, he cackled as he put the phone down. Yeah, I grinned, curling my hand into a ball, replaying my fight with Seamus; and *this* is a fist!

By the time I got back, we'd chalked up another victory, making the score 2-3. A couple of brilliant performances later and we were one up. We had the momentum now. The lads were well and truly up for it, ensuring we battled, scrapped and fought for every point of every remaining round to keep our noses in front, eventually securing a 6-4 victory, as unlikely as it may have seemed early doors. A humongous piss up followed, all the British and Irish lads together, with not a hint of hostility, as you'd expect from a bunch of fine, young, respectful martial artists. While we may have triumphed on the mats, however, we didn't stand a chance when it came to boozing. Seriously, every single one of the Irish mob spilled more down their shirts than any of our lot supped; a feat they would doubtless regret come morning.

Wishing dad had hung around, after all, I suddenly realised I'd no means of getting home. Luckily, Sean and Phil came to the rescue, kindly offering me a lift back. Before we left, however, there was one last piece of business to take care of. Kit bag slung over my shoulder, I was taken to one side by Tony, who informed me there was a return contest on the island of Ireland, a little over eight weeks from now, twin bouts at separate venues, and that I'd been selected to participate. I was completely bowled over at the news, punching the air and whooping with delight. As soon as he confirmed the dates, however, I deflated like a pair of over-sized bellows, palms bared like I was out checking for rain.

"I'm afraid I can't attend, Tony. It's…it's the same weekend as our Bev's wedding."

Tony immediately commenced the task of talking me round. Unsurprisingly, I capitulated instantly. I didn't like it, mind. Not one bit. But Bev would have to understand. Alright, so it was the biggest day of her life; but it was also mine, the opportunity to represent my country on foreign shores and I wasn't passing it up for anything. As soon as I told him I was in, he disappeared as fast as his legs could carry him, probably before I changed my mind again. The blonde in the short skirt reappeared. All over me like a rash, it was obvious I'd pulled. I asked if she'd like to come back to mine and take a look at my ceiling. It was then I spotted Sean's red Ford Capri, steering for the exit. Without so much as a by-your-leave, I set off running, traversing the grounds like the *Six Million Dollar Man*, waving my kit bag around, desperately trying to make myself heard. And, the faster I ran, the more Sean accelerated, engulfing me in great clouds of stinking petrol fumes. A few seconds later, he was through the gates, leaving me red-faced and breathless in the middle of the drive. Glancing my watch, I cursed and swore and stamped my feet: ten o'clock. *Now* what was I going to do? I didn't dare ring my dad. Not having packed him off home, anyway. Well and truly stranded, I sighed so hard, I made a noise like an express train, passing through a deserted railway station at midnight. All fell silent. Until the welcome sound of Phil's beery baritone materialised, that is, cutting through the cool night air like a red-hot knife through butter.

"Come on, Jack," he yelled, hanging out of the window. "Get in and make it snappy. We haven't all night, you know. There's a pint in The Potter's Wheel with Jack's name on it. And guess what…you're paying, Jack."

8. Ireland Away

In the weeks leading up to Ireland, I trained like crazy, same as I always did, a mix of personal work-outs supplemented by supervised team training at Dearneside. In between time, I also spent lots of time with my mates. Touching eighteen now, the days of twenty a side football matches had finally been consigned to history. The big thing nowadays was endless beer swilling nights in the village. Hoyland had a thriving night scene, eight or nine licensed premises within close proximity of one another, perfect for a good old fashioned pub crawl, inevitably starting and finishing at The Potter's Wheel. One night, Chris Oldfield joined us after returning home on leave from the army. An intrinsic member of the original raggy lads' gang, he never made any secret about his ambition to join the forces. A few months out of school, he fulfilled his dream, accepting the Queen's shilling. Brought up on war films and with a fascination for military history, I very nearly followed him, eventually bailing out, using my blossoming taekwondo career as a get-out clause. Listening to Chris, however, regaling the tap-room with exciting tales of squaddie life, I suddenly found my interest rekindled. He'd completed his basic training and had seen active duty in Northern Ireland, manning checkpoints and even being ordered to return fire after coming under attack during a foot patrol in bandit country. He'd made mates from every corner of the UK and went out on the piss with them when and wherever possible, habitually chatting up girls and getting into scraps with the locals. His stories left me feeling extremely envious, reigniting my captivation to the point where I intentionally went out of my way to visit the Army Recruiting Office in Barnsley bus station. The recruiting sergeant took my details, asking for a bit of background information; what was I about; what were my hobbies and interests? Sport, I replied, confidently, letting it be known I'd had football trials for Barnsley and was a taekwondo martial artist, who had competed internationally and also won the British championship. His face lit up like an angler, bagging up with a record haul of fish. He suddenly came over all pally, throwing an arm round me, extolling what a great life it was in between a couple of phone calls to his superiors. He couldn't give me the news quick enough when it came: I was lined up for a guaranteed place in Parachute Regiment training. All I had to do was get my parents to sign the approval forms and I was in. I told him I'd have a think about it and think about it I did. Overnight was all it took. The prospect of becoming a Red Devil and donning the coveted maroon beret was just too much. Mum, on the other hand, was far from convinced, doing all she could to talk me out of it. She failed, miserably. Well, nearly, anyway. When she offered to cough up the cash for a brand-new, state-of-the-art Commodore Amiga computer, I yielded instantaneously. The army would have to look elsewhere for its next Johnny Rambo, because I was staying put on good old Cloughfields. Good old mum. She did exactly the same a few years previous. When I broke my bike chain, I borrowed Phil's racer to do my paper round, coming off when the brakes failed on a downhill stretch. I broke my wrist and had to go through to A&E for a pot on. Returning the mangled frame later, I gave him a right old roasting, challenging him over why he didn't tell me about the faulty brakes. His response was simple: you never asked, Jack. The week after, I'd been due to fight top local competitor, Alan Riley, at Sheffield's Crucible Theatre, a competition in which, coincidentally, Phil became the stand out contestant, bolstering his growing reputation by battering anyone who dared to stand in his way. Alan ribbed me endlessly when he heard my news, declaring I'd broken my arm on purpose to avoid having to face him. Imagine the look on his face, then, when I offered to cut the pot off, enabling the fight to go ahead. Luckily for him, mum found out. Knowing what a desperado I was, she reached for her purse and offered me a tenner not to do it. Needless to say, I took her up on the offer. Put simply, I snapped her bloody hand off.

A big positive to come out of the period leading up to Ireland was that our Bev was totally cool about me not attending her wedding. She said she would have preferred me to be there, naturally; but she also made it clear she understood how much my martial arts career meant to me and wouldn't do anything to hinder my progress. I loved my big sis, still do, an emotion clearly reciprocated; otherwise, we wouldn't have been able to arrive at such an amicable agreement. As anticipated, one or two niggles erupted elsewhere. Nothing serious, though. And, thankfully, it all blew over quickly, especially when I agreed to have a picture taken in my best suit, standing alongside Bev in her wedding dress. I was so relieved when it was all sorted. The last thing I wanted was any festering rifts at home while I was away on international duty. I needed to have my mind fully focused. I couldn't afford any distractions and neither could the team. Ireland away was as tough a gig as imaginable and everyone needed to be fully focused and fighting fit. Team Great Britain and a couple of dozen supporters travelled overnight by car and mini-bus, arriving in Holyhead in preparation to catch the morning ferry to Dublin. I travelled in the same transport as Sean and Phil. Another local fighter, Paul Oxtoby, was with us, as were Tom and Mick Bracken. It may have been mid-August, but there was a proper storm brewing as we boarded. None of us possessed sea legs and so knew what to expect when we got going. In typical Barnsley fashion, we approached the situation head on, ordering a full English breakfast, washing it down with a couple of pints of beer. Big mistake. The weather was rough as toast, ensuring the ferry pitched and rolled the entire voyage, almost six hours in total. I'd never seen anything like it, scores of people, staggering around, being sick. Puke was everywhere. On the decks. In the corridors. All over the toilets and blocking up the sinks. At one point, I found myself hung over the pot, watching a length of sick, swinging pendulum-like from my chin. Now, everyone who knows me will vouch for the fact I have an extremely fertile imagination. Little wonder then a couple of adjacent piles of vomit raised my creativity to unprecedented levels. As my head came over all woozy, I envisioned the mounds deep in conversation. Don't ask me how, or why, or where it came from, because I genuinely haven't a clue; all I know is it happened. One pile said: we're lost, aren't we? And the other replied: are we heckers like lost…I was brought up round here. I may have passed out after; I'm not altogether sure. I just remember a big, bear-like hand, rattling my shoulders and a familiar sounding voice, assaulting my eardrums.

"Alright, Jack? Waken up. We're here, Jack. We're here. Are you coming, Jack, or what, Jack, are you coming…?"

An hour later, we arrived at the hostel, our accommodation for the next three nights. We checked into a shared dormitory and enjoyed a well-earned shower. Then we went for a walk round the town alongside a few pals from Doncaster. We were international martial artists and fit as fuck. We were also very young. We knew we shouldn't. Try as we might, though, we couldn't resist it. The competition wasn't until tomorrow and so we hit the pubs and hit them hard, arriving back five or six hours later, completely rat-arsed. Everyone else was in bed and didn't appreciate the boisterous intrusion, lots of screaming, singing and shouting. As the lights went on, one lad sat up bolt straight, glaring angrily across the room. With a pale complexion and greased, jet-black hair, he looked Dracula, rising from the grave. He referenced Grandmaster Sutherland, a renowned disciplinarian who was in charge of team affairs, stating he wouldn't stand for such misbehaviour and would quickly restore order upon his return. Phil told him where to get off and we eventually turned in, banking a decent night's kip. It must have worked wonders, because, next morning, we were all fresh as daisies, even partaking in a pre-breakfast jog around the local neighbourhood. Sutherland arrived and gave a team talk, reminding us of our responsibilities as sporting ambassadors. We should display integrity, respect and self-control at all times, he insisted, not partaking in any activity which could bring our country into disrepute. Dracula opened his mouth to speak, but zipped it when Phil treated him to a stare which was nothing short of pure evil. If he'd uttered so much as a word of dissent, he would have been heading back to his grave for good.

We were transported to the venue, a nearby working men's club. Getting straight changed, we warmed up in a flag-draped, voluminous concert room, where the competition was taking place. Things moved fast. Before we knew it, we were lining up for the national anthems, enthusiastically supported by visiting and home fans alike. It was an incredible atmosphere and looked like being a cracking contest, underlined when we were personally introduced to a bunch of particularly rough-looking opponents. I'd expected Seamus, but he hadn't been selected after such a comprehensive defeat in Doncaster. Instead, I was fighting a scrawny looking red belt with a pimple laden face to match. He didn't look confident and I swear he was trembling when we shook hands. I could have been mistaken. Somehow, though, I doubted it. There was an unmistakable look of trepidation in his eyes, confirmed a few minutes later when I spotted him loitering in the background, watching me doing a spot of pad-work with Sean. Shortly after, I received a notification from Sutherland, passed on to him by the organisers. The Irish lad had decided he didn't want to fight me and I'd been given a bye, with the points going to Team Great Britain. Word soon broke that he'd discovered I was British champion and simply didn't fancy it, even more so after watching my work-out. He'd gone home with his dad and was going to spend the day trout fishing instead. In all my years, I'd never known anything like it. It was so untypical of martial artists per se and left everyone totally perplexed. On the positive side, it did my reputation no harm whatsoever. I became the hot topic on everyone's lips and was even asked for a few autographs in between coaching the lads and watching the contest unfold from the sidelines.

With an emphatic 7-3 victory in the bag, the next morning we headed by coach to Gorey, County Wexford, to complete the second part of the encounter, fighters and supporters embarking together upon a journey across seventy miles or so of the greenest countryside I'd ever seen. It was even greener than the fabulous greenbelt of land surrounding Hoyland, if that were possible; but at least now I knew why they called it the Emerald Isle. We had a guest along, a hardy-looking local chap going by the name of Patrick. No one knew his surname or even why he was there; but we would, eventually. And we'd be glad of his presence as well, forever grateful to Sutherland for having the foresight to invite him along. Upon arrival, we had a walk around the town, doing a spot of window shopping, eyeing up mementoes and souvenirs. Not that anyone bought anything. Nobody understood Irish punts and everyone was shit scared of paying over the odds for things. The locals didn't seem particularly enamoured by our presence. Everywhere we went, people scowled or made sure they gave us an extremely wide berth. There was a fairground in operation with rides also priced up in punts. One of the lads decided to ask a woman how much a punt was worth in pounds and she reared straight up at him, spitting in his face and calling him an English bastard. A large group of males started to gather in the aftermath. With trouble in the air, we tactically retreated. If it had all kicked off, and fortunately it didn't, we would have absolutely kicked the shit out of them: they just didn't know it, that's all.

The event was being held in a sports hall. Gym equipment had been removed for the duration of the encounter and was currently lining corridors, leading to toilets and changing rooms. As ever, seating had been arranged around centrally located mats with judges positioned adjacent. It hadn't gone unnoticed that the atmosphere of the streets had followed us inside. The only flag on display was the Irish tricolour and we were quickly informed there would be no rendition of *God Save the Queen* only *Amhrán na bhFiann*, national anthem of Ireland. As a protest, we refused to enter the fighting arena until the formalities were over. Our move went down like the proverbial lead balloon. Did we give a shit? Did we bollocks! The wind suddenly got up, driving pouring rain against the windows, mimicking conditions on the way over, adding to the inauspicious atmosphere. Expressions of local spectators and fighters alike were immovably grim, harsh and unforgiving. The Irish team was a totally different set of lads from the ones we took on in Dublin. We tried to make conversation, lending our opponents customary levels of politeness, courtesy and respect. We needn't have put ourselves out. The response we received was curt at best, a series of mumbled replies, principally unintelligible grunts, moans and groans. As for the competition, I may have received a bye in Dublin, but I would definitely be fighting today. My opponent was the 48-52kg Irish Champion, setting up a clash of titans. Older than I was, he had a big height advantage. It mattered not. I had my game plan and intended sticking to it: he was going to get some of what Seamus got and that's all there was to it. First up, I battered him, winning every single round with ease. Irish Champion or not, he never stood a chance, beaten by superior skills, speed and stamina. Going against the grain, he was totally magnanimous in defeat. He knew he'd not so much been beaten by the better man, but totally annihilated. It's just a shame the Irish supporters didn't take a leaf out of his book, booing and jeering as I circled the mat, taking a bow north, south, east and west.

My victory set the tone for the night. A more one-sided encounter, I couldn't begin to imagine. Every single one of the lads fought magnificently, bringing home the bacon. The only loss of the evening came during the final bout, which concluded when our man was almost decapitated by a flying drop kick. Boos and jeers trailed us all the way back to the dressing room. Normally, we'd have taken a leisurely shower; perhaps retired to the bar for a couple of swift ones. Not tonight, though. Genuinely worried for the safety of all concerned, we were washed and changed in record time, gathering in a meeting room to the rear. Through the window, we could see the bus waiting for us at the top of the car park. When a scout returned, reporting a baying mob outside the front entrance, we made the decision to escape via the adjacent fire exit, heading single file and in silence across the tarmac. By the time we'd boarded and completed a head count, the coach was completely surrounded by locals. There must have been three or four hundred of the buggers, predominantly aggressive males, snapping, snarling and scowling with rage. Age range was mid-teens right through to late-fifties and I seriously think if anyone had been stupid enough to alight, they would have been torn limb from limb. They were banging on the windows and rocking the bus to such an extent it felt like it was made of balsa. Irish flags were flying and they were singing republican songs: *Go on Home British Soldiers* and *The Boys of the Old Brigade*. Sitting in the front seat was our guest, Patrick. We still didn't know why he was present, but had every intention of finding out. With the situation continuing to deteriorate, a group of us approached him and demanded answers. Who was he? What was he doing here? What was going on outside? Could things get any worse? And, most importantly, was there anything he could do that might make a difference?

"Come on, mister," I asked, shooting from the hip. "What's the score? Are we going to get out of this alive, or what...?"

Patrick peeled back his jacket, revealing a shoulder holster and pistol. It was the first time in my entire life I'd heard Hoylanders, gasping with shock. Normally, *we'd* be the ones handing out nasty surprises. He slowly got up and the driver hit a button on the dash. The door whooshed, then concertinaed open, allowing him to step down and confront the mob ringleaders head on. The door closed, denying us the opportunity to hear what was being said. Whatever it was, it was obviously serious stuff, lots of bared teeth and finger pointing, mainly from Patrick. He had it sorted in no time. Climbing back aboard, he waved a hand, dispersing the crowds like Moses, parting the Red Sea. The coach departed and an enormous cheer went up as we finally left Gorey behind.

Back in Dublin, Sutherland awarded me my red belt with a black stripe as reward for my efforts. One more big push and I'd be black belt. I could hardly believe it. Well, I could, because it was never in doubt from day one; not with immeasurable amounts of talent and belief, coursing through my entire being. It was what I'd been put on earth for: it was my destiny.

9. The Carroty Kid

I absolutely *loved* martial arts. A part of my life for six or seven years now, it was an intrinsic component of who I was, an integral feature of my make-up, as important as ancestral genes, the blood coursing through my veins, or an unyielding devotion to my family. I was British champion. I had fought internationally, recently defeating the Irish champion. I was young. I was fit. I was virile. I trained daily and was at the absolute top of my game. I was also determined to improve myself at every turn, obsessively practising and refining techniques, slowly but surely perfecting my art. Woe betide anyone who came up against me in competition. Because it wouldn't end well. Not for me. For them. Because I'd batter them. Well and truly. Not because I had anything against anyone. Not one iota, in fact. I'd batter them for one reason and one reason only: because they were there; because they had the temerity to step out and challenge me in competition. That's was I was like, I'm afraid. I couldn't help it. I possessed an insatiable desire to succeed; a fire which couldn't be extinguished and still burns as brightly today as it did way back yonder.

Always ready to try something new, I accompanied a martial artist pal of mine on a Saturday afternoon trip to a karate open tournament at Concord Sports Centre in the Firth Park area of Sheffield. John Harper was his name, or Beaujolais as we preferred to call him, on account he was a fancy licker. Interpret that as you wish. All you need to know is Beaujolais was as hard as nails and I was happy he was at my side as we trapesed a maze of terraced streets en route to the venue. I'm not saying it was rough, like, but Rottweilers were walking about in pairs and the rats were carrying flick knives. A taekwondo black belt by this stage, I'd never had a bash at karate, but was of such a standard now, I was convinced I could handle the discipline with ease. I'd read up on it extensively and so wasn't going in totally blind. While taekwondo concentrated on kicking techniques, the focus of karate was on hand strikes, which I'd been working on obsessively since the infamous visit with Phil to the Wicker's muay Thai gym. As ever, the competition was taking place in a voluminous hall, the biggest I'd encountered yet, in fact, decked out in the usual format, with rows and rows of seating, rising high to nestle against perimeter walls, overlooking squares of interlinked blue and red mats. Beaujolais and I registered for competition and were directed to a holding area where we would be categorised by weight. British champion or not, I was amongst the youngest present, with the majority of competitors aged twenty-five plus. I won't make any bones about it: there looked to be some right hard bastards about; men who looked like they had been hewn from pure granite, engaging in rumbustious warm up sessions, fine tuning karate moves likely to have decapitated someone had they connected. Don't ask me how, but word quickly spread about who I was; my achievements and spiralling reputation. As I was lining up to be weighed, I became conscious of innumerable sets of eyes, staring me down alongside a cacophony of whispered comments. One or two ventured up close, purposely barging into me, attempting to instigate a reaction. Remaining calm, I refused to take the bait, winding up the impromptu audience even further. All of a sudden, every man and his dog wanted a piece of me. I found myself bombarded with all manner of physical threats, much to the amusement of Beaujolais, who responded to the taunts with a series of fast-moving tongue pokes, underlining his fancy licker reputation. The weigh-in was a breeze. I'd been training hard and knew I was right on the mark for my category. Imagine my shock then, when it was announced by officials that I was a couple of kg overweight. Smelling a rat, I vehemently protested. Unfortunately, they were having none of it, dissing my objections outright, insisting the scales were properly calibrated. Unless I could make the weight, I was out, period. And, so, I did the only thing I could think of, making a beeline for the bog, taking up residence on the pot, shitting for England to the point where I could kak through the eye of a needle. It did the trick. Several pounds lighter, I was grudgingly given the green light to compete.

Donning my dobok, I commenced my warm up under the supervision of Beaujolais, a long stretching session followed by an intensive period of pad and bag work. Every kick and punch connected with power and precision, attracting a crowd of forty, fifty or more; a mix of officials, contestants and spectators. The taunting mob of earlier suddenly started to disperse. Looking like a young Burt Reynolds, with curly, dark hair, good looks and magnificently toned body, it seemed no one wanted to fight me anymore. The development worked wonders for my confidence. The sight of numerous karate brown, red and black belts, scuttling off like rats, fleeing a sinking ship, didn't half give me a boost. It made me realise what a threat I posed to long established exponents of the sport and convinced me more than ever I could make a serious impact on the afternoon.

The draw was made and I was amongst the first to fight, stepping out to perform in front of a crowd which must have numbered a couple of thousand or more. The noise was deafening, lots of hand clapping, screaming and shouting, as partisan groupings vociferously bellowed support for their preferred contestant. I must have generated a healthy backing because, the instant I raised my hand in salute, the volume turned up even higher, hundreds of people I'd never even met, roaring me on. Competing minus hogu, I was summoned by a pair of surly looking referees, laying down the law in advance of a bout of two three-minute rounds. Wearing gum-shield and shin pads, I vividly recall closing my eyes, revising basic rules before the fight got underway, drumming it into myself not to forget that punching and head shots were permitted, with points awarded for strikes. I was paired against a black belt with a pale complexion and a shock of ginger hair. No one told me his name, so I immediately nicknamed him the carroty kid after learning he fashioned himself upon bullied teenager turned martial artist, Daniel, in *The Karate Kid*. He was a right ugly bastard, not a pretty boy like yours truly. Last time I saw a face like his, Frankie Dettori was whipping it. And I was about to make it look even worse, if that were possible, kicking and punching seven bells out of him, knocking him down twice in what was probably the easiest fight I'd ever had. Beaujolais informed me afterwards that the crowd roared approval from start to finish. I must have really been in the zone, because I couldn't remember a thing; but the huge round of applause I received at the end is something which will stay with me forever. I met the carroty kid in the middle and we touched fists, bowing with respect. He'd done his best. Unfortunately, it hadn't been anything like good enough. Poor kid, he had so many bumps and bruises across his face and head, he looked like freak show exhibit John Merrick in *The Elephant Man*.

Mind already in the next round, I was about to receive the most bizarre of knockout blows. Not a physical blow, an immaculately placed kick or strike; but a metaphoric blow, resulting directly from the referee's decision. Boos rang through the hall as the contest was duly awarded to the carroty kid, who immediately spread his palms in embarrassment. He knew the score. He knew he'd lost. He knew it was a fix. He knew there was only one winner and that the last thing the organisers wanted was a taekwondo champion waltzing in, showing the karate lads how it was done. To his credit, he marched straight over and had his say on the matter, verbally communicating his objections to karate's equivalent of Maradona's hand of God. He was wasting his time. The reaction of the referees said it all, a nasty, snarling, tell-tale volley of abuse, causing him to wheel off in humiliation, slamming the door as he disappeared into the changing room with an almighty huff on. Determined to make my feelings known, I confronted the crooked pair head on, giving them a right piece of my mind. As anticipated, it didn't make the slightest difference. The result stood and I stormed off in the foulest of moods. It must have shown, because people were scattering like I'd just pulled the pin on a hand grenade. With the fancy licker in tow, I got changed, pausing for a parting word on the way out, offering to take the illicit judges outside and thump their ears for them. They politely declined my offer and I can't say I blamed them, either. Make no mistake, I'd have gone through the pair like a dose of bloody salts.

I soon got over it. Nothing a few beers wouldn't sort out, I had a shower then got my glad rags on and popped round to Phil's house, tapping twice on the door. It opened in a flash and there was the big man, leaning on the jamb, looking like he'd lost a bob and found a tanner. I asked if he fancied a few jars in the village and he shook his head, vigorously, as if I'd just invited him to a bingo night out the local Darby & Joan club. He picked a bogie and flicked it. I swerved it like Spiderman, dodging a bullet, while admiring an inch long scar on his index finger, accrued several years earlier in our hallway. What a laugh that was. We used to keep a piranha fish in a bowl and would often engage in a worm dangling game, seeing whose bait lasted longest. On this particular occasion, the piranha inadvertently latched on to Phil's finger, feasting on flesh before he was able to prise it free, using a hurriedly requisitioned butter knife from the kitchen. Peering back at him, I spread my arms in disbelief.

"But you've *got* to come out, Phil."

"But I can't, Jack. I'm skint, Jack."

"Skint, my arse. I wish I was a bob behind you. Besides, it's my birthday, isn't it? You wouldn't let me down on beer day, would you…?"

The sympathy card worked a treat. Fifteen minutes later, we were propping up the bar at The Potter's Wheel in advance of a raucous pub crawl with the lads. Come closing time, we got a taxi into town and went clubbing at popular night scene, Japanese Whispers. A couple of scraps broke out while we were there. Nothing serious and we did our best not to get involved. It was never going to happen, though. Big Phil attracted trouble like dog shit attracted flies and he was soon involved in a major fracas in the middle of the dance floor. I was at the bar when it kicked off and it was all over before I got there. Needless to say, we were summarily ejected, unceremoniously dumped in the street, rolling around on the pavement, laughing our heads off. As we clambered in a taxi for the return journey, Phil turned to me with a puzzled look on his face.

"That was great fun, Jack. But I *do* need to mention something. Remind me: what's today's date?"

A big, beaming smile, spreading inexorably across my face, I shrugged, nonchalantly, knowing full well what was coming next.

"The twenty-second, isn't it?"

"Of what though, Jack? Of what?"

"September, isn't it?"

"Yeah, that's right, Jack. And your birthday's not until November. So…how come we're out celebrating your birthday tonight?"

The taxi cornered a bend, force of gravity throwing us together, instigating a little wrestling match on the back seat. The great pillock. I swear, he'd have believed the moon was made of green cheese if I'd told him.

10. A One in Ten: A Number on a List

Another day went by. Another week. Another month. Before I knew it, my real birthday had been and gone, celebrated with another heavy night on the piss with Phil. Christmas was gone in the blink of an eye. A new year dawned, 1991. I was getting old now. In a year, I'd be twenty. And I didn't like it, already starting to worry my best years were behind me. Little did I know, but the wonderful roller coaster of life had mapped out a spectacular and tumultuous journey ahead, a series of exhilarating and sometimes scary events, which I could never have imagined during my formative years. Looking forward, I made myself a promise: a sincere vow to make the most of every single day and push myself as hard as possible to be the best I could possibly be. Life wasn't a rehearsal: it was a one-off gift and I needed to make sure I milked every waking second. Everything was going along hunky-dory; until, typically, disaster struck. Well, it didn't really. It just felt like it at the time. In a bolt from the blue, my position at Cowan & Barrett was made redundant. I was gutted beyond belief. It was my first proper job. I'd met some brilliant people and fully expected to be there until retirement. After an intense period of reflection, however, predominantly drinking The Potter's Wheel bar dry, I realised there was no cause for remorse. Alright, so it wasn't what I wanted to hear; but I was a firm believer everything happened for a reason and that this was just another twist and turn along life's long and chequered journey. All roads led somewhere. And, for the first time ever, mine led to Hoyland dole office. With deindustrialisation of the surrounding area continuing unabated, it's fair to say there wasn't a lot going. And, so, as the old song alluded, I was a one in ten, a number on a list; nobody knew me, but I was always there, a statistical reminder of a world that didn't care. I didn't let it get me down, though. Not a chance. There was no lagging about in bed all day. Not for me, thank you very much. I was up and out and about, going for long walks, keeping fit and staying focused in advance of the highlight of the week: a series of nightly taekwondo classes.

One day, I got a call from my good friend and mentor, Arthur O'Loughlin, aka Locky. All-round good guy and living legend, Locky was a Barnsley born, multi-weight, British and World kickboxing champion. He ran a Wombwell gym, which I'd frequented on numerous occasions. He was quite simply the fittest man I'd ever known and possessed all the attributes you'd expect of a world champion: skill, speed, power, courage, dedication and determination. Locky introduced me to kickboxing and I'd become reasonably proficient at it, winning a few fights and attaining a sufficient standard where I was kindly invited to occupy a place on a team he'd put together for a forthcoming competition in Hamburg. An incredible honour, I immediately said yes. That was before I discovered the cost: a hundred and fifty quid, including flights, accommodation and fees. With spending money on top, it would double the investment and was cash I simply didn't have at the time. I should have bailed out there and then; but I didn't like. I respected Locky immensely and didn't want to let him down, foolishly going along with things, assuring him I'd be there on the date stipulated. As soon as I put the phone down, I started to worry, experiencing sleepless nights, the lot. I desperately wanted to participate, but couldn't think of any way to raise the necessary funds. I very nearly asked dad to lend me something, but couldn't bring myself to do it. It wasn't right. Not at this moment in time, anyway. Something infinitely more important was bound to crop up in time. I'd no idea what; but it would. I could feel it in my bones. And, so, I continued to bottle it, stupidly paying Locky lip service every time we spoke instead of coming clean and telling the truth. The weeks ticked by and the date of the trip finally arrived. Burying my head in the sand, I went to the pub with Phil, arriving home steaming several hours later, hoping and praying things would blow over. I was about to be disappointed. The instant I stepped inside, dad collared me and I could tell by the look on his face he was concerned.

"There's a bloke called Arthur been on the phone for you."

I collapsed in the nearest armchair. Stomach full of ale suddenly performing somersaults, I put on a brave face.

"What did he want, like?"

"What did he want? He said you were meant to be going to Germany with him but never turned up. A kickboxing competition or something."

"That's right. I didn't have the money."

"I see. Well, perhaps you should have let him know, because he's not happy. Far from it, in fact. He says he's going to thump your ear 'ole for you…"

At that precise moment, I wanted the earth to open up and swallow me. As if I didn't have enough problems without upsetting a good old, salt-of-the-earth character like Locky. I knew he'd send for me when he got back and I was right. Summoned to his gym, I was given a right old dressing down for my idiocy. If I'd contested matters, there could have been trouble. Instead, I sensibly took it on the chin, doing my best to diffuse the situation. He was right and I was wrong and that's all there was to it.

As the weeks and months ticked by, I was getting more and more desperate. Still out of work, I was only on twenty-five quid a week and it was nothing like enough to sustain my often-flamboyant lifestyle. Then, finally, my luck changed. Mum pulled a few strings with a couple of influential friends of hers, who worked in the offices of local wood-stain, paint and preservative manufacturer, Ronseal, pleading with them to put me a good word in. Daz Kilner and his sister, Andrea, also had prominent contacts within the company and chipped in with a character reference, landing me a Monday morning interview. Unbelievably, I passed with flying colours and started the day after, a production line job which paid pretty good money compared to other factory environments in the area. I was back in business. And, with my change in fortunes, opportunities suddenly appeared left, right and centre. I was soon teaching taekwondo at multiple locations, six nights per week, with schools at Jump, Rotherham, High Green, Hoyland and Sheffield. It was hard graft on top of a full-time job, but I didn't care. I loved it. Absolutely lapped it up, in fact. Martial arts were my life and I would have gladly tripled the number of classes had I been able.

I remained in close contact with Locky, continuing to hone my kickboxing skills under his expert guidance. I desperately wanted to repay him and the opportunity eventually presented itself, albeit the best part of a year later. At short notice, he asked if I'd make the numbers up in a Sunday morning semi-contact kickboxing competition, which he was organising at Hoyland Sports Centre. I couldn't say yes quick enough. As ever, though, there was a problem. I'd a long-standing night out with Beaujolais arranged for the night before. I tried my hardest to cancel, but he was having none of it. I knew what was coming next and wasn't wrong. In true fancy licker style, he got me pissed as a fart, taking me clubbing, before dumping me home at three in the morning. How I got up I'll never know. Suffice to say, though, I managed it, somehow. That said, I was in a terrible state. With a mouth like sandpaper, I could easily have drunk the tap dry. I had a searing headache and was suffering terribly with acute feelings of nausea. Consequently, it wasn't looking good as I entered the dressing room, changing into my dobok. Seeking a psychological boost, I borrowed a 3rd dan belt, tying it firmly in place. It was a bit naughty, but I didn't care. I was going to need all the help I could get if I was to emerge in one piece. It was then I realised uncle Pete and aunty Maureen had finally fulfilled a long-term promise, turning up to watch me compete. Today of all days, I could have done without it. Maureen was a panicker at the best of times and I couldn't bear the thought of how she'd react if I was to take a beating. I gave the pair a quick wave then went to meet my fate. I'd moved up a weight now and was fighting in the 58-62kg category. Luckily, I got a bye in the first round, receiving a free ticket to the semi-final. I couldn't have been happier. It gave me valuable recuperation time; the chance to swallow a couple of paracetamols and guzzle on water. My eventual opponent was an undefeated, thick-set black belt, who commanded a fearsome reputation. I soon understood why. Fast on his feet, I couldn't catch him for love nor money. He was way too slippery, a situation not helped by the fact it was a kickboxing competition I was involved in, which obviously wasn't my natural game. He continued to lead me a merry dance. Not for long, though, getting the shock of his life when I changed tactics, switching to south paw, right foot forward, leading with the right. Almost immediately, I caught him with a peach of a spinning hook kick, knocking him off his feet. Semi-contact meant no excessive force and I was lucky to avoid disqualification. Undefeated, maybe; but the fight sailed straight out of him in the aftermath, allowing me to continue to press home the advantage and coast to an easy win.

With the final looming, I disappeared to the toilet to be sick. When I returned, the challenger was ready and waiting, a tall fellow with rippling muscles and enormous dreadlocks. The referee must have been dizzy by the end of the bout, because I ran rings around him, letting loose a constant barrage of kicks and punches. Same as my first opponent, however, he was as slippery as an eel and I struggled to lay a hand upon him, while soaking up several sucker-punches. It was enough for the judges, one of whom was Locky's daughter, Vicky, to award the decision the other way. Beaten by a point, I suddenly found myself embraced by the victor, praising my performance, saying I was one of the best fighters he'd faced, while admitting he was nervous throughout of what might have transpired if I'd landed properly. The look on his face when I revealed I was suffering from a raging hangover was priceless and I departed reasonably content with my performance. As an added bonus, I hadn't let Locky down, meaning I could hang on to my teeth a few more years, plus which uncle Pete and aunty Maureen could rest easy on account I hadn't been beaten to a pulp.

A week later, I was out on the piss again, this time with Daz Kilner's elder brother, Roy. A good eighteen or twenty years my senior, Roy was six-foot-two with eyes of blue and weighed a good sixteen or seventeen stone. Ex-military and a powerful martial artist, he was a real hard man, boasting a searing local reputation. Nobody messed with Roy, and I mean *nobody*. It wasn't worth the risk. Not unless someone had a hankering for eating through a straw for the foreseeable future. Not that Roy looked for trouble. He wasn't like that. He would rather walk away than become involved in fisticuffs. By the same token, though, he wouldn't shy away if push came to shove. And woe betide anyone who got in the way of one of those giant haymakers. We had a few pints round Hoyland then headed to Birdwell WMC, a couple of miles up the road. There was a heavy-rock band playing. Roy loved his music and was merrily head-banging away when a scrawny-looking youth came scampering over, bleating there was a gang of lads picking on him, threatening all sorts. I knew the kid from somewhere and he obviously knew me; but could I heckers like place him. Clearly not the type to cause bother, he pointed the gang out. I recognised them instantly: they were well known in Hoyland and Elsecar for making a nuisance of themselves, hanging about on street corners and verbally abusing anyone and everyone. It wasn't what I needed, but I felt compelled to intervene or the poor kid was going to get a right kicking. I made a conscious decision to leave Roy out of it. The last thing I wanted was the big man reducing the club to matchwood in a scene reminiscent of the famous saloon brawl in classic cowboy film, *Shane*. I did get him to hold my pint, though, ensuring I could keep my mitts free, just in case. Sauntering over, I told them to calm it down a bit, an intervention which spawned exactly the opposite effect. The moment the words parted my lips, a gang member performed a quick Ali shuffle, then smacked the youth straight in the mouth. He went down like a sack of coal and the others jumped in like a pack of raging hyenas, stamping and sticking the boot in. I reacted with lightning speed, swatting a couple of assailants off him. Properly getting into my stride, I pirouetted, preparing to launch a flying kick, but slipped in a puddle of beer, landing heavily on my right ankle. In terrible pain, I instinctively curled into a ball and made ready, waiting for the kicking which never came. It never came because Roy appeared, lamping one, two, three hyenas in a row, dropping them like ninepins. As the others skedaddled, he picked me up, threw me over his shoulder and carried me outside, sitting me down on a wall. I couldn't believe how bad it was. My foot had rotated one hundred and eighty degrees and was now agonisingly positioned back to front.

"Bleeding hell, Greenie," he grinned, showing off chafed knuckles. "You look like something out of Ripley's believe it or not. I suppose we'd better get you sorted…"

With no time to waste, he ordered a taxi, taking me home. Dad wasn't exactly thrilled when the front door clattered open. It was Saturday night and he'd just settled down for *The Two Ronnies*. Instead, he had to make do with the two cronies, Charlie and Roy, pissed as farts and slobbering all over his kitchen. As ever, though, he stepped straight up to the plate, just like he'd always done. He'd always been there for me when I needed him and always would be. What worried me was that, one day, positions would be reversed: it would be my turn to look after *him*. I just found it impossible to imagine in what circumstances, that's all; no doubt I'd be fully aware when the time arrived. Without complaint, he got the car out and drove Roy home, before taking me through to A&E. I'm not saying the waiting times were excessive, like, but I'm sure there was a bloke in front of us with a particularly nasty musket wound.

What seemed like an eternity later, we were back home. I had my leg in a pot from the knee down, which naturally kept me off work for a couple of months. It didn't stop me teaching taekwondo, though, albeit in the foulest of moods. As a means of exorcising my frustrations, I relentlessly beasted my students with rigorous fitness training; endless push ups, sit ups, burpees and lunges. Protests were commonplace and I responded by tearing agitators a new arsehole. If that didn't do the trick, I'd invite them on to the mat and make my point in slightly terser fashion, basically kicking the shit out of them. It didn't matter I only had one leg. Hopping around like Long John Silver, I was still way too fast and nimble, plus which, there was method in my madness. It hardened my fighters up, providing perfect preparation for the stresses and strains of looming competition. Everyone in the game agreed my fighters were brutal. It was how I rolled. And, if students didn't like it, there were plenty of run-of-the-mill classes out there that would be delighted to accommodate them. Go and train with mister insignificant, I'd remark, bluntly: see where it gets you...

11. Land up Yonder

I soon discovered a fresh passion: lads' holidays abroad. Over the next couple of years, I visited Majorca and Ibiza several times over, arduous and hilarious booze laden trips that came and went in a flash. Memories were mostly a blur. I could barely remember who I went with, let alone what happened. I do recall my old pal, Tommy Nicholson, playing a major role, however, like betting me a tenner that I couldn't take a sleeping bloke's socks off on the trip out. It wasn't difficult and the entire plane erupted with laughter in the aftermath. He never paid me, of course; but then I knew he wouldn't. As ever, it was all about the competition; the challenge and capacity to see a task through to a successful conclusion. In between time, my martial arts development continued unabated. A black belt 2nd dan now, I was heavily into teaching, mentoring a long line of students, men and boys, who passed through my classes like attendees of Brookfield School in the heart rendering film, *Goodbye Mr Chips*. I was also big into girls. One memory I *do* have of the holidays abroad is a conveyor belt of young ladies, eager to hook up for a bit of fun with the lads. If you want all the sordid details, why not give my old mates Chris Rodney and Dave Hesling a call? I'm sure they'll be delighted to expand, reeling off a whole string of X-rated tales; ear muff protection strongly advised. I remember once pulling a bird at The Potter's Wheel. A good fifteen or twenty years older than I was, she was ubiquitously known around the village as surrender Brenda. Well, she took me back to her place and…hang on a sec'. What? What was that? Alright, alright, calm down. There's no need to get personal. Get a grip, can't you? Don't even go there, because there's *no way* this is turning even remotely sleazy. It's a book about my life and times as an international martial artist. I'm merely trying to relate what an incredible ladies' man I was. Still am, in fact. I can't help it if I'm Hoyland's answer to Burt Reynolds, can I? Now, if you don't mind, may I continue? It is my book, you know. As I was about to say, before I was rudely interrupted, I was in the boozer with a few of the lads one Sunday night. It was turned midnight and we were engaged in a spot of after-bird, which translates to after-hours drinking for the uninitiated. Sean O'Neil was the landlord. He'd barred Phil on Sundays on account he was bad for business, constantly falling down drunk and knocking people over, most especially on the day he sank forty-three – *yes, forty-three* – pints of John Smiths. Suddenly, there was a bang on the door. Convinced it was the boys in blue, we skedaddled into the back with our beer, leaving Sean to tiptoe across the lounge, sticking an ear into the jamb, enquiring who it was. The response left us creased up with laughter.

"It's me, Jack. Can I come in, Jack?"

"Can you fuck, Jack. You're barred. It's Sunday, remember."

"It's not now though, Jack. It's ten past twelve. We're into Monday now. So, can I? Can I come in, Jack? Can I…?"

Sean opened the door and Phil tumbled across the threshold, a stupid smile embossed upon his features. He'd brought Steve Taylor with him, an old school pal of sorts, but not someone I was particularly friendly with. Little did I know that, after tonight, we would become incredibly close in the months ahead. While Phil drank the bar dry, we enjoyed a good old chinwag on all manner of things, rapidly discovering we had lots in common. It turned out Steve was also big into sport and fitness, so much so we arranged a few gym visits together, keeping fit alongside endless rounds of excruciating weight training. A few weeks later, Steve told me he'd been offered a big money mining job in Western Australia and suggested I accompany him. I was shocked, flabbergasted and gobsmacked, all rolled into one. Did I hear him right? Australia? *Moi*? Was he having a laugh? What could Australia possibly have that I didn't have right here in sunny Hoyland? I turned him down, obviously; it would mean packing my job in and all sorts. That stated, the seed was very firmly sown. Off Steve went and, lo and behold, a couple of months later, I was on my way to join him, proud bearer of a twelve-month working visa. It would mean a year's sabbatical from my beloved martial arts and I'd also been forced to resign from Ronseal. But it was a price I was more than willing to pay in order to embark upon the trip of a lifetime. Unlike Steve, I didn't have a job lined up for when I landed. *Que sera sera* was the attitude: whatever would be would be. I'd work things out when I'd settled in, plus which, I wasn't exactly going empty-handed, having saved a good few bob to take with me, albeit predominantly beer money. I flew from Manchester via Cathay Pacific, a non-stop flight to Hong Kong, where I would be staying overnight, pending an afternoon connection to Perth. I was seated beside a well-dressed and extremely well-spoken chap called David, a diplomat from Guinea. If I'd have been him, I'd have asked to swap seats rather than endure a twelve-hour beasting from a raggy lad from Cloughfields. He was way too polite for that, though, even holding his nerve when I took full advantage of a free in-flight bar. A conversation which had started out quite mundane gradually increased in volume and intensity as the alcohol did its job. I talked endlessly about football, lecturing him upon the prowess of the mighty Reds. After that, it was a chat about Kes followed by a resumé of my martial arts career. He didn't seem particularly interested; or at least until I mentioned my achievements, becoming British champion and fighting internationally. Then he quizzed me incessantly on every aspect of the sport to such a point that even *I* got bored. He soon quietened down when I began talking about my love life, though, turning red as a London bus at my stories, especially when I turned the tables, asking him to relate a few tales of his own. I thought I was being clever. Little did I know, but the man from Guinea had a trick up his sleeve. When I enquired if he had any painkillers to counter a raging headache, the bugger popped me a couple of sleeping pills. Next thing, I was waking up in the toilet, totally paranoid about an awful dream I'd just had; a dream in which I'd vomited in the diplomat's lap. I freshened up, then headed back to my seat, arriving just in time to witness an air hostess, assisting David in scraping alcohol-laced airline food from his trousers. Shit! Engaging reverse gear, I swiftly disappeared back the way I'd come, assuming a standing position at the rear until he'd been ushered up front somewhere. Then I timidly made my return, snuggling up against the window, gluing my face into the plastic oval, keeping a low profile, while watching over our descent; lots of low cloud then a concrete jungle of skyscrapers and high-rise apartment blocks, with piles of washing, straddling the street. I can't deny I was disappointed with the view, initial feelings which, unfortunately, set the tone for the remainder of the visit. It was like being on a different planet. I didn't care for the traffic and constant flow of people. A Chinese buffet I attended was the worst food I'd ever had and I couldn't believe how many people were wearing facemasks. What were they playing at? What *were* they thinking? How could a flimsy piece of cloth, slung across the face, seriously guard against anything? Surely breathing holes would be infinitely larger than air-bound infectious spores masks were meant to protect against? Surely they would cause extreme anxiety and long-term mental health problems? Surely wearers would suffer exponentially as a consequence of continually breathing in exhaled waste products? What a joke. Masks were a comfort blanket and nothing else and I made a vow there and then that, if the damned blasted things ever hit the streets of the UK, then I, for one, would refuse point blank to support the idiotic trend. About the only good thing to come from the stop-off was a ferryboat ride around the harbour, during which I came over all emotional, eyeballing various locations used in the filming of Bruce Lee's classic, *Enter the Dragon*, an experience which took me right back to my youth, practising kicks in my bedroom mirror. That apart, I couldn't board the connecting flight quick enough, waving a sarcastic goodbye through the window, while making a firm pledge never to return.

Australia was an absolute blast by comparison. Perth was quite simply the most amazing place I'd visited in my life. There was so much to do: a trip to Rottnest Island, for one, a popular getaway with its white-sand beaches, secluded bays, scenic bike paths and vehicle-free atmosphere. Whale watching or swimming with dolphins in the incredible Indian Ocean was another. Winery visits, or extended trips inland, experiencing a vast and predominantly uninhabited wilderness. World class beaches abounded. Star-gazing was popular, as was a cruise along the Swan River, or a day out at the spectacular Elizabeth Quay. Most of all, though, Perth had a multitude of bars and restaurants, frequented by an abundance of young, fit, nubile females. Like a cat at a pigeon fayre, I had every intention of making the best of it. And make the best of it I most certainly did.

It was boiling hot as I exited the airport. Steve was there to greet me, driving me the fifteen miles or so to digs he was co-sharing with a trio of other ex-pats; a Scouser, a bloke from Wigan, another from the north-east and a big, butch Kiwi to boot. Located on the outskirts of the city, the apartment was littered with evidence of its bachelor pad status. Empty beer bottles were everywhere. Overflowing ashtrays. Unmade beds, discarded clothes and a sink full of pots. There was even a bra, trailing from a ceiling fan; pink lace, 36DD, as I recall. After brief introductions, we made a beeline for the boozer, watching English football on the telly. A beer swilling pub crawl inevitably followed. We pulled a few birds and took them home with us. Smiling ear to ear, I was convinced I'd hit the jackpot. I had as well; to all intents and purposes, I'd died and gone to heaven. Especially when the same thing happened the next day and then again, and the day after that. Week in and week out, it was more of the same. In between time, I'd visit the beach, catching a few rays and swimming in the ocean. I soon had an incredible tan, sun-bronzed body perfectly complementing my Burt Reynolds lookalike status. I learned to surf. With a sporting pedigree, it was an activity which came naturally, so much so I was soon riding waves alongside all the top locals. I absolutely loved it, particularly the female attention associated with the sport, scoring with numerous young ladies along the way. Whenever I found myself being chatted up, which seemed to be every five minutes, the first thing that got talked about was my broad, almost unintelligible Barnsley accent. Inevitably, they'd ask where I came from and I'd instantly respond with a song I'd dreamed up, sung to the tune of Men at Work classic, *Down Under*: *I come from a land up yonder. Her Majesty's Y-O-I absconder. When I got home, I went and shunned her. I'd better watch out, she's gonna send her brother…*

On the downside, I must confess I didn't care much for the shark net. Two hundred metres out, it permitted bathers to enjoy the water without fear of attack. Stray outside the zone, however, and you were potentially in danger. Not that shark sightings occurred on a daily basis; far from it, in fact. Moreover, it was an absolute rarity. When sharks did appear, though, it was big news. People would rear up from sunbeds and stare anxiously out to sea, as swimmers and surfers alike splashed and dashed for the shore, scrambling to avoid a nasty encounter with a marauding bull shark or sandbar. Every so often, a shark would venture so close in-shore, its tail and dorsal fin could be clearly seen, cresting the water, fetching gasps, screeches and screams from terrified onlookers. Gasps invariably turned to cheers when the rescue copter appeared, though, side door slung open, a crew member leaning out, dispersing the creature with a highly persuasive prodding stick. Compulsive viewing, I often wondered what would have happened if I'd owned a dog called Shark and taken it to the beach to practise recall. Shark! Shark! I reckon my popularity with the locals would have dissipated instantly.

As weeks became months, the holiday high life continued and my finances began to crumble as a consequence. I'd turned down a few jobs, most notably as a bartender on a cruise ship, touring the Indian Ocean. I must have been mad. It would have opened up all kinds of opportunities and would have been the perfect life for a raggy lad like me. I knew I'd have to find work eventually, but was determined to hold out as long as possible. In between time, my sporting instinct had cajoled me into accepting a trial for top local football team, Dianella White Eagles, a club largely made up of Polish immigrants. It was a great set up, as good if not better than anything I'd encountered in the UK, approaching professional standards in terms of outlook, ambition and facilities. That said, my reserves run-out was more like a scene from the football match in Kes, an experience made all the more surreal by the fact the manager was a Brian Glover lookalike, short and dumpy, sporting a thinning, blond crew-cut. In an even bigger coincidence, he was also called Sugden, mirroring the surname of the insufferable on-screen games master. He found me some kit and a pair of boots to wear. Lo and behold, everything was a size too big, leaving me looking like a bedraggled Billy Casper and making me wish I hadn't bothered. At least he didn't ask me to play in goal, which was a major bonus, sticking me out on the wing and telling me to stay out of trouble. Because I wasn't registered, I was playing as a ringer. If the referee asked my name, I was to tell him it was Zbigniew Kwiatkowski. Some chance, I thought: I couldn't even remember it, let alone say it. My first touch was a complete disaster. Badly fitting boots caused me to stand on the ball and fall over. Even worse, the opposition went straight upfield and scored. I quickly made amends, though, netting a brace and laying on another, before losing my temper, kicking a chunk out of a sassy midfielder who was trying to take the piss. The referee promptly produced a yellow card, asking my name. Fuck knows, I replied, pre-empting the inevitable, marching off as fast as my legs would carry me. It was left to Sugden to unravel. What he said, I've no idea. All I know is I was soon firmly entrenched in the first team. Scoring tons of goals, I was even being paid for my services. While the cash was useful, though, it was nothing like enough and Sugden knew it wasn't. Starting to get bored, he did everything he could to retain my services, lining me up with a part-time job in a supermarket and even offering me free board and lodgings in his own home. We were due to play in the Western Australia Cup semi-final.

Much to everyone's dismay, I jacked it all in the week before. In retrospect, I should have taken him up on his very generous offer and played on. Semi-final participation would have probably led to a full-time professional contract, as I'd learned several top clubs were watching me closely. Turn the clock back a few years and it would have been everything I'd ever dreamed of. Not now, though. I wasn't a footballer; I was a martial artist and deliberately went out of my way to rediscover my roots, searching out a local taekwondo club, attending a series of training sessions, albeit purely as a spectator. Each visit, I attracted more and more attention from a group of inquisitive instructors, constantly looking over and talking about me. Eventually, one of them came across and asked if I was Charlie Green. A fellow Yorkie, he said he'd watched me fight in a competition at Doncaster Dome the previous summer. He invited me to attend forthcoming classes and I promised I would. I'd brought my dobok along, just in case, but couldn't be arsed when it came down to it and so never even turned up. As a way of making myself feel better, I blamed non-attendance on the fact my back was troubling me again. It was weak excuse and one which made me question what I was doing, sacrificing everything I'd ever worked for on an extended jolly on the other side of the world. Don't get me wrong: Australia was magnificent. I could quite easily have emigrated, settled down and set up home there. The problem was my lifestyle. As much as I was having a whale of a time, I knew I couldn't sustain it long term, mentally, physically and financially. And nor would I want to, either. The booze; the women; days at the beach and lazy mornings in bed: the whole shebang was combining to impact negatively upon everything I was or aspired to become. For the very first time, I'd ceded my love of sport, a development aptly illustrated by my passing up on martial arts training and a potential professional football career. What *was* I thinking? What had happened to *don't stop believing*? For the first time in my life, I started to feel down. It was a state of mind which lasted all of five seconds. In true Cloughfields style, I brushed myself down and made ready to go again. The penny had finally dropped and I knew what I had to do. Down to my last few cents, I swallowed my pride and got on the blower to dad, asking if he'd send some money over to get me home. He agreed, just like I knew he would; the only condition was that I'd pay him back in full. To be honest, I wouldn't have had it any other way; there was no way I'd see him out of pocket on account of my own shortcomings. The money landed next day, nestling in the bank account I'd wisely opened upon arrival. He sent far more than I'd expected as well, a couple of grand, roughly equating to five thousand Australian Dollars. It was a good job really. I'd borrowed a few quid off the lads, which would need paying back, and I also required living expenses for the remainder of my time in the country. By far my biggest expenditure, though, was the ticket home. I'd done my sums and worked out that, after everything else, I just about had enough to fit in a couple of nights stopover in Singapore. It was a tantalising prospect and a nice carrot to finish off what had been an unforgettable trip. Determined to make it happen, I booked my tickets and accommodation straight away, while I still had the money, fearful I'd blow it all on a series of wild nights somewhere, a very strong possibility given how insufferably incorrigible I was.

An unfortunate consequence of my financial position meant I had to give up my digs. We'd always shared rent and food costs, but it didn't come cheap and my current position meant I was in no position to continue such a level of contributions. The lads said I could stay as long as I wanted for free; but I politely declined. It simply wasn't me. I'd always paid my way. It was one of my core principles and wasn't something I was willing to forfeit on a whim. Besides, I'd agreed to spend my final week in Perth with a Scottish pal I'd made, a witty, effervescent, hard drinking Glaswegian going by the name of George. In advance, however, I made sure I had one final night out with the lads. We went out and had our usual skinful of amber nectar, then grabbed a couple of slabs of beer from the offie, sixty tinnies in total, returning home to enjoy a pre-arranged evening, watching a few of our favourite DVDs. The Kiwi selected *Once Were Warriors*, a story of an unemployed Māori, battling to survive in Auckland's slums. We sat through *A Hard Day's Night*, which wasn't bad, then *Get Carter* and *Lawrence of Arabia*, neither of which did a great deal for me. Then it was my turn. Needless to say, I put *Kes* on. Steve had obviously seen it and so had the Scouser, but none of the others had even heard of it. The good news was they all agreed it was brilliant, though they invariably struggled with the harsh dialogue, meaning I was constantly having to act as interpreter. It was a daft move on my part, putting my fave on. It may have painted a bleak picture of my home town; but it didn't half leave me feeling homesick, making me wish I was back in Hoyland, kicking a ball around with Phil, Daz, Chris and the rest of the gang. Not that I'd any real cause to fret, because in a few short days that's exactly where I would be heading.

Bags packed, I said my goodbyes, taking a taxi to George's. It was a big old bungalow, five bedrooms, with an open plan lounge and kitchen. With a beautifully manicured lawn and surrounded by a host of similar properties, it felt like I'd just landed a part in *Neighbours*. George invited me inside and introduced his dad, Jock. Sprawled on the settee in a string vest and tartan boxer shorts, he had a roll-up in one hand and a can of McEwan's Export in the other, watching Scottish footie on telly. Much to my delight, Celtic were playing Rangers and the Hoops were 2-1 up with only injury time to play. The referee blew his whistle and I jumped up and down in celebration. That was my first mistake. My second was opening my mouth to speak.

"Who's this English bastard," he roared, tipping ash into an empty can.

"It's Charlie," George reassured him. "You know…the lad I was telling you about. The one who's coming to stay."

He asked who I supported. I answered Celtic. He promptly declared he was a Gers fan, saying he didn't want any Irish bastards in his house. Unable to do right for doing wrong, I randomly blurted I also followed Barnsley. Armpit hair blowing in the breeze of the ceiling fan, a huge smile spread inexorably across the big man's features. Waving me over, he gave me a mighty bear hug and then handed me a tinnie.

"That's alright then, son. Get some ale down you. And don't worry…there's plenty more where that came from."

Already pissed as a fart, I was suddenly about to get a whole lot worse. I felt good, though, and was happy to be sharing my final days in Perth with my lovely Scottish mate. Jock wouldn't take anything for board and lodgings, no matter how hard I tried to pursue the matter. In the end, I simply gave up, getting down to doing what I'd been doing from the moment I arrived: having the best time possible. Australia had been a blast. A perfect pick-me up for a lad from up yonder, I'd recommend it to anyone.

12. Back to Reality

I arrived at Singapore's Changi Airport in a state of panic. I'd slept most of the five-hour flight from Perth, a fitful, disturbed sleep, anxious my time in Oz was over amidst growing concerns about what was round the corner. It was nothing to do with Singapore. I was looking forward to my stopover in the city-state immensely. It was what was awaiting me back home I was worried about, principally my disastrous financial position and the fact I no longer had a job to go to. As previously intimated, Australia had been amazing and I didn't have a single regret about the time I spent there. In retrospect, though, I knew I should have boxed clever prior to departure. For the life of me, I couldn't understand why I'd so nonchalantly resigned my position at Ronseal, disappearing into the sunset without a thought for potential repercussions. I was more than well in with the management, having been told a few times I was being groomed for promotion. If I'd asked nicely, I'm sure we could have come to some kind of arrangement, a few months sabbatical, for example, with my position mothballed until I got back. That would have been too easy, though. Same as always, I had to do things the hard way. It was just the way I rolled. Well, whether I liked it or not, the time had arrived to eat a portion of humble pie. After fighting my way through customs, I went straight to a payphone and called home, speaking with mum, asking her if she could work her magic and try and wangle me my job back. It was a big ask; but she unhesitatingly said she'd give it a go, just like I knew she would. Whether she'd succeed or not was a different matter. It just seemed highly unlikely, that's all. All I could do was keep my fingers crossed and wait and see.

I checked into my hotel then embarked upon a pre-planned sight-seeing tour, eating out at Newton Circus and window-shopping at Orchard Road, before taking a taxi to the world-famous Singapore Zoo. It was really busy when I arrived, so I decided to give it a miss. Not only that, it was really expensive, way in excess of the amount I'd budgeted. The only problem was I desperately needed the toilet, meaning I had to employ all my charm to persuade a security guard to permit me temporary entry in order to relieve myself. He followed me every inch of the way, even standing outside the toilet block while I did the business. Imagine my shock when I re-emerged to discover him doing an interview with a camera crew, filming a documentary about the attraction. Realising I was in shot, I stopped and smiled, pointing a finger at the WC sign, while thinking: Michael Caine, eat your heart out, because old Greenie boy has just landed the starring role in Zoo-Loo. Back in the city, I had a few drinks with a couple of intoxicated Kiwis, who persuaded me to accompany them on a visit to a dubious sounding establishment called Four Floors of Whores. The clue was in the name and I knew in advance it wasn't my scene. I was well capable of generating my own fun, but couldn't resist having a look all the same. There was a problem, though. It turned out there had been a mass brawl earlier in the evening involving rival groups of English lads. As a precaution, door staff were temporarily refusing admission to anyone from Blighty. The Kiwis got straight in, but I was stopped and asked where I came from.

"Hoyland," I answered, instinctively, smiling my best smile.

"Ireland, eh?" came the reply. "No problem with anyone from the Emerald Isle. In you go, son. Next, please. Next…"

Head filled with Anglo-Irish-Hoyland-Ireland pronunciations, I laughed my way to the bar and ordered a drink. I wasn't laughing long, though. In typical Yorkshire fashion, I screamed: *how much*? A couple more at that price and I could have visited the bloody zoo three times over. As the Kiwis disappeared to conduct a spot of *business*, I walloped my drink then took my leave. Full of misfits, it reminded me of the cantina scene in *Star Wars*, albeit somewhat weirder. A taxi ride deposited me at Raffles, the most celebrated hotel in Singapore, infamously occupied by the Japanese top brass during the war. I made straight for the Long Bar and ordered a Singapore Sling, a gin cocktail mixed with various liqueurs, pineapple, lime, bitters and sodas. It blew my head off and made a hole in my wallet. But at least I was able to snack upon hundreds of peanuts, littering the bar and floor, supposedly a throwback to when Raffles was first built and the building was overrun with cockroaches and shells were deliberately scattered so patrons didn't know if they were stepping on nuts or roaches. After Raffles, it was a few jars at Hooters, famous not only for food and beer but also revealing waitress uniforms. Charlie being Charlie, I was soon regaling staff and customers alike with my natural wit and raconteur. Alright, alright, pipe down. If you think funny is the *last* thing I am, here's one for you: what do they call a Frenchman in sandals? Phillipe Phillope. Get it? Flip-flop. Oh, behave. Go play marbles on the M1 if that's how you want to be. Anyway, Hooters walls were decorated with numerous pieces of sporting memorabilia. American football gear. Baseball, cricket and basketball items. A South African rugby top. Then I spotted it: a red Barnsley FC shirt, neatly folded in a frame, unbelievably the only football top in the building. I explained Barnsley was my team, not forgetting Celtic of course. Before long, the discussion had progressed to a discussion upon my martial arts career. They were ever so impressed, constantly pouring drinks down my throat and fussing round me like I was some kind of superstar. I was a bit embarrassed by it all to be fair and responded in the only way I could think of, by offering to donate my dobok. My offer was duly accepted and, next evening, before leaving for the airport, I was back with the aforementioned garment. I signed it to a fanfare of claps and cheers, a flourish of permanent marker alongside a glass of bubbly, a flurry of handshakes and repeated back-slapping. It was framed and in pride of place fifteen minutes later, proudly declaring: *All the best, Charlie Green, SM.* All over me like a rash, a flirting waitress asked what SM meant. If I'd been staying a few days longer, I'd have gladly enlightened her. Instead, I simply replied: Superman…what do you think? If only she knew. She'd have run a mile; or perhaps not. Unfortunately, I'll never know.

Somehow, I managed to blag an upgrade for the return journey, spending fourteen luxurious hours in business class, endlessly troughing on champagne, steak and cheese boards. I soon came down to earth with a bump at Heathrow, however, literally as well as metaphorically. Aside from experiencing the worst landing ever, I inadvertently joined the international arrivals channel instead UK citizens. Three hours later, I was finally through the airport and on my way, a horrendously long Sunday afternoon journey back up the M1 to sunny Hoyland. It was pouring down as I arrived, the first proper rain I'd seen in months; but at least there was good news waiting for me when I got in. Mum had worked her magic and I'd only got my Ronseal job back. What? Really! Grateful beyond belief, I hugged and kissed her, then collapsed in an armchair, sipping on a relaxing cup of Yorkshire tea, fielding question after question from all and sundry. I did my best; but it wasn't easy. My head was still in a spin at the news, plus which I was totally and utterly jet-lagged and looking forward to a well-earned lie-in. Stretching and yawning, I made ready for bed. Mum ruffled my hair, following me to the foot of the stairs.

"Get a good night's sleep, our Charles. I'm not up till eight, but don't worry…I'll leave your sandwiches in the fridge."

I looked at her like she'd just stepped off a rocket ship from Mars.

"What sandwiches are these, like?"

"For work. Didn't I tell you? You start back tomorrow and you're on earlies. Don't you go overlaying now, do you hear me…?"

My guts sank. Back tomorrow? *What*? This couldn't be happening! Could it? The look on her face never altered and I knew it was true. Feelings of euphoria vanished. All of a sudden, I felt thoroughly and utterly depressed. Talk about back to reality. Face like wet weekend, I went straight upstairs and did the only thing I could think to do: I sat on the bog and had a right good shit. Miraculously, I got up and even clocked in on time. Culture shock, or what? A few days ago, I was living it up in Australia and Singapore and now I was undergoing a refresher course before making my return to the production line. Depressed beyond belief, I made myself a promise there and then I would return to Oz at the earliest opportunity. In the meantime, though, I steeled myself and got stuck in, fully immersing myself in the task in hand. It was the only way. I might be fed up, but I was also a realist. I needed money to fund my lifestyle and pay my dad back and a steady wage packet was currently top of my list of priorities. At least all the lads were glad to see me back, which was nice. It helped me settle back in and I was soon up to my old tricks, winding up the management and making mischief at every opportunity. I'd only been back a week when the company introduced production line safety goggles. Outraged, I protested, vehemently; we all did. While everyone else swiftly succumbed to the instruction, though, I continued to fight it, even going so far as to remove the glass, walking around in empty plastic frames, doing a passable impression of *Benny Hill*. I managed to keep up the façade for the best part of a fortnight, until I was grassed up by one of the lads, a relative newcomer with illusory career aspirations. Summoned to the office, I was given a verbal warning and instructed to toe the line or be prepared to face the consequences. Caught bang to rights, my first instinct was to knock the slimy bastard's teeth down his throat. We were Barnsley lads. We hailed from pedigree mining stock. We were a community which had displayed unswerving solidarity during the year-long strike. We stuck together through thick and thin and would *never* sell out to the management. A smack in the kisser was the least he deserved for his actions. Unfortunately, it couldn't be. I'd be out on my ear if I resorted to violence and so sensibly started looking for other ways of getting my own back. It didn't take me long to find one, either. Grass worked on the line, mixing and canning varnish. While he was on his break, I sabotaged his machine, changing labels, altering tin sizes and recalibrating settings so the apparatus poured 5L into 250ml cans. Grass promptly arrived back at his machine and recommenced work, pressing buttons and pulling levers. An enormous cheers went up as the surrounding area suddenly drowned in varnish, pouring across the floor and creeping under partition doors into adjacent corridors. If looks could have killed, I'd have been six-foot under. He knew it was me but couldn't prove it, disappearing for a mop and bucket to clean up the mess. As we left for home that night, I treated him to a condescending wink in the car park: one nil to the lad! He didn't say a word and it was a good job, otherwise I'd have followed him home and made it two.

Back in the world of martial arts, I'd thankfully restored my mojo and was heavily into training and teaching. I had some good young students who I was pushing hard and had big hopes for. I trained every day, pounding the streets and spending an overt amount of time in the gym. I also took up Brazilian jiu jitsu, attending numerous training sessions to the point where I was more than competent, adding another valuable string to my bow. I had a few girlfriends. Moved in with one then straight back out again, returning home. I went out boozing with Phil, bailing the great big pillock out of no end of trouble as usual. Chris Oldfield came home on leave again, temporarily reigniting my interest in joining the military. It didn't last long, though. I dismissed the idea as quickly as it came, refocusing upon my current course. Work, rest and play, I was in a particularly good vein. Every week, I drew my wages and every week I paid off a bit more debt until dad finally confirmed it was all clear. Then I started saving for the return trip to Australia I'd promised myself. It took an age, but I eventually had enough put aside to make the booking. It was here before I knew it, a repeat of the first trip, meeting up with my old pals and hitting the beaches and bars of the most fabulous and vibrant of cities. Twelve months later, I was back again, returning like the proverbial boomerang to commence round three. Steve Taylor was due a few days after I arrived, taking up renewed employment at the mine. His partner, Karen, had learned through the grapevine that big Phil was also on his way, joining me along with another couple of old mates, Tony Fowler and Pepsi Pete, for what would inevitably become the mother of all piss-ups. Terrified about Phil's drinking reputation, she made Steve promise to steer clear of him at all costs. Of course, he agreed; why wouldn't he? Perth was a huge city with a population approaching two million, meaning there wasn't a cat in hell's chance of dropping on the big lad by chance. Or at least that was the theory. Crossing the road towards his hotel, he looked like someone had just walked over his grave when he felt a hefty tap on the shoulder, immediately followed by the immortal words:

"Hey up, Jack. How's it going, Jack? Imagine seeing you here. You coming for a pint with us, or what…?"

He could hardly refuse, could he? Six hours later, he was propped up in a chair, fast asleep, dribbling from the corner of his mouth, totally oblivious to Fowler, lining up another round, while Pepsi Pete sought a marker pen to treat him to penny glasses, a beard and moustache. To the best of my knowledge, Karen never heard a whisper of what had happened. Let's hope she's not reading this then, eh? No, let's hope she is; because we had a great time, didn't we, chaps? The time of our lives, in fact. Enjoy the read, Karen. Hopefully see you again one day soon…

13. Even the Best-laid Plans

One day, I bought a motorbike off a kid on our estate. I soon wished I hadn't. First time out, a car pulled out of a junction and knocked me off, necessitating a trip by ambulance to A&E. The bike was a write-off and I was left with numerous cuts and bruises and a nasty case of whiplash. I put a claim in and was duly awarded five grand in compensation. With the insurance coughing up the value of the bike, it left me in a very nice financial position indeed. It was a good job really, because the travel bug had well and truly stuck. With Christmas approaching, I decided I was going to take advantage of the factory shutdown and head off somewhere exotic as opposed to embarking upon the traditional series of nightly pub crawls round Hoyland with the lads. The only question was: where should I go? I found the answer during a browse through the Sunday papers, a bargain return trip to Hawaii, including accommodation and incorporating a two-night stopover in LA on the way back. I had it booked before Phil Rudd could say Jack Robinson. Hawaii was a martial arts hotspot, boasting numerous famous gyms. I'd long harboured a desire to train there and this was an opportunity to fulfil my dreams, while soaking up a few rays and hopefully pulling a few birds at the same time. The internet was still in its infancy back then and cumbersome at best. Using dial-up, it took an age to connect to my gym of choice. I got there in the end, though, securing a block-booking of pre-paid training sessions to accommodate my stay there. Amazing news, I simply could not wait. The last few shifts at Ronseal didn't half drag as a consequence; but at least I'd had the good sense not to throw it all in this time and would still have a job to go to upon my return.

Flying out a few days before Christmas, I had a few hours to kill before my train to Manchester and so decided to nip to The Potter's Wheel for a couple of pints. A few old pals were in, enjoying a good old session. Richard Ogden was one. Paul Footitt was another alongside Mark White and Chris Reynolds; Les Hannighan and James and Simon Turner.

The Stewart brothers arrived a few minutes after I did; Chris, Wayne and Matt, with Mark and Ian Stephenson trailing faithfully in their wake. A big audience, I took great pleasure in announcing my trip. Needless to say, the piss-taking commenced immediately. Make sure you don't burn your Hawaiian pizza, Charlie: if you do, it will need to go on aloha heat. *Funny ha-ha*! I see the US football results are in: Hawaii won 5-0. *Funny ha-ha*! Apparently, there's a city in Hawaii which pays an annual tribute to a sixties female Scottish pop star: every year they like to honour Lulu. *Funny ha-ha*! You visiting Pearl Harbour, Charlie? Is he heckers like: there's only one kind of pearl he's interested in and that's necklaces. *Funny ha-ha*! On and on it went, until I brought my fist down on the table with such force that ale spilled down the sides of glasses, flooding the table.

"Right, you set of wankers. I'm off. Enjoy Christmas, won't you? Have fun. Get pissed. Spend the entire holiday rotting in here while I'm off seeing the world. I'll catch you all when I get back…sitting in the same old seats, no doubt, and at the same bleeding table!"

I was only joking. Well, I was and I wasn't. They were old school pals. We'd never fall out. Not under any circumstances. I was just making a point, that's all. The Potter's Wheel was great. But it wasn't the epicentre of the universe, like some would have you believe. I guzzled my beer then left, making a mental note to pop back in a fortnight and see if I was right. Several hours later, I was at the airport and boarding the first flight of my journey, a trip to Newark, New Jersey. It was a free bar as usual and it would have been rude not to take advantage of it. That stated, I didn't forget what happened on the trip to Hong Kong and was extra careful not to go OTT. It was a good job, because I didn't half need my wits about me upon arrival. I had to fill out a US Customs landing card and got it badly wrong, requiring several repeat attempts before it was finally accepted. Then another problem: my luggage had gone missing. I was gutted. Practically every item of clothing I owned was in that case, including my dobok and hogu. I reported it, but to no avail. No one seemed to be interested and I was quickly sent packing; no pun intended, of course. Suitcase free, I was soon boarding a plane to LAX, worrying myself sick every minute of a nearly three-thousand-mile journey, wondering what on earth I was going to do. Upon arrival, I attended the carousel and waited and waited, and waited. When it didn't show up again, I filled in a few forms, then spent a long, sleepless night at the LA Hilton. After a hectic scramble to locate my bus next morning, I was back the lost property counter, filling out even more forms, for compensation this time, several hundred dollars-worth, in fact, a pleasant surprise which at least softened the blow of the disastrous episode. I was about to disappear into the sunset with the dosh when a porter appeared, hauling a trolley load of suitcases. I was summoned back to the counter and asked if my case was black with a red stripe. Eureka! I punched the air with delight, then settled back and listened to the explanation: I should have been informed at source that my luggage was being automatically transferred between carriers and I wouldn't see it until I reached LA. Did I care? Not one bit was the answer. It was as if all my Christmases had arrived at once. And at least I'd got all the bad news out of the way early doors, before the holiday properly got underway.

Hawaii was marvellous, just like in the movies. White sand beaches and beautiful turquoise seas with big waves. High rise buildings. Lots of green spaces with a plethora of shops, bars and restaurants. The sun was blazing and happy, smiling tourists and locals were wearing shades, shorts and traditional, multi-coloured Hawaiian shirts. A soon as I'd checked into my hotel, I was one of them, strolling the streets of Waikiki, looking and feeling like Steve McGarrett in Hawaii 5-0. Spotting a couple of dangerous looking teens on a street corner, clearly dealing something or other, I randomly imagined myself and big Phil, sauntering over and clobbering the pair, before sticking them in handcuffs. Book him,

Danno! suddenly became replaced by: book him, Jack! Moments later, we whisked the offenders away, dumping them in the rear of the famous Ford Mercury Park Lane Brougham in advance of speeding off down the famous strip, ubiquitously known as Kalakaua Avenue. I was absolutely loving it, until I realised how expensive things were. Like anyone from Barnsley going on holiday, I always compered the price of beer to the equivalent back home and was shocked to find it was almost double. The food wasn't cheap either and I knew it was going to be a struggle to survive a week let alone two. Not with the funds I had available, anyway. If the lads back home found out, they would laugh their bloody socks off. Not that there was a snowball's chance in hell of that happening. Not a soul knew my financial circumstances and I certainly wasn't going to tell anybody. Hang on a second. What if they're reading this book? What if they're poring over this page? What if they're pissing themselves laughing? Well, if they are, they'll know all about it now, won't they? So what? Who cares? Twenty odd years is a bit late to be taking the piss, isn't it? Just remember one thing: like Bryan Mills in the film, *Taken*, I have a very particular set of skills. Skills I have acquired over a very long career. Skills that make me a nightmare for people like you. And I'd certainly know where to find you. I mean, let's be honest: it wouldn't be difficult, would it? Probably sat at the same blinking table in the same flipping boozer, drinking flat lousy beer.

Next morning, I grabbed my kit and caught a bus to the gym in Honolulu. It was located in a grassy-verge laden side street, close to the harbour. It was a modern, prefabricated building, a couple of stories high with tinted glass windows. I entered reception and a girl who looked like a Barbie doll directed me upstairs to the training area. I was greeted by a couple of instructors, who showed me where to change. There was no beating around the bush: I was immediately asked if I wanted to fight. Still acclimatising and jet-lagged from what had been a horrendously long journey, I chose not to. Tomorrow,

I said, warming up with a few basic exercises before commencing a lengthy period of bag and pad work. They watched me intently throughout. It was obvious they had done their research and knew who I was. After all, it wasn't every week they had a British champion come to train, was it? At the end of the session, I had a lengthy chat with the pair. I could tell they were impressed; so they should have been as well, because I'd pummelled the stuffing out of heavy bags for the best part of an hour, leaving them dimpled, distorted and misshapen. And that was just for starters: wait until they saw what I could do when there was meat on the table.

Time to relax, I returned to Waikiki and treated myself to a burger before heading for the beach. Spawled on a towel, I struggled to come to terms with the sheer beauty of my surroundings. Aside from sun, sea and sand, there was the stunning backdrop of Diamond Head State Monument to admire, Hawaii's most recognised landmark, a huge, saucer-shaped volcanic crater, formed a staggering three hundred-thousand years ago. I was astonished by the magnitude of it all and struggled believe I was actually here, thousands of miles from home in one of the world's most desirable locations. As an added bonus, it was almost Christmas. I couldn't begin to imagine the splendour of what lay ahead, partaking in festivities which were bound to be interplanetary compared to what I'd come to expect back home. I'd just need to make sure I didn't get any facial injuries during my forthcoming fight, especially if I wanted to score with one of hundreds of bikini-clad, miss world lookalikes, parading up and down the beach, performing like they were auditioning for a part in *Baywatch*. Time for a swim, I bought the cheapest, nastiest surf board I could find, then hit the water, determined to rekindle skills I'd perfected in Perth. I paddled out a couple of hundred yards, riding waves flat on my belly, before very carefully rising to my feet, standing atop the flimsy, fibreglass board. A sizeable wave picked me up, sweeping me rapidly back towards shore and I celebrated by leaping in mid-air, landing feet first in the water like a one-man synchronised diving team.

"Jesus-H Christ!"

I knew instantly I'd done serious damage. Searing pain tore through my leg, causing me to scream with agony. A young couple swimming nearby peered over in anguish and I had to signal to them I was okay, lest they thought I'd been stung by jellyfish or, even worse, had my leg torn off by a shark. Cursing my stupidity, I refocused. What the *fuck* had I done? It didn't take long to work it out: my foot had landed full force on a shard of razor-sharp coral. As the sea around me turned blood red, I headed for the beach to check the damage, hoping and praying it was merely superficial, while already expecting the worst. I could have cried when I checked the bottom of my foot. Stretching from big toe to heel was a single, elongated cut, bizarrely reminding me of the San Andreas Fault, a couple of thousand miles away in nearby California. Absolutely pouring blood, I immediately sought the help of a lifeguard. A proper beach-bod, he started tugging at his hair, clearly more than a bit concerned; not for me, unfortunately, but for the love of his life, a stretch of beautiful, white sandy beach.

"Hey, man…don't bleed on my sand!"

He advised me to go straight to hospital. I told him I'd love to but that I didn't have insurance. He sighed and shook his head in disbelief, pointing out a neighbouring drug store, telling me to invest in a roll of sticking plaster, bandages and butterfly stitches. Taking his advice, I limped back to the hotel, patching myself up as best I could. Straight after, I had a kip, drifting into the deepest of deep sleeps, dreaming of swimming in red wine of all things. When I woke, I discovered the bedsheets were soaked in claret. Terrified of being charged for replacements, I ordered a jug of coffee and deliberately poured the lot all over the bed, disguising the bloody morass. It worked a treat. I reported it and a maid arrived, unquestioningly fitting fresh sheets. The full enormity of what I'd done was slowly sinking in. What was the old saying? Even the best-laid plans? My foot was so sore, I could barely walk, let alone perform martial arts, the principal reason for the trip, honing my skills under the guidance of foreign masters. Neither could I enjoy the resort. Not now, anyway. Getting from A to B would be nigh on impossible under the circumstances. There was no way I could afford taxis everywhere and the local bus service wasn't the best, meaning I was pretty much confined to the hotel for the remaining eight or nine days. With money incredibly tight, I put a small amount aside for LA, dividing what was left by the duration. My choices were simple: eat like a king every day or get totally and utterly bolloxed. Anyone who's ever spent time in my company will already know which option I chose. Morning, noon and night, I was at the bar, making the best of a not so very merry Christmas, fighting a continual battle with an arse of a bartender, who kept asking me to prove my age, purely because I refused to tip him each time he refilled my glass. Every day I showed him my passport and the next he asked to see it again, testing my patience to the absolute limits. I kept repeating to myself: don't forget that quaint old Barnsley saying, Greenie. *Fuck him*! I was at the point of planting the arrogant little shit when a couple of Aussie pals I'd made intervened and did the job for me. A big, blond, burly, beer guzzling bloke from Brisbane went right up to his ear, threatening to bury him in the Pacific. Great blokes, the Aussies and it upsets me I never got chance to say goodbye properly. So, if by some quirk of fate, you're sat up in bed reading this, somewhere over by Bill's mother's, cheerio, cobbers. Oh, and have a couple of tinnies for me.

As my time in Hawaii drew to a close, I couldn't deny I was disappointed to be going home. Alright, so things mightn't have gone exactly to plan. I damned nearly killed myself, meaning I had to cancel the remainder of my training sessions and didn't get a sniff of a bird. But that didn't mean it wasn't an amazing location to visit, overflowing with attractions and incredible things to see and do. I was leaving with loads of memories and sincerely hoped to return one day. For now, though, I had to be content with a couple of nights, slumming it in LA. Not easy, I know, but hey; I suppose somebody had to do it, lol. Before I departed, however, the Aloha State had one final surprise in store; or at least the hotel did. I'd phoned home a few times, detailing my accident and wishing everyone Merry Christmas and the like, with the calls inexplicably racking up an eye-watering hundred-dollar bill. I paid it without question. What else could I do? The problem was it left me penniless to the point where I didn't even have enough cash for a taxi from LAX to the hotel, meaning I had to spend forty-eight hours dossing around the airport terminal, scraping together a few dollars here and there for drinks and sandwiches. I arrived home totally exhausted a few days later and went straight to bed. When I couldn't sleep, I got ready and popped down to The Potter's Wheel for a pint. As I walked in, a huge cheer went up from the back. Lo and behold, it was my entourage of pals. And, yes, they were sitting in the same old seats at the same old table. I couldn't stop laughing; wait until I told them I was contemplating a trip to Mexico in the near future.

14. Master Charlie Green

As the months and years rolled by, the martial arts career continued unabated, as did my obsession with sport in general. I'd determinedly risen to 3rd dan and was eager to make 4th upon which I'd attain the kudos and stature of becoming a taekwondo master. Out of the blue, I was invited to Rotherham to complete my grading, an event scheduled ridiculously early on Saturday morning to enable people time to get home to watch Australia versus England in the 2003 rugby world cup final. Tony Quigley was doing the honours and I was looking forward to the experience immensely. Unfortunately, my back was playing up again and I was also suffering a repetitive strain injury from months of non-stop teaching and training, leaving me incapable of performing the thirteen poomsae patterns I'd been instructed to perfect for the occasion. I wasn't in a position to fight or spar either and so took the decision to sit things out, reluctantly putting my 4th dan celebrations on hold until a later date. It wasn't all bad news, though. I thoroughly enjoyed watching thirty odd other students being put through their paces. Everyone passed and it was fantastic watching men and boys receiving belts of various colours. Only afterwards did the reality of the failed occasion hit home. Bitterly disappointed, I was meant to be joining Tony, Phil and Daz for world cup food and drinks at the Rockingham Arms, Wentworth. An affluent little village on Hoyland's southern flank, it was where the legendary Grandmaster was staying overnight. I could easily have bailed out. No one would have blamed me if I had. Not under the circumstances, anyway. I chose not to. My grading mightn't have turned out as envisioned, but I couldn't see any point crying over spilled milk. What was done was done and that's all there was to it. We enjoyed a beautiful steak lunch, then settled down in front of the rugby, screaming, shouting and applauding the boys on, while partaking in eternal pub-wide renditions of: *Swing low, sweet chariot. Coming for to carry me home.* Standing room only, the Rock was packed to the rafters by the time Jonny Wilkinson's famous drop goal went over with just twenty-six seconds left on the clock. England had done it and the pub erupted, people hugging, singing and shouting, showering everyone in the vicinity with wine and beer. We celebrated in typical fashion, getting some more beer in. Another round quickly followed. Then another and another, and another. The Beach Boys were on the juke-box, singing: *Round, round, get around, I get around.* I wish they would get a round, I remember thinking, because my pocket was emptying at an unprecedented rate of knots. Soon, it wasn't the only thing empty. I'd consumed so much ale by this stage, I took myself outside and threw my guts up in the beer garden. Leaning on the wall, swinging spittle, adorning my bottom lip, I suddenly felt a slap on the shoulder.

"Nothing changes, Master Green. Come on, lad, let's get you sorted..."

Tony's choice of words reverberated around my subconscious like a herd of galloping elephants as the full enormity of his address slowly sank in. Had I heard him correctly? Was I dreaming? Was I imagining things? Or had I died and gone to heaven? The answer was no on all counts. After almost a decade of blood, sweat and tears, I finally had my 4th dan. The Grandmaster had decreed it on the grounds that my expertise, experience, energy and enthusiasm was *more* than adequate. In short, I had nothing left to prove. He'd already made out the certificate and would present me with my belt later, black with four gold stripes, meaning I was now officially instructor class, attaining a level where I was able assess and grade students as I saw fit.

Not long after, I proudly accompanied Team GB on an international jaunt to the Netherlands. I was meant to be coaching a friend of mine, an up-and-coming martial artist called Lee England, who was fighting in the competition. Unfortunately, he sustained an injury in the run-up and had to pull out, meaning my role was now merely as an observer. Lee still travelled, however, albeit with a nasty limp, accompanied by his elder brother, Darren, a top lad who eventually went on to find fame as a Premiership referee. Also on the trip was head coach Gary Sykes, another ex-British taekwondo champion, and a famous name of the future, Doncaster's Sarah Stevenson MBE, the phenomenally successful taekwondo world champion and Olympic bronze medal winner. Staged in a giant Eindhoven sports hall, the event had been advertised well in advance as being shown live on Eurosport. As such, I made sure the family tuned in, promising I'd find a way to get on the telly, somehow, however unlikely it might seem. I wasn't talking a wave, either, but something infinitely more substantial, though what I'd no idea. My room wasn't ready when I arrived at the hotel, so I was given a couple of complimentary drinks while I waited. All sorted, I headed for room 326 and couldn't believe the sight which greeted me when I unlocked the door: an unmade bed, towels strewn across the floor and dirty food trays here, there and everywhere. I was back down at reception in a flash, handing out bollockings left, right and bloody centre. The manager was summoned and immediately awarded a free bar as compensation, a gift which I took full advantage of, a prolonged drink to celebrate my recent grading. A gallon or so later, I was taking my seat in the arena, three sheets to the wind and absolutely stinking of ale. Located several rows back, I had a fantastic panoramic view of the action. One fight followed another in what was a closely matched contest, several bouts taking place simultaneously across four or five rings. TV cameras were sited directly opposite. I must have featured on-screen numerous times over, but was still awaiting the opportunity to get on telly proper. Then I got my chance. As a referee prepared to take charge of an upcoming bout, I frantically began waving my arms in the air, succeeding in attracting his attention. He instinctively waved back and I cupped hands around my mouth, yelling he had something on his shoe. Full weight on one leg, he twisted at the hip, raising a heel to check, upon which I yelled once more, *hello sailor* on this occasion, causing him to sigh and shake his head in disbelief. Unbeknown to me at the time, the incident was shown live on Eurosport and beamed to fifty-four countries across twenty different languages. Result, or what? By all accounts, the family absolutely lapped it up. And who could blame them?

A couple of months later, I was on my travels again, to Madrid this time, purely in a spectator role for the world championships. It cost me a few quid but I didn't mind. I was earning good money at work and my taekwondo schools were fetching in a decent second income, meaning I could comfortably afford it. I shared a room with a couple of lads from Jump, top notch taekwondo instructors Kev Carnell and his son, Gary, who complained incessantly about my infernal snoring. Several years previously, we'd have been on opposite sides of the stone-throwing, Elsecar-Jump raids. Now we were best of pals, martial artists and boozing partners extraordinaire. It was a quiet trip by previous standards, other than the fact Sarah Stevenson claimed silver in the middleweight division. That was the good news; the bad was that we missed the bout on account of a delayed flight. Alright, alright, I know what you're thinking: only us. And you'd be right. But at least we got plenty of beer down our throats, enjoying a bloody good laugh in the process, making the best of a bad situation. During a fun-filled and thoroughly hectic few days, we took in lots of competition and engaged in plenty of sight-seeing, predominantly bars and restaurants in what was a freezing cold trip. One of the highlights was meeting an Aussie film director, whose grandma lived in Jump. He gave us all the details and we actually knew her; where she lived and where she went on her nights out, playing bingo at Jump WMC, under the watchful gaze of ever popular steward, Andy Hodgkinson. I don't know what the odds on that were, but there must have been more chance of Phil Rudd breaking the habit of a lifetime and getting a round in. Yeah, right. In my dreams, maybe. As Jud famously quipped in *Kes*, the bugger was as tight as a camel's arse in a sandstorm.

Another world cup rolled round. Not taekwondo this time, but football. And it was being held just across the water in Germany. A group of us signed up to go, thirteen in total, exclusively martial artists, travelling by minibus through France and Belgium to our Frankfurt destination. In advance of the trip, I worked every hour God sent, saving up a shed load of money to keep me in food and drink for the duration. A few days before we were due to leave, however, everything went Pete Tong. And I mean big time! I took my passport to the travel agents in order to change a large wedge of pound sterling into Euros. Straight after, I headed to nearby Wath-Upon-Dearne, where I was holding a weekly boxercise class. I made sure I took the cash inside with me, just in case; but foolishly left my passport in the glove box. When I emerged at the conclusion of the class, the car had gone. I'd never been a flapper. Not up until that precise moment, anyway. Not until I realised I hadn't a clue what I was going to do now; how I was going to travel across Europe without a flipping passport. The easiest thing would have been to knock the trip on the head and stay home and watch it on the telly. Not a chance. Old Greenie boy was made of sterner stuff than that and quickly determined to find a way. Slowly but surely, I hatched a plan. First job was to inform the police what had happened. Second was to book an appointment at HM Passport Office, Durham, to obtain a replacement document. This was fixed for 10am Thursday, meaning an early start, cadging a lift off dad to Doncaster, then a train up to the north-east. Half way there, my phone rang. It was South Yorkshire Police. My heart leapt. Please let it be good news, I prayed; please let them have found the car and recovered my passport, meaning I could about turn and go to the pub instead. I confirmed my details and they informed me they had, indeed, located my vehicle. Punching the air in celebration, I was soon brought back down to earth with a bump. The car had been burned out in nearby Wombwell Woods and was currently being recovered. Don't ask me why, but it was only then I remembered I'd left valuables in the boot: an Armani suit and a brand-new set of golf clubs, recently purchased to satisfy a resurgence of interest in a sport I hadn't played since childhood. My heart sank, but nothing like as much as it did when I was informed the replacement document might take a week or so to process on account of a backlog of applications brought about by recent strike action. I huffed and I puffed and I blew the house down, painting a no-holds-barred picture of my predicament. I explained I was going to the world cup. I was travelling Tuesday and, if I didn't get my passport, I wouldn't be able to go: it was as simple as that. The young chap behind the counter sympathised, unashamedly. The north-east was football mad. *He* was football mad. A Middlesborough fan for his sins, he said he would speak with his supervisor and see if anything could be done. It caused a right kafuffle, raised voices and a thump on a table strong enough to make cups and saucers rattle. Luckily for me, it finished one-nil to the Boro. I could have my passport, but it wouldn't be ready today because my application would need to be certified professionally, requiring the signature of a doctor, policeman, accountant or the like. I booked another appointment for Friday morning, then made the long trudge home, pulling a few strings in transit, getting a copper pal of Sean's to do the honours in exchange for a bottle of whisky. A quick night's sleep and I was back again, grinning ear to ear that the end was finally in sight. Little did I know, but I would soon be sporting a face like a wet weekend. I was duly informed it wouldn't be ready till Monday now, necessitating another horrendous round trip and associated expenses. I can't pretend I was happy, but I remained philosophical as ever. Contesting the decision might easily upset the apple cart and so I kept schtum and went with the flow, praying nothing went wrong this time, largely because I didn't have any more holiday days remaining on top of those already booked for the world cup.

My pleas were answered. Monday was a breeze and Tuesday afternoon we were on our way, catching the overnight ferry, before weaving our way through the near continent in a minibus filled with fun, laughter and endless piss-takes. We had a fridge on board. Where it came from or how it was wired up, I never discovered. Needless to say, though, it was the perfect companion for countless cases of beer, accompanying us on the trip. We didn't have any match tickets. I don't think we even tried to get any, either. What would have been the point? Prices were extortionate in the extreme, plus which we had better things to spend our hard-earned brass on. Like beer, beer and more beer. It was red hot as we arrived at our Frankfurt campsite. Tent-city didn't come into it. It seemed to stretch forever, reaching out towards a skyline littered with skyscrapers. The site demographic was ninety per cent English, with a few Poles, Italians, French and Americans thrown in for good measure. The flag of St George was everywhere. It was draped over tents and toilet blocks; campervans and perimeter fencing. A party atmosphere was immediately evident. Alcohol was flowing and groups of rival football supporters were happily engaging with one another, putting aside decades-old rivalries in support of a common cause. Spurs fans rubbed shoulders with Gooners; Mancs with Scousers; West Ham with Chelsea. There wasn't a sniff of trouble anywhere, exactly how we liked it. It was a pity the local polizei weren't embracing the congeniality. As we headed into the Frankfurt for a few sherbets, the streets were lined with officers in riot gear, standing alongside strategically positioned water cannon and fleets of lock-up vans. Fans were funnelled in different directions to dilute numbers, ensuring strung-out groups of friends were split up. I finished up with a prominent kickboxer I knew called Andreas Joannou. Lee England was also with us alongside his dad, Dave, who'd come along just for the laugh. We ended up in a bar packed with Germans. We got along brilliantly, sharing beers and a few laughs, with Joannou in particular having a whale of a time. Resembling a Greek God, he had pretty fräuleins swarming all over him, inadvertently ruffling quite a few feathers. All of a sudden, the atmosphere changed. A couple of glasses were thrown and the Germans started chanting anti-English rhetoric. Penned into a corner, it looked like we were in for a right good kicking. Lee got on the phone to the others, explaining the situation. By some miracle, they managed to locate us, pouring into the bar like the 7th Cavalry just a few minutes later. The only thing missing was the bugler, sounding the charge. The Germans weren't stupid. Confronted by a dozen of the roughest, toughest, fittest looking bunch of Brits they were ever likely to encounter, they retreated to a safe distance and left us to it. We were unbelievably relieved. Alright, so we were practising martial artists. But that didn't mean we wanted trouble. Suffice to say, though, we'd have responded vigorously if provoked. And I suspect it very clearly showed.

By the end of the day, we were safely back on the site. The partying continued throughout the night in advance of England's opener versus Paraguay the following day. We hoped we'd have plenty to celebrate come full-time. A one-nil win was all we got. But it would do for starters, a nice precursor to another raucous night out in the city. The day after was more of the same and then the day after that. Still boiling hot, we were permanently dressed in short-sleeved England football shirts, shorts and flip-flops, ubiquitously known as Jerusalem bovver boots. We eventually found ourselves in a bar filled with England fans, watching the second group game versus Trinidad & Tobago. Once again, we struggled to impress, grinding out a scrappy two-nil victory. It mattered not. The after-match celebrations were wild. *Eng-er-land, Eng-er-land, Eng-er-land,* rang through the streets for hours afterwards. I vividly recall breakdancing with a group of South Koreans. The Ten German Bombers song reared its ugly head. Flags were waving. Beers were flowing. And there we were, right in the mix, merrily rubbing shoulders with the boys from the Mersey and the Thames and the Tyne. The sun went down. Night fell and I got another round in. I was so pissed now I was almost out of it, disappearing to the bog to chuck my guts up. When I returned, everyone had gone. With my phone dead, I asked a group of Turkish supporters if they'd seen any English lads leave. Things quickly got lost in translation. And *I* got lost in Frankfurt, inadvertently winding up in the red-light district. Desperate for my bed, I waved down a taxi and gave the driver the name of my campsite.

Twenty minutes later, he was still driving circles round the local area, deliberately running up the bill. I ordered him to stop and he pulled up adjacent a canal, demanding forty Euros. I gave him ten and told him to go and jump in the cut if he didn't like it. I could tell he didn't understand a word; but he *did* get the message. Realising he was a millisecond away from a thick ear, he hoofed me straight out, speeding off, clouds of thick, black smoke trailing from the exhaust. That sorted, I was dismayed to discover I was now being aggressively stalked by a group of menacing-looking youths. There was no way I was in any fit state to make a run for it. And, so, I clenched my fists and made ready, bracing myself for the forthcoming beating. Luckily, I'd totally misinterpreted the situation. As the group drew closer, I realised they were English, a real mixed bag if ever there was one; three Geordies, a Scouser, Bristolian, Cockney and Brummie, combining to make it feel like I'd just stepped into an episode of *Auf Wiedersehen Pet*. We got talking and discovered we were stopping on neighbouring campsites. Also lost, we were busy discussing options when a polizei van pulled up and a couple of armed officers jumped out, asking what we were up to. We explained the situation, detailing where we needed to get to. Absolutely miles away, they said we'd struggle to make it across the city so late at night and that our best bet was to get a room at the hotel down the road, which they assured us would have vacancies. We knew why when we got there; the rooms were just awful, filthy with dirty sheets and cold-water showers. Somehow, though, I managed to get my head down for a decent period, a miracle considering the door wouldn't lock, meaning I spent half the night sleeping with one eye open. By the time I got up, my new found pals had done one; but not before paying my bill for me, an amazing gesture from a crowd of total strangers and testament to the love I'd experienced throughout my stay to present. I ordered a taxi to the railway station. A short train ride later, I was back on home turf and having the pissed ripped out of me by the lads, par for the course really, as predictable as fish and chips for Friday tea or a Saturday morning hangover.

The days rolled by and I got to thinking I couldn't believe I'd willingly put my body through such an ordeal. I was a martial artist; a British champion; an undefeated international athlete. And it didn't sit well with me. I would need to get back training as soon as I arrived home. First and foremost, however, there was a couple more days of fun and frivolity to get through. We headed for Cologne to savour the atmosphere of England's final group game versus Sweden. Our new campsite was hosting an inter-camp, seven-per-side football tournament, including the participation of several local teams. I've no idea how many rounds were played, but it started at nine and was still going on early evening. Lee picked our team and stuck me straight on the bench. Nobody could believe it. I'd had trials for Barnsley and turned down the chance of a professional career in Australia, but was only selected as sub in a boozy, ad hoc competition on a German cabbage patch of a pitch. When things started going wrong, he soon brought me on, putting me up front, where I seemed to score with every touch, including a scissor-kick which would have put Pele to shame. Against all the odds, we made the final. It was destined to end in disappointment, though. We lost 7-6 to a team of locals, but at least went away with our heads held high. In the evening, we watched England draw two apiece with Sweden. The atmosphere was fantastic with no sign of animosity, exactly how it should be. England fans were predictably in full flow, dreaming up endless hilarious chants, constantly taking the piss out of opposing supporters. On a busy street lined with bars and restaurants, to the tune of *Go West* by *The Pet Shop Boys*, everyone started singing: *You're shit but your birds are fit. You're shit but your birds are fit. You're shit but your birds are fit. You're shit but your birds are fit...*

I couldn't have agreed more. Like a kid in a sweet shop, I was spoiled for choice, genuinely not knowing which way to turn. As for the football, we'd qualified for the round of 16, which we would unfortunately have to watch at home. No matter. We'd had a fantastic time and not encountered any trouble; until an enlarged group of German fans pelted England supporters with bottles, that is, forcing the polizei to move in en masse with batons and water cannon. We took shelter inside an Italian restaurant, enjoying a fantastic meal, during which I crept up behind one of the lads and dumped my old man on his shoulder while he ate. Everyone was screaming with laughter, especially little old me. I was soon laughing on the other side of my face, though. The person in question, who shall remain anonymous, cottoned on to my antics and stuck my pride and joy with a fork, skewering it like a German sausage. Then another disaster. Crossing a crowded room, gripping four or five flaming sambucas, I swerved to avoid a table and burning liqueur spilled down the side of the glass, igniting my fingers. I instinctively swayed the other way and the same happened again, setting my other fingers on fire this time. A film must have formed across the affected areas because I didn't feel a thing. I'd become as instant celebrity, though, tables filled with customers, roaring with laughter, screaming comments in a variety of languages, pointing me out like I was some kind of freak show. As soon as the film burned off, it was a different story. The pain was so intense, I was forced to stop and kneel, setting the glasses on the floor while I blew and wafted my fingers out. Then the shout went up:

"Watch out…the bloody carpet is on fire!"

Back home, we watched the boys beat Ecuador 1-0 in the next round, then lose on penalties to Portugal, bowing out with an inevitable whimper. An instantly forgettable tournament for England, it was one which would remain emblazoned upon my subconscious for all eternity.

15. A New Hope

Quite abruptly, my time at Ronseal came to an end, just like I knew it would eventually. Destined for bigger, better, brighter things, I convinced myself it was meant to be and was merely commencement of the next chapter in life's journey. The only regret was it all finished a bit more acrimoniously than I would have preferred, a crying shame really after such an enjoyable and successful tenure. I'd long since waved goodbye to the production line and was now firmly entrenched in a new position as trainer's trainer, instructing line and departmental mangers upon how to get the best out of new and existing staff as a means of improving production and profitability. I had my own office. Please knock and wait, it said on the door. I liked that; liked it a lot, because it meant no one could burst in and catch me red-handed, clandestinely formulating future plans, principally setting up my own martial arts clothing brand. I hadn't come up with a name for my venture as yet and so gave it a working title, *A New Hope*, because that's essentially what it was, a play-on-words reference to *Star Wars Episode IV*, the inaugural film in the series. I did my planning during working hours because I could. I was hardly overworked. I just pretended I was, that's all, making sure I hummed and hawed and sighed and shook my head whenever discussing new training initiatives, overplaying the time and work involved in getting things up and running. I had it off to an absolute tee. I could make mashing a cup of tea sound complex and the management invariably fell for it, sanctioning far more time to complete individual projects than was ever required, freeing up countless hours for extra-curricular activities. My Ronseal troubles were nothing major. It was more an accumulation of niggly encounters, such as being reprimanded for eating on the shop floor. Straight after, I went on the sick with the bad back which had haunted me throughout my sporting career. The company decided I was swinging the lead, throwing my toys out of the pram in retaliation for my recent disciplinary. I wasn't, of course; nothing like it, in fact. It was giving me more gip than ever, so much so that I even booked an appointment to see a chiropractor. Next thing, I'd been referred to the hospital for an X-ray, where I was worryingly informed the problem had its roots in the fact I'd fractured my spine at some point in the dim and distant past. I didn't need to think too hard to pinpoint the incident, reliving the fall from the Tarzan swing, landing on my head and crawling all the way home. I asked what the prognosis was and they told me there wasn't one. What was done was done, unfortunately. There was no miracle treatment. The only advice was to take things easy, an instruction which naturally fell on deaf ears, as it would have done for any self-respecting martial artist. I eventually returned to work, but was off again a few days later with food poisoning this time, news which went down like a lead balloon in the corridors of power. I was recovering on the settee when human resources turned up, banging my door down. Fully conversant with employment law, I wasn't happy and told them so in no uncertain terms. I knew they couldn't just rock up uninvited and so involved the union to fight my case. As anticipated, I was ordered to attend another disciplinary hearing. The GMB union representative attended with me. He told me they had it in for me and warned me to expect the worst. Imagine his surprise then, and mine, when the gaffer backtracked on absolutely everything and even offered me improved hours and a hefty pay rise. I could and probably should have accepted it, but very politely declined. A fortnight later, I'd chucked it all in and departed those hallowed, wood-stained corridors for the final time.

The good news was that I'd made decent progress on my clothing brand. I'd finally settled upon a title and registered the trademark. Still going strong today, *Musa* was the name, translating as warrior in Korean and Moses in Arabic. I was also in conversations with a Korean taekwondo equipment and clothing company named Mooto, who were seeking a UK distributor. I was eventually invited to fly to Seoul to bid for the franchise. It was a terrific opportunity, but one I sadly had to decline. I had a bit of money put aside, but the cost of the trip would have pretty much skint me and there were no guarantees I would be awarded the contract. In between time, I had a short spell on the shop floor at B&Q, before starting work at Ventura, a local call centre, training to handle incoming technical support calls for internet provider, Wanadoo, a division of mobile phone company, Orange. By my own admission, I struggled to begin with. Way out of my comfort zone, I wasn't expected to survive my probationary period. The company knew it and so did I. Luckily, I had an amazing manager to fall back on, a bloke called John Fitzsimmons, who took me under his wing, helping me at every juncture with assistance from a couple of lovely ladies, Gemma Haigh and Brooke Harrison. I eventually survived what was colloquially known as the cabbage patch, a four-week training and development course for the crazy brave, designed to weed out all non-hackers who didn't pack the gear to serve on the beloved call centre floor. Once qualified, I was put to work with a guy called Lee Mills, who rapidly converted me into the finished article. If you're reading this, mate, you have my eternal gratitude. One of these days, you watch, I'll turn up at yours with a case of wine and a straw basket filled with fruit, Oskar Schindler style. And, if you believe that, I'm currently employed as a bus driver, working from home. Without doubt *the* most notable event which occurred at Ventura, however, was that I met my new partner, Nicola. A few months later, we'd moved in together, sharing a house in Low Valley, a small settlement sandwiched in between Wombwell and Darfield. As if that wasn't enough, we were soon expecting a child. Yup, incredible as it may have sounded at the time, Charles Richard Green, Cloughfields raggy lad, was about to become a daddy.

As far as Ventura was concerned, I was getting along great and quickly gained promotion; but I still cradled ambitions of my own and was pouring much of my spare time into development of *Musa*. Eventually, I visited BBIC, Barnsley Business Innovation

Centre, where I was coached upon various aspects of running a business; sales and marketing; profit and loss; accounting and taxation. In time, I was interviewed to check my suitability for a grant. The lady concerned rubber-stamped my application without hesitation, describing me as a go-getting, forward thinking, ambitious entrepreneur. My ensuing smile said it all: I'd have taken that. I was awarded five grand, but under the strict condition I didn't use it to purchase stock, which seemed fair enough. After much deliberation, I used a large portion of the cash to set up an all-singing, all-dancing ecommerce website, a one-stop shop for anyone seeking good quality, highly affordable taekwondo gear. Next, I embarked upon the task of looking for a supplier, a foreign based sporting goods manufacturer who could produce equipment and garments at the right price. It was a daunting assignment, involving literally hundreds of back-and-forth emails to factories in far-flung countries such as India, Turkey, Malaysia, Vietnam and China. I eventually set up a UK meeting with a promising lead from Pakistan. I was looking forward to it immensely. Everything went well and I placed a nice little order, parting with a sizeable deposit with the balance payable upon receipt. Unfortunately, the guy was nothing but a shitester. Months passed without delivery and I was really beginning to worry. I'd tried calling him numerous times without luck. Then, miraculously, one day he answered. I leapt down the phone at him, first introducing myself and then demanding my money back. He tried fobbing me off, feeding me all kinds of garbage. It didn't work. I threatened to expose him on a supplier website he used and finally buckled, forwarding a full refund. With a sharp intake of breath, I started over again, endlessly burning the midnight oil, revisiting previously contacted potentials while determinedly unearthing new connections.

Back on the martial arts circuit, I was still teaching across multiple schools. Phil and Sean had their own taekwondo schools by this time and there was a friendly rivalry between us regarding who produced the best fighters. It was the hot topic each time we met;

until I revealed my news about *Musa*, that is. All of a sudden, the hot topic became *me*, a million and one piss-takes alongside relentless questioning of my plans. I gave as good as I got, naturally; the bastards couldn't pillock one who'd pillocked thousands and never would. Best pals, maybe; but I could tell they were green with envy at my ambitions, a situation which made me all the more determined to succeed. Every training session, it was more of the same. All the students would rip the piss out of me, assailing me from every conceivable angle. It was a good job they didn't attempt it on the mats, or I may well have popped one or two of the buggers.

The clock continued to tick. Weeks became months and Nicola's due date drew ever closer. Then it happened. Summoned to the hospital, I was more nervous than I had been before any of my fights. In the ring, I only had myself to worry about. Now I had Nicola and our unborn child on my mind. Not that you'd have known it. As usual, my anxiety manifested itself in flamboyant humour. I put on a show for all the medical staff, making them laugh throughout the entire procedure, sharing funny stories and singing a few Celtic football songs along the way. In the end, it all came down to a C-section, expertly performed by a doctor with mitts as big as Kenny Everett's oversized stage hands. Mother and baby were announced as doing fine. We were proud parents now, blessed with a beautiful, bouncing baby boy, who we duly named Harley.

In more good news, I unearthed a firm *Musa* lead, this time from a supplier in Quanzhou City in the Fujian Province of southern China. We exchanged numerous emails and eventually agreed a price for various items, subject to the supply and acceptance of a range of pre-production samples. The samples arrived bang on time and were exactly the quality I was looking for. All I had to do now was decide whether or not I was going to proceed and place the order. My contact was a gentleman called Wang Shuang, who used the English name of Jase for simplicity. He was a decent bloke was Jase. He insisted I take my time, which was really appreciated and a smart move on his part. I wore my heart on my sleeve. Everyone knew that. But I would *never* fall for a hard sell. Not after last time, anyway, especially when it meant parting with thousands of pounds up front. In the end, I decided to go for it. That was the easy bit. The hard part was collating the stock order and dividing it into my budget of roughly fifteen grand, accrued from savings and what was left from the lump sum I received after being knocked off my motorbike. I got there in the end, though, making an order which ticked all the boxes, giving me a decent spread of kit across all product categories; adult and kid's versions of hogu, dobok, head-guards, shin-guards, paddles, hoodies and T-shirts. All I had to do now was go ahead and place it.

First things first, though: it was Harley's christening in Darfield, a precursor to a much-needed holiday in Greece. All the family were present and we had a great day with a good old drink at the end of it. We were so proud and Harley looked the business in his christening outfit. Except there was a problem and a big one as well: dad wasn't well. Hadn't been for a couple of days to be fair. Everyone was worried about him. A shadow of his former-self, he looked shocking, gaunt, struggling to walk and slurring his speech. Never once, though, did he let his guard down. God bless his heart, it must have been terribly difficult, making all the right noises and joining in whenever called upon. By mid-afternoon, he was so exhausted I had no other choice but to order him a taxi home. I remember shepherding him to the car like it was yesterday, one arm slung around his shoulder, the other cradling Harley. Dad had *always* been there for me. And I'd long been aware that, one day, the roles would inevitably be reversed. Sadly, it dawned on me that that day was now. A tear trickled down my cheek as he ruffled my boy's hair, bidding him cheerio. Harley chortled in response, trying his hardest to enunciate his beautiful grandad's name. *Wuss*, he kept saying: Wuss, Wuss, Wuss. Ironic really, because *wuss* was the last word anyone would use to describe dad, a rough, tough, straight-talking, strait-laced, no nonsense, salt-of-the-earth Yorkshireman. He clambered into the back and I closed the door for him. Fingering his beard, he smiled and waved. Then he was gone, speeding off down the road, a diminishing figure, silhouetted in the rear window. By some miracle, I managed to hold myself together. I don't know how, because something deep inside of me said I'd never see him again. Praying I was mistaken, I took Harley back inside and immediately informed Nicola of my feelings. She told me not to be silly, insisting it was just my imagination, playing tricks. Far from convinced, I ordered another pint. It was all I could think to do. Needless to say, by the end of the evening, I was well and truly plastered.

Two days later, we were in Dassia, Corfu, drinking cold beer and making bucket and spade sandcastles on a sun-soaked beach. Nicola had persuaded me not to take my mobile. She said I'd been working too hard, what with Ventura, *Musa* and martial arts classes, and needed a complete rest from it all. I couldn't agree more and so did as I was told, leaving stock order placement in the hands of a Ventura pal of mine, a chap called Simon, who I asked to send email confirmation first thing Monday morning, ensuring it didn't get lost in scores of other weekend correspondence, clogging up Jase's inbox. The days drifted by, slowly at first then speeding up as the holiday progressed, just like they always did. We had a nice little routine going and everything was good; breakfast on the terrace; sunbathing round the pool; a leisurely lunch; a trip to the beach for beer and a swim. After evening meal, we'd have a walk around the resort, stopping off at various bars, eating, drinking and making merry. It was what life was all about and I can't deny I was lapping it up; but I still couldn't shed repeated premonitions I was having about dad's well-being, consistently waking up in the middle of the night, panting for breath in a cold, cold sweat. Nicola invariably did her best to calm me down. It wasn't enough. Nothing she could say or do made the slightest difference. Whatever was happening, I knew it was real. I couldn't just sense it: I could feel it in my bones. Something bad was coming. The only thing I didn't know was what? And when?

One evening, we were in a sports bar, watching tennis on the telly. Harley was asleep and Nicola had her nose stuck in a menu, studying pizza toppings. A waiter happened by and I stopped him, ordering another round of drinks. As he disappeared to the bar, the most incredible thing happened: the entire room illuminated and I glimpsed a powerful lightning bolt, walloping the widescreen, ethereal plasma, splashing and distorting, an unmistakable message from heaven. I stood up and gazed around. The bar was half full, but it was obvious no one else had seen anything. Not Nicola. Not the waiter. Not the group of youths on the next table. Only me. I sat back down, blowing hard. I realised instantly what it meant. The clock on the wall said 6pm precisely and I cried, because I knew it was the exact moment dad had passed. No matter how many times Nicola tried to convince me otherwise, I wasn't having it. It had happened and that's all there was to it. I immediately wished I had my phone. Then again, I was glad I hadn't, because it would have provided the means with which to confirm my fears. And, when Nicola offered me use of hers, I backed off like she'd just offered me a tablet of cyanide flavoured chewing gum.

After a fraught final couple of days, we arrived back in the UK and were picked up at the airport by Nicola's parents. Neither spoke a word until we were in the car and on our way up the motorway. Again, I knew what was coming. The words I'd been dreading finally surfaced: dad had died. I asked when: date and time? Monday at 4pm came the answer. The response threw me; but only momentarily. Including time difference, it was the exact moment the lightning bolt struck. Such a profound moment, I came over faint. Then I cried, shamelessly; just like I knew I would when I received confirmation.

16. The Iceman Cometh

As if losing dad wasn't distressing enough, there was more bad news awaiting when I got home. The next few days were naturally spent mourning with family, trying to come to terms with the passing of the finest human being I, we, all of us, ever had the pleasure to know. Back online, I rang Simon to get an update on the *Musa* order, eager to discover when it would be delivered. All I can say is, it was a good job it was a phone call and not a face-to-face meeting. My Ventura colleague suddenly accrued a new nickname: *Simple Simon*. He'd only forgotten to place the order, hadn't he? Blood up, I got straight on it, whizzing my requirements across. An anxious couple of days later, an email popped up from Jase, confirming goods would be manufactured and despatched within the next week or so, conditional upon receipt of payment. I bank transferred the invoice total the same day and received another email by return, confirming receipt and saying everything was in order. That evening, I attended a kick boxing training session and was immediately ribbed by Phil, Sean and the lads, poking fun, asking where my gear was. It was getting boring now and I let them know it, before taking out my frustrations on the heavy bag. By the time the session was over, word of my news had finally broken. The result was an outpouring of love, an immense show of affection, fetching a fresh round of tears, as if there hadn't been enough of those already.

Next morning, I realised I'd dropped a bollock. I urgently needed premises for *Musa*. As it stood, the stock order would be delivered to my home address. Fifty grand at retail, it would have filled every room and cubby-hole, so I went straight out and rented a cut-price industrial unit in the Carlton area of Barnsley, emailing Jase the change in instructions. The day after that, I returned to work, an awful, mind-numbing period, leading up to the funeral. Not unexpectedly, it was the worst day of my life when we laid Russ to rest. It came and went, though, same as I knew it would and we didn't half give him a good send off, getting pissed as farts afterwards, celebrating his life. The weeks crept by and the *Musa* delivery finally arrived, a forty-foot shipping container, overflowing with stock. It took us a full weekend to check everything off and put it away. And that was only the start. We then commenced the laborious task of manually photographing and listing items on the ecommerce site alongside price and product descriptions. A week later, it was all sorted and we were ready to go live. Or would have been if I didn't need to be back at Ventura.

Realising I was at a crossroads, I had to decide which direction to take: carry straight on and endure a humdrum nine till five existence, or take a gamble and go left, setting up on my own. It took me all of five seconds to make my mind up. How did it go now? Don't stop believing? Well, I never had and never would, either. I resigned forthwith, working my notice. Then I opened a gym on an industrial estate in Wombwell, leaving Nicola as the main breadwinner. I was teaching taekwondo at nearby Darfield WMC at the time and took all my students with me, meaning I wasn't starting entirely from scratch. I still had a few quid left over and used it to buy a job lot of second-hand exercise equipment; weights; exercise bikes; rowing machines; leg trainers and the like. I called the new gym *Musa*, closing the original unit and transferring stock across, meaning everything was under one roof. I was selling a fair bit of product now, but openly admitted I didn't have a proper plan. I was one hundred per cent winging it, making things up as I went along, pretty much as I had done my entire life to be fair. On a whim, I decided to start teaching Brazilian jiu jitsu, a self-defence martial art and combat sport based on grappling, groundwork and submission holds. I'd practised the discipline on and off down the years and had become reasonably proficient. As such, I'd hoped to be given official recognition and exclusivity to teach in the Barnsley area. An old friend of mine, Ben Poppleton, was close to the Gracie Barra Brazilian Jiu-Jitsu Association, which administered over a thousand worldwide schools, and I hoped he'd be able to pull the necessary strings. Unfortunately, some bugger had beaten me to it. It was a body blow, for sure; but it wasn't all bad news. Another old friend, Steve Marsden, who had gained official accreditation in the Sheffield area, kindly agreed to conduct twice weekly training sessions at *Musa*. Don't get me wrong, I'd much rather have been supervising the sessions personally; but I remained philosophical about the situation. Beggars couldn't be choosers and at least Steve's commitment and cooperation provided another guaranteed income, further supporting the fledgling business.

The months ticked by. I was selling *Musa* items daily and the gym was thriving, gaining fresh members on a weekly basis. I was content with my lot and slowly but surely settling into a routine which would have been easy to maintain indefinitely. Then a call out of the blue from Steve changed my life forever. I thought I was hearing things at first. Royce Gracie was *the* number one name in martial arts. A living legend, he was the finest practitioner of Brazilian jiu jitsu the world had ever seen. And he was coming to South Yorkshire, hosting a seminar in Rotherham just a few short weeks from now. Even better, Steve, who was one of the organisers, asked if I'd like to attend. His offer prompted an instant response: is the Pope catholic? Course I would. Why wouldn't I? It wasn't every day of the week I was presented with the opportunity of a lifetime and there was no way on earth I was turning it down. The big day couldn't come quick enough. Every day seemed like a month in the run-up; every month a year. Same as everything, though, it came round eventually and I arrived at the venue overflowing with confidence after an intensive period of practise and training. The hall was filled with a real mixed bag of martial artists, experts in taekwondo, karate, kickboxing and, of course, Brazilian jiu jitsu, undoubtedly inspired by the UFC, the Ultimate Fighting Championship, or cage fighting as it was commonly known, which was becoming increasingly popular not only throughout the UK but around the world. It soon became apparent only rising stars and perennial achievers had been invited, patently obvious from the way they expertly warmed up and preened themselves.

Athletes to a man, we were told to pair up with fighters of roughly the same height and weight. There were no preliminaries: we were immediately ordered to fight, utilising jiu jitsu submission and grappling techniques. I make no bones about it: I'd always been the best on the mats. Just not this day. Time after time, I was submitted in seconds by different opponents, forced to tap-out in the face of excruciating chokes and exquisitely performed leg, shoulder and wrist locks. All I can say is I kept going, refusing to throw in the towel, making a silent pledge to improve my skills over the weeks, months and years ahead. Ubiquitously pronounced *Hoyce*, the Portuguese speaking man o' war was barking instructions alongside the unbelievably talented Eddie Kone, a superb martial artist who went on to carve out a fantastic career in the sport. I doted upon every word, picking up every little tip I could. Some I'd put into practice there and then; others I'd mentally store and refine later. I adored Royce. He was everything I'd dreamed he'd be and more. I learned so much and thoroughly enjoyed every minute, painful as it was. At the end, Royce conducted a lengthy Q&A, then posed for photographs, which were printed straight off, permitting personalised signatures. Mine said: to Harley from Royce. I shook the great man's hand and that was it. Time was up and I departed, devastated I'd never meet him again. Or so I thought; little did I know.

The relationship with Steve continued to blossom. I discovered he'd learned jiu jitsu in the States and famously fought and tapped-out Michael Clarke Duncan, who played the part of giant John Coffey in one of my all-time favourite films, *The Green Mile*. Imagine that! His son, Tom, was also a prominent martial artist and a proper chip off the old block, one of life's eternal good guys. A few months later, I got another important call from Steve, explaining that Royce had been in contact. He was coming back over to the UK and was looking for a seminar location in South Yorkshire. With only six weeks' notice, I instantly offered up *Musa*. While Steve's response was courteous, it was also very much to the point.

"No disrespect, Greenie," he said, "but *Musa* is freezing cold and damp. It used to be a car workshop. It stinks of grease and engine oil. *Hoyce* is the most famous martial artist in the world. I would imagine he'd be looking for somewhere a trifle more salubrious…"

There was no point arguing the fact. *Musa* was my first gym and clearly had issues, which I'd deal with in the fullness of time. On the flip side, I refused to give up on the idea. Somehow, I needed come up with a plan; a ruse to lure Royce to our neck of the woods. In a classic light bulb moment, I made a beeline for Barnsley Sports College, asking if I could use the main hall to hold a Royce Gracie Brazilian jiu jitsu seminar. Just my luck, the manager had never heard of him. He sat up and listened when a young lad in the background whistled between his teeth, however, explaining how he hero-worshipped Royce and would love to meet him, as would half his mates by the sound of things. Half an hour later, it was all booked for the dates stipulated and for a very reasonable price as well. Understandably, I flew into a right panic in the aftermath, wondering what would happen if Steve shot the proposal down. Luckily, I caught him in a good mood and he was straight on board with the idea. All that remained was to ascertain Royce's financial demands. I made immediate contact, agreeing a two-and-a-half grand fee plus overnight accommodation. That sorted, we were all set, finalising the itinerary and putting plans in place to ensure we made a healthy profit on our investment. We hit Facebook hard and secured a write-up in the Barnsley Chronicle and a couple of other local rags. Soon, we had people banging our door down for tickets, which we'd priced at seventy quid for participants and forty for spectators. In addition, Nicola employed the services of a sports photographer she discovered online. A Mancunian with a big grin and a dodgy Mexican-style moustache, his name was Pete Spensley. Not for long, though. Looking like a bandit out of classic western, *The Magnificent Seven*, we immediately christened him Pedro. Selling signed photographs for a tenner apiece, we offered him a fifty per cent cut on the proviso all material costs were his responsibility. Needless to say, he couldn't say yes quick enough and we welcomed him on board.

We arrived at the venue early, making sure the hall was properly laid out, arranging mats and seating and setting up a refreshments area. When Royce arrived, I was absolutely bursting with pride. A large crowd had gathered and he was constantly stopping to sign autographs on the way in. He couldn't have been more obliging, mirroring the gentlemanly, generous reputation which preceded him. I greeted him with a smile. He smiled back and we shook, heartily. He was tall. He was lean. He was beautifully tanned and incredibly good looking; almost as handsome as me some would say. Alright, alright, I can hear you, Lisa Rudd. I know what you're thinking: face like a blind cobbler's thumb. Just keep your nose out and go and get Phil's tea ready or something, can't you? As we entered the college, I had to pinch myself to make sure I wasn't dreaming, briefly casting my mind back to those heady days in Shaftesbury Drive, when I first discovered my love of martial arts, making a racket on the bedroom floor as I practised hell for leather in front of the mirror. Not in my wildest dreams would I have imagined that, one day, I'd be the centre of attention, hobnobbing it with the most famous martial artist in the world. As for the seminar, it couldn't have gone any better if I'd scripted it. The hall was jam-packed and there was a real party atmosphere about the place. With spectators seated around the outside, participants were formed into pairs and instructed to engage in bouts of jiu jitsu. Mirroring the Rotherham seminar, Royce was hands-on throughout, instructing, assisting and advising, engaging in one-on-one sessions where applicable, playfully grappling with participants and manoeuvring them into submission holds. The Q&A was equally brilliant, lots of genuine, heartfelt responses to intelligent, well thought out questions from a horde of wannabe martial artists. Before we knew it, it was over. Royce was out the door and the event sadly came to a close.

We were all on cloud nine in the aftermath; myself, Nicola, Pedro, Steve and Tom, plus everyone else who chipped in with assistance along the way. We'd made a few quid into the bargain and all was good. Our only regret was we couldn't do it all over again. Little did we know that, a few weeks later, this incredible rollercoaster of an experience would take another amazing turn. Steve received an early morning call from LA. It came from Royce, hugely praising the event and saying a mixed martial artist friend of his was due to tour the UK imminently and had a spare date to fill. He'd told him all about the Barnsley seminar and he was very interested in doing something similar. That was the good news: the bad was that the date was just four weeks away. I asked who it was and Steve's response didn't just knock me for six, it hit me clean out of the ground. We were talking Chuck Liddell, a UFC light heavyweight champion, widely credited alongside fellow UFC fighter, Randy Couture, with bringing MMA into mainstream American sports and entertainment. He wanted five grand for a two-and-a-half-hour session with the customary Q&A thrown in at the end. I was honoured, blown away and flabbergasted, all at the same time. Chance of a lifetime, I immediately went for it, but on the condition Chuck couldn't slag us off if things didn't quite match up to his expectations. After all, we only had a month to get things organised, which wasn't long by any stretch of the imagination. I also negotiated a better price, shaving five hundred quid off the asking price. Everything was agreed and a contract was hurriedly drawn up, which all interested parties signed. Barnsley Sports College was free on the required date and so we booked it without hesitation. We got Pedro involved again and went down the familiar Facebook and local newspaper route of advertising the event. Even though Royce Gracie was the chosen one, the chiselled figure of Chuck Liddell was definitely more in vogue. Everyone but everyone had heard of him and tickets were snapped up no time, folk eager to come and meet the legendary fighter affectionately known as The Iceman. As previously, the big day arrived in an awful hurry.

We endured a very early start, making sure everything was shipshape and Bristol fashion; mats; seating; refreshments; Pedro's photographic area and multi-coloured wrist bands, denoting visitor status, be it participant, spectator, Q&A, staff or guest. Then came a big surprise: an ESPN camera crew showed up unannounced. The director explained they were doing a documentary on Chuck and asked if we minded them filming key aspects of the event in return for a spot of name-dropping at key junctures. Did we mind? Did we buggery! There was no such a thing as bad publicity, remember. News the big man was only ten minutes away gave me goose bumps, especially when I saw the amount of people waiting outside, a feeling accentuated when the crowds erupted into cheer as his car turned the corner, pulling up adjacent. As Chuck threw open the door, clambering out, I was overcome with awe. He looked just like he did on the telly. A big old unit, he was dressed in jeans and a T-shirt and was sporting his trademark mohawk. He greeted me and we shook hands with such intensity, I'm convinced I felt my fingers crack, reminding me of an imaginary encounter with scouse hardman, Shake Hands, on dad's favourite 80s TV drama, *Boys From The Blackstuff*. We had a few minutes alone, discussing the itinerary. He did most of the talking to be fair. But I didn't care. Not by this stage, anyway. I was just happy to be in his company and finally getting to know him. Then we were straight into it, replicating Royce's recent seminar; lots of hands-on instructional work intertwined with one-on-one discussions. Chuck didn't half know his stuff, giving powerful demonstrations upon kickboxing, wrestling, muay Thai and jiu jitsu. My favourite bit, though, was his take upon boxing techniques, especially his interpretation of an overhand right; thumb and palm down with a big, swinging, far reaching hook. I practised the technique endlessly afterwards. It stayed with me and is something which is still part of my repertoire to this day. After the Q&A, we enjoyed a nice cup of tea and I made him smile a few local stories of *Kes* and Barnsley FC and the perils of life growing in Hoyland. I've often wondered what he thought. I love my hometown, but it must have seemed incredibly spartan compared to the sights and sounds of his native LA. As he climbed into the back seat of his car, I began singing, to the tune of the classic *Sparks* record: this town ain't big enough for both us Chucks. He liked that. Liked it a lot, in fact, raising a clenched fist and smiling blithely at me through a mouthful of pearly whites, before treating me to an affectionate nod and a wink as the car slowly pulled away.

All in all, it couldn't have gone better and, once again, we'd turned a nice little profit. On a roll now, I immediately began to think who could be next, opening up a big discussion point during the ensuing pub crawl round Barnsley. Only time would tell with that one, if, indeed, it happened at all. It seemed unlikely, to be fair. All the same, I was allowed to dream, wasn't I…?

17. The Axe Murderer

Bathed in success, I was relaxing in the conservatory Sunday afternoon, considering my next big move. It was raining so heavily, it sounded like someone was pouring bags of rice on the roof from an upstairs window. I was swigging on a bottle of Stella. If I'd smoked, which I obviously didn't, there would have been a big, fat cigar, dangling Winston Churchill like from the corner of my mouth. I had my laptop open, resting on a cushion on my knee. I'd been surfing the web for the best part of an hour, desperately seeking inspiration, though not getting very far. More to stop myself falling asleep than anything else, I randomly typed: Wanderlei Silva. A couple of million results instantly assaulted the screen. Infamously known as The Axe Murderer, Wand was a UFC fighter of the highest calibre, holding the record for the most wins, knockouts, title defences and the longest winning streak in MMA history. In footballing terms, he was Pele, Messi and Ronaldo all rolled into one. Next thing, I was logged on to his page and staring at contact details for his US management team. Bit between my teeth, I sent a carefully worded email, tentatively asking if Wand would be interested in hosting a series of UK seminars, with an exotic tbc foreign destination tagged on at the end. I backed up the email by detailing the highly successful Gracie and Liddell sessions, attaching pictures and video content from the ad hoc ESPN visit. If I'm honest, I never expected to hear anything back; but that doesn't mean I ever stopped believing. It was the only way. It was my mantra. Always had been. Belief was power. Sheer power. Believe and good times would inevitably follow. It summed up my entire life; then *and* now, a philosophy which was about to come up trumps once more. After getting a polite rebuff from an identical email sent to Randy Couture, who I was informed was away filming *The Expendables*, I received an extremely positive response from Wand's manager, a Las Vegas attorney, indicating he would definitely be interested. Email discussions commenced with vigour, concluding with an hour-long midnight call to the States, where agreement was finally reached, initiating intense feelings of euphoria for both myself and Nicola. A contract was drawn up, which both sides signed, a mutually beneficial document, permitting both parties to earn a good few bob from the initiative. For each seminar, Wand would receive three-and-a-half grand. Appearances only would earn him fifteen hundred pounds. We also had to cover the cost of all flights, transportation and accommodation for Wand and his wife, Tea, and his eight-year-old son, Thor. For our part, we could invoice venues whatever amount we needed to generate a profit, eventually settling upon five grand for seminars and three for an appearance, with Wand's fees to be deducted from the overall figure. We also had free reign to let Pedro run amok with his camera, taking as many pictures as possible, which Wand would sign as required. Additionally, Wand had agreed to do the Barnsley seminar free of charge, enabling us to recoup a few costs and pocket a couple of extra quid into the bargain, a marvellous gesture which was gratefully received.

That was the easy bit. The hard part was getting everything organised. Nicola was a champion at information gathering, collating contact details for pretty much every single gym across the UK and Ireland. We then ran a massive email campaign, detailing Wand's visit, providing dates and costs and inviting interest. Needless to say, the response was phenomenal. We could have sold the gig two or three times over if we'd had sufficient time. As it was, the visit would be strictly limited, spanning 13th October to 5th November. The full itinerary was duly announced, predominantly seminars with a couple of appearances sandwiched in between. Cork was first then Belfast and London, which, purely by chance, was hosting a UFC conference and fight the same day. Then it was two days in Hastings followed by Leicester, Derby, Manchester, Barnsley, Newcastle and Paisley. The final seminar would take place at St Andrews Golf Club, before jetting off to a yet to be confirmed foreign destination.

For reasons of illness, specifically a horrific bout of man-flu, a debilitating condition that anyone of female persuasion can only *begin* to imagine, I was unavailable to meet and greet Wand upon his arrival, thereby bequeathing Nicola to do the honours. She picked him and the family up at Heathrow, staying overnight, before accompanying him on an onward flight to Dublin and then a road trip to Belfast, both of which proved to be incredibly successful seminars, dutifully attended by hundreds of budding martial artists, eager to learn from the best of the best. Recovered now, I finally hooked up with the legend at the Earl's Court UFC Conference, an indoor event incorporating dozens of martial arts stalls and displays, promoting manufacturer and distributor goods and services. Wand was at our beck and call, engaging with the public, keeping Pedro on his toes, printing reams of fan photographs for him to sign. I couldn't believe how much cash we were taking. Money had never been my driving force. Never would be, either. But I can't deny I had pound signs in my eyes. That evening, we were at the O2 Arena, watching UFC 120, a night of brilliant full-on scraps, featuring Michael the Count Bisping versus Yoshihiro Akiyama as the main event. Bisping was victorious and celebrated his win with an after party in the function suite, a dedicated food and drinks concourse with tastes to suit every palate. We were also present, wining and dining Wand and Tea. We'd secured a VIP area in a Brazilian bar. Up a flight of steps and roped off to prevent intrusion, we were enjoying a fabulous meal of seafood and barbecued meats, washed down with copious amounts of wine, beer and spirits. Entry to the VIP area was by ticket only, while the bar area remained open to the general public and had quickly filled with hundreds of awestruck MMA supporters, magnetised by the mystical presence of the shaven-head Brazilian. As such, the bar a couple of doors down, where Bisping was hosting celebrations, was all but empty as word spread and more and more people entered *our* bar, hoping to catch a glimpse of Wand and his entourage. Nicola was there. So was Pedro and a few specially invited friends, as much piss artists as martial artists; father and son, Kev and Ricky Stables; Mike Bird; Kent's number one son, Chicken Legs, aka Lee Cutting, plus a couple of others. Wand was such a draw, I swear if he'd taken a walk along the embankment, hordes of hypnotised fans would have followed Pied Piper like and promptly taken a dip in the Thames. Strange but true, I even witnessed Ricky, purposely dropping his baseball cap in advance of disappearing beneath the table. When I looked, he was stroking Wand's foot like it was a pet cat, such was his adoration for the legendary man from Brazil.

The night wore on and it was soon time to head back to the hotel. Wand and Tea had already gone and we were determined we wouldn't be far behind them. As we turned to leave, the bar manager appeared and walloped us with an enormous food and drinks bill. Fuming, I immediately contested the charge, demanding it be waivered. We'd already coughed up a small fortune for the VIP area, plus which, we'd filled the bar for hours on end with our presence, earning the business what must have been an obscene amount of money. Unfortunately, my words fell on deaf ears. Adamant the amount must be paid, he disappeared back to the bar while we sorted ourselves out. All the cash we'd taken was back in the hotel for safe keeping, leaving us no other option but to copper up. No one possessed a credit card, or at least weren't admitting it if they did. And, so, we all chipped in with whatever we had on us, a few notes of various denominations alongside piles of copper and silver. About thirty quid in total, we dumped it in the middle of the table and made ready. I was up first, heading for the fire exit. The others weren't stupid. They knew what I was up to and quickly followed suit, disappearing in all directions to make their escape. Seeing what was happening, the manager chased Kev and Ricky down the adjacent corridor, repeatedly shouting: Bill! Bill! All he received by way of response was:

"My name's Kev not Bill and you can fuck off…because we're not paying!"

We left Wand sight-seeing in London over the weekend. When we returned, it was secure in the knowledge we'd finally booked the foreign trip, a destination which we decided to keep top secret until the tour was complete. We followed a meticulously formulated schedule, heading down to the south coast, then back up to the Midlands and Lancashire, before hitting South Yorkshire, better known to one and all as God's country. Every single appearance and seminar went down brilliantly and Barnsley was no exception: a couple of addictive hours on the mats followed by an enthralling Q&A. Pedro really milked it on the photos front, adding huge value to the five grand freebie Wand had agreed as part of the deal. Afterwards, we'd arranged a three-course meal at Barnsley Metrodome, with Wand's famous Michael Bisping fight playing on a big screen in the background, a rumbustious bout which Wand won in round three and was ultimately voted the best MMA fight of 2010 and the greatest middleweight encounter of all time. Wand did an absolutely marvellous speech, following this up with a brilliantly conducted Q&A, which lasted the best part of an hour. As organisers, we were afforded complimentary drinks status for the duration of the function. It was a good job really, considering how much booze we got through. Having developed a taste for Guinness on the Cork leg of the tour, Wand didn't half go for it, downing five or six pints of the black stuff in rapid succession, much to the dismay of Tea, who was doing her best to haul him off to bed, totally unaware I was passing him refills underneath the table. He'd also developed a love for English fish and chips, taking full advantage of the plethora of choice on Whitley Bay seafront prior to the Newcastle seminar. After the event, I made sure he overheard me asking Nicola if she wanted me to pick up cod and chips on the way home. He jumped straight in, saying it was a great idea and could he have some, please? When Nicola declared it was the biggest mistake of her life, allowing me to name the twins, he looked at her like he'd just sat through a lecture in advanced algebra. We did our best to explain the play on words, but failed miserably. All we received was repeated demands for food, to the point where we were left with no other option than to divert to the nearest chippie in order to satisfy his craving.

Paisley and St Andrews were a breeze, after which I arranged a visit to a highly talented sports artist going by the name of Geo Thompson. A big Celtic fan, he majored on commissions and prints, producing paintings of famous footballers and sport stars in general. He'd painted an unbelievable picture of Wand, fighting Michael Bisping in the UFC. It had already been personally signed by The Count and The Axe Murderer added his own signature during our visit. I don't know what happened to the painting afterwards. All I'd say is, if it's still in circulation, it must be worth a fortune now. With Scotland done and dusted, it was finally time to head off to sunnier climes, a visit to a brand-new gym named The Contender, owned and run by MMA starlet, Tam Khan. Even better, it was located in the beautiful, sun-drenched surroundings of downtown Dubai, where myself, Pedro, Wand and co would be heading for an incredible week-long stay, with Nicola sadly having to stay home to mind Harley. Tam and I had spoken extensively in advance and he was under no illusions of the significance of hosting someone of the prominence of Wanderlei Silva. It was an amazing opportunity and the positive effect it would have upon his business couldn't be overstated. I have to say, I liked Tam from the start. I found him pleasant, polite, interested and engaging. He was also meticulous in his planning, making sure every box was ticked in order to get the absolute best from this once in a lifetime visit. Terms were agreed in no time. In addition to a generous fee, Tam would also supply hotel accommodation, including breakfast and evening meal alongside all in-country transportation costs. In return, Wand would make several publicity appearances at The Contender and partake in a one-on-one session with the Sheikh of Dubai, with whom Tam was personal trainer.

We flew out from Manchester on Qatar Airways, transferring flights at Doha for the final hour into Dubai. Unbeknown to us at the time, there had been a security alert at East Midlands Airport, involving a suspected explosive device hidden in a printer; an identical model to the one Pedro was transporting. Nothing happened, obviously. If it had, my life story may well have taken a very different course indeed. As we disembarked, trotting down the steps towards the tarmac, it was so hot I thought the engines were still operating. Wiping a hand across a perspiring brow, I soon worked out the explosion of heat was, in fact, the outside temperature. The sun was blazing down in the most brilliant blue sky I'd ever seen, with a temperature gauge on the runway bus indicating a searing 42°C. We collected our luggage, then headed for arrivals. A couple of Emirati men in traditional, single-piece, ankle-length kandura and shemagh headdress were holding up paddle boards with Green and Silva scrawled upon them. The men introduced themselves as Yasser and Moad, close associates of Tam's, who I discovered later were in the oil business. Both sporting gleaming Rolex, I'd no idea how much they were worth. I didn't dare hazard a guess, either. I just wished I had a penny for every penny they had. We were escorted outside to a pair of gleaming, black Range Rover Sports of the type Prime Ministers and Presidents would ride around in. Standing adjacent was a tall, lean, muscle-bound man in shorts and T-shirt. Wearing the coolest set of shades I'd ever seen, I recognised him instantly as Tam. He greeted me with an enormous bear hug and I hugged him back, struggling to get my arms all the way round his back on account he was so big. The connection was instant and I knew straight away I'd made a friend for life. He quickly introduced another fellow, a UFC TV commentator and practising martial artist called Rio Altaie. Again, I was immediately taken by the man, a tall, distinguished looking chap with short-cropped hair and beard. I introduced Wand and his family and hugs and handshakes were exchanged all round. Pedro came next and then we were off, the two northern monkeys and Rio in one vehicle with the Brazilians and Tam in the other, heading down Sheikh Zayed Road, the main arterial highway of the city, flanked either side by unbelievably tall buildings, casting thick, black shadows across the ultra-rich, urban metropolis. With Yasser driving one car and Moad the other, it was like being in a film; *Men in Black* or the latest big budget offering from *James Bond*. We discovered we'd been booked into the Sheikh's hotel, the Emirates Grand, a towering, glass-fronted building, overlooking the Persian Gulf. We were given a sim card each and provided with a number to call if we got lost or had any trouble, further adding to the mystique of what had been a breath-taking start to our visit. Then another surprise: the quality of the hotel rooms was nothing less than magnificent. Pedro was screaming at me to come and view his allocation; bedroom, bathroom, kitchen, sitting room and balcony. Mine was all that and more, a penthouse suite with multiple rooms and bedrooms, including a fully functioning study, accentuated by mahogany fixtures and fittings, marble floor and stunning views across the water and city. I've no idea what Wand's was like, but can only imagine it was even better; the best of the best, totally befitting of a man of his standing.

We fended for ourselves that evening, a nice steak meal out, while Wand went off to do his own thing. Next day, we got a call from Yasser, saying he would pick us up at six. Right on the button, the Range Rovers arrived, transporting us and Wand and co to the world-renowned Pai Thai Restaurant, the final leg of which was conducted by abra boat, a gondola-type vessel which had been the city's principal form of transport for centuries. Tam was there, as was Rio, hosting an occasion which turned into a proper bonding session, dining alfresco in the most scenic of settings, a meal of crispy beef, chicken dumplings and prawn curry, overlooking fabulous waterways, frequented by pretty boats, ferrying happy, smiling people to and fro. How much the meal cost I'd no idea. I was just happy I wasn't the one picking up the tab, because I doubt there would have been much change from a couple of grand. Good old Tam did the honours and I'm proud to say that, by the end of the evening, we'd firmly cemented our blossoming friendship, regaling one another and treasured friends with endless tales of fitness and martial arts.

Next day, we lounged round the pool, child minding Thor while Wand and Tea disappeared for a spot of retail therapy in Dubai's ultra-modern malls. Not that we'd cause to complain. A private waiter took care of our every need, making sure we were well fed and watered throughout another burning hot day. Sunmbool Syed was his name. We became firm friends and I'm proud to say we are still in contact to this day. Later on, I visited The Contender with Wand, a preliminary visit prior to commencing his contractual duties. Now, I know a good gym when I see one and, let me tell you, this was top class, gleaming with brand new, state-of-the-art equipment and overflowing with people. I was offered the chance to train, but politely declined. I was in peak physical fitness as it was and had already determined Dubai was going to be a well-earned rest period, the opportunity to unwind amidst beautiful weather and surroundings. The following day was the same and the day after that as well; copious amounts of fun and laughter from start to finish. My only professional involvement was attending the seminar, minding Wand and dealing with the paparazzi and accompanying film crews. Pedro, meanwhile, was busy coining it, milking invited guests and gym members with wads of signed photographs. I was informed afterwards that Wand's one-on-one with the Sheikh went exceptionally well. I wasn't surprised. It was only ever going to be a rip-roaring success. How could it be anything else with The Axe Murderer in charge? The day after, I got another call from Yasser, saying there was a private party later at the world's tallest building, the Burj Khalifa, an incredible feat of engineering which epitomised the heart and soul of the city. Commencing at 9pm, only a twenty or so people were invited and Pedro and I were amongst the chosen few, attending alongside a very special guest. I asked who it was. If Yasser knew, he did an excellent job of disguising the fact, batting me off with a nonchalant shrug of the shoulders. I said we'd be there, naturally; but that was before the beer started flowing and the football came on. It was too late by the time the game was over and so we had another drink then went to bed. Next morning, Yasser was on again, firstly asking where we were and, secondly, revealing the name of the special guest. It was only Tom bloody Cruise, wasn't it? In the region, filming a scene for Mission Impossible 4, I was gutted I'd missed him. One of my favourite film stars, I swear I wouldn't have let him be until he'd promised me at least a bit part in the film. Bugger me, I thought: imagine that: Charlie Green, actor. Who knows? A couple of years on, I could have been offered the lead role in a remake of *Kes*. Now that *would* have been something, wouldn't it? Kes! Come on, Kes!

The time to go home came round way too soon. Tam settled mine and Pedro's hotel rooms. I don't know the night-rate, but I caught a glimpse of the bill and it was fifty-three thousand Dirham, about twelve grand in pounds, shilling and pence. It was then I discovered Wand had decided to stay on another week. I wasn't happy because he never mentioned it. Even worse, he didn't bother to pop round and say goodbye. Responsible for the family's air-fares, we'd already booked and paid for flights back to the US, with no hope of cancelling at such a late stage. I took it on the chin, same as I always did. What else could I do? And at least we'd had a good trip. No, I take it back: we'd had a *brilliant* trip. What would come next, I wondered. I supposed I'd have to wait and see on that one…

18. The World's Most Dangerous Man

With memories of Gracie, Liddell and Wand gradually fading, I began looking for the next big thing and it didn't take long to find it, either. Using the same tried and tested formula, I emailed the Lion's Den, an MMA training facility in Susanville, California, founded by The World's Most Dangerous Man, UFC heavyweight hall of famer, Ken Shamrock, a former professional wrestler and one of the most instantly recognisable fighters on the planet. We exchanged a series of emails and the vibes weren't good. The legendary four times UFC champion and world champion wrestler didn't seem particularly keen on visiting, shooting down every facet of my proposal in a string of curt responses. I didn't beat myself up about it. What would be the point? If he wasn't interested, there wasn't a lot I could do about it. All I could do was keep plugging away and hope for the best. Then, bingo! Completely out of the blue, Ken agreed, signing up for a series of seminars on similar fiscal arrangements to previous visitors. As usual, we agreed to pay all air fares and accommodation. All he had to do was book the flights and we would reimburse him upon arrival. We'd only just commenced the planning stages when we received another email, saying he was arriving the day after tomorrow. Instant panic set in. We had a few things pencilled in but nothing definite and suddenly found ourselves running around like headless chickens, desperately trying to get things organised. In reality, we should have pulled the event. As it turned out, we bashed on regardless, pulling out all the stops to cobble together a full itinerary at extremely short notice. What other choice did we have? It was Ken bloody Shamrock we were talking about, not some second-rate, journeyman fighter no one had ever heard of.

A prominent programme at the time was *The Ultimate Fighter*, a series in which professional fighters from around the globe trained and competed against each other in a mixed martial arts competition to win the coveted title and a UFC contract. Teams were coached by esteemed UFC fighters, big names such as Chuck Liddell, Tito Ortiz, Forest Griffin and, yes, you've guessed it, Ken Shamrock. I always felt the programme didn't paint Ken in a particularly good light, portraying him as dour, difficult and somewhat arrogant. Wrong. Meeting Ken and his lovely wife, Tonya, off the plane at Heathrow, I rapidly came to the conclusion that, if there was a more friendly, polite, kind, interested and funny person anywhere on the planet, I'd yet to meet him. We checked into the hotel, then drove round the local area for what seemed like forever, trying to find a place to eat. I'd brought Kev Stables along for the ride and he did his best to keep the couple entertained as I nipped in and out of various restaurants, sussing things out. Try as we might, we couldn't find anywhere suitable and I was mightily relieved when Ken politely suggested we return to the hotel and eat there. With the Shamrocks settled in the dining room, Kev and I did what we did best, disappearing to the pub. A hefty session later, we were back in our room with a couple of takeaway pizzas, three sheets to the wind and absolutely loving life. I asked Kev if he wanted his pizza cutting into six or ten pieces. Six, he replied: I'd *never* eat ten. I might have found it funny if it was a joke; but the daft bastard actually meant it! The last thing I recall, before turning out the light, was dumping a couple of leftover slices on the floor. What must have been three or four hours later, I was rudely awoken by the sound of Kev, calling me every name under the sun as he hopped barefoot around the room, caked in tomato puree. I laughed until my ribs were sore. Promptly nicknamed Pizza Toes, I can still see him now, draped in ham, cheese, pineapple and pepperoni. For one awful moment, I thought he'd topped himself.

Forty-eight hours later, we were attending a BAMMA, British Association of Mixed Martial Arts, event in Manchester, a TV production which aired on channels throughout Europe, Africa and Asia. In the UK, it was shown live on ITV4 and Bravo. I'd offered Ken up for an interview on the show on the condition that wherever he went, I went. There were no grumbles from the producers on that count. Looking back, I should have demanded more, whatever took my fancy, in fact, because I'm certain I would have come up trumps, such was the incredible draw of a man who always reminded me of Major Chip Hazard in action-comedy movie, *Small Soldiers*. Imagine the shock my mates back in Hoyland got when, after sitting through bouts featuring the likes of Tom Watson, Rico Rodriguez and Katie Price's partner, Alex Reid, I suddenly appeared on-screen, standing side by side with Ken as he gave an in-depth post-fight analysis. My phone was red hot in the aftermath. What were *you* doing there? How did you pull that one off? Can you get me Shamrock's autograph? Are you fetching him to The Potter's Wheel for a couple of jars? Kev and Ricky were also in attendance and, next morning, the three of us regaled the Shamrocks over breakfast with endless funny stories, to the point where we soon had a large audience of restaurant-goers, gathering round, listening in. It wasn't all one-way traffic, mind. Ken was a very funny man and chipped in with quite a few stories of his own. My favourite related to his Japanese wrestling career; an hilarious and brilliantly articulated tale of how junior wrestlers had to wash the backs of senior competitors after training. A few days later, the story magically resurfaced. After a superb seminar at Barnsley Metrodome, I bumped into Ken in the shower, chilling after a particularly strenuous work-out. I didn't mince my words, telling him he wanted bleeding milking if he thought he was getting a back wash from me. I thought my remark might have been lost in translation. Not a chance. Ken was a smart cookie and we roared with laughter in the aftermath. The seminar was such a success that the Events Manager, a nice young man called Richard Bailey, pinched a selfie with Ken and Tonya, plus Nicola, Harley and myself, a picture which was eventually framed and wall-mounted in pride of place, where it still sits today. The next seminar took place in ever-popular Newcastle. After that, it was Huddersfield. then Wakefield, the latter of which was topped off with a superb Italian meal filled with laughter and engaging, two-way conversation. I think it's fair to say neither hosts nor visitors wanted the evening to end. But end it did. Then, sadly, it was time to say goodbye. The World's Most Dangerous Man winged it back to the States, while myself and Nicola headed home, already busily contemplating the next stage of our development.

We eventually made the difficult decision to close *Musa*. The reasons were simple: I didn't have enough time to dedicate to the gym and sales had slowed dramatically as a consequence. In an attempt to thin out a plethora of stock, clogging up the conservatory, we engaged Sunderland fighter and UFC veteran, Ross The Real Deal Pearson, to judge a highly entertaining ring-guy-and-girl contest at Barnsley's Royston Civic Hall, an interesting precursor to the lively seminar and Q&A session which followed. The winners would join us at Birmingham's NEC the following weekend, wearing *Musa* clothing and handing out cards and promotional leaflets. A couple of girls were duly selected and turned up as promised, while the guys never showed. It didn't really matter. Alongside the indefatigable Mike Bird, we had enough bodies on hand to achieve our goals, departing early Saturday morning with a distinct air of optimism. The event was being held in a voluminous exhibition hall, bigger than the biggest aircraft-hanger imaginable. Trade stands were organised in a maze of neat little rows, one after another after another, each manned by happy, smiling, engaging staff in corporate uniform, busily interacting with endless swarms of people, attending the event. Some were handing out freebies and information leaflets. Others were selling MMA clothing and protective equipment. Numerous demonstrations were also in progress; mats and rings, overflowing with martial artists, showing off a mix of text-book techniques and rarely seen fancy moves. While the ring-girls handed out various pieces of paraphernalia, Ross was busy signing hundreds of autographs, talking up *Musa* products at every opportunity, promoting the fact he'd be using them at the seminar we'd for him in the morning. We bumped into illustrious

American martial artist, Bill Wallace, who famously took Elvis Presley to karate black belt. He was there alongside world champion martial artist, Cynthia Rothrock, who was also a star of the silver screen, having performed in countless films and TV programmes, both at home and abroad. Always thinking ahead, I had a long chat with Bill, explaining everything we'd done over the past few months, dropping in all the big names. I could see he was impressed, even more so when I introduced him to Ross. Seizing the opportunity, I left a card and took his contact details, basically setting him up for later. He didn't know it yet; but I'd be in touch, for sure, and sooner rather than later.

Back at the hotel, we bumped into none other than Gok Wan, fashion consultant and television presenter, who was staying over with brother Kwoklyn, himself a prominent martial artist. We had a good old combat sports chinwag, with special emphasis on the professional chef and restauranteur's favoured disciplines; Shotokan karate, kung fu and Chinese boxing. Afterwards, Ross suggested a few bevvies in Brum. Not anticipating a big night out, I only had my day stuff; trackies and trainers, meaning I would need to borrow shoes and trousers if I was going anywhere. Cue Mike, who lent me everything I needed. It was really good of him, except I was only size seven and he was a ten, plus which, the pants he gave me came right up to my chest, making me look like a cross between Coco the Clown and Billy Casper in the football scene in *Kes*. Off we trooped, leaving the girls back at the hotel, a boys' night out on Brum's famous Broad Street, packed to the rafters with revellers, enjoying a multitude of bars, nightclubs and restaurants. We were pissed as farts by the end of it all and how we made it to Ross's morning seminar was anyone's guess. Make it we did, though, and very good it was as well. Shortly after lunch, Ross disappeared to Manchester for an appointment, messaging me later, asking if I could bank transfer his fee over. There was nothing I would have loved more; but there was a problem. The seminar administrator did one, vanishing off the face of the earth without paying us. I'd forked out a fortune on this and that and the other and was well out of pocket. Even worse, I couldn't afford to pay Ross and had the unenviable task of explaining the situation to him. He wasn't pleased. But what was I meant to do? I could have paid him in Monopoly money, but that was about it. And, so, we didn't part on the best of terms, which I'm desperately sorry about.

Home again, Nicola and I set about planning our next big push and it didn't take us long to come up with something, either. In another bold move, we succeeded in luring Marcus The Irish Hand Grenade Davis over to perform a series of seminars. A former professional boxer turned UFC fighter, he was big friends with Dana White, president of the Ultimate Fighting Championship. Not many people can boast that, I can tell you. And, lo and behold, he was on his way over to the UK to meet little old Charlie Green from Hoyland. Needless to say, I was proud as punch when I arrived to pick him up from Manchester Airport. Worryingly, though, I was waiting ages in arrivals. His flight landed on time and all the passengers had emerged, making me fear he'd missed the plane or backed out at the final moment, despite sending me a text to say he was boarding. Just when I'd given up hope, it happened: the rugged, chiselled features of the former law enforcement officer finally surfaced, totally stressed out after a lengthy, unexpected and unnecessary immigration delay. He spotted me immediately and we made an instant connection. That was the good news. The bad was that we had a five-hour drive ahead of us, all the way down to the south coast, Poole, Dorset, to be precise, for the first seminar in the morning. Nicola was driving. Harley was also in the car and we enjoyed a thoroughly enjoyable conversation on the way down. A large chunk was naturally martial arts related, but we also spent a significant period of time comparing the UK to the US. Driving on the left came first. Then the weather. Language peculiarities. Regional accents. British football versus US. Cricket and baseball. TV and cinema. History and literature. We even talked extensively about *Kes*, though I could tell Marcus didn't get it. Not properly, anyway. How could he without actually seeing it? And, even if he had seen it, I doubt he would have fully appreciated it. It was a culture thing, a yawning abyss, separated by three thousand miles of unforgiving ocean. All I know is that, at the end of it all, he reached out and offered me his hand.

"I really respect you, Charlie. You're some dude, bro, and I'm really glad I came over. Really glad we met and looking forward to spending some *serious* time with you…"

I heaped praises back at him, squeezing his fingers so hard, it must have felt like I was trying to nick his wedding ring. And, all the while, I was filling up with pride, overcome with emotion at his kind words. Here I was, an average Joe from a South Yorkshire backwater hardly anybody had heard of, sharing words and feelings with one of *the* most famous fighters in the world. I could have cried, truly I could. Not unsurprisingly, though, I managed to keep it together, just like I'd been indoctrinated, maintaining a stiff upper lip like generations of stout, working class Hoylanders before me.

We eventually arrived on the south coast and headed for the local holiday park chalet we had booked. While Nicola and Harley rested up, Marcus and I went out for a few pints, watching the Wladimir Klitschko versus David Haye heavyweight IBF, WBO, IBO unification fight. The boozer was filled with screaming combat sport fans, vociferously shouting on the Londoner. Incredibly, not one recognised the champion in their midst, unbelievable given how famous Marcus was. Unsurprisingly, the bout went to form: Haye lost and we drowned our sorrows with a few more pints, before heading off for a late-night pizza. It was just what the doctor ordered. As ever, though, there was a problem. All the local taxis were booked up, meaning we had a ninety-minute walk ahead of us to get back to the park. Fortunately, one man in Poole *had* recognised Marcus and that was the pizza shop owner. He treated us to a couple of glasses of vino while he closed up and then voluntarily drove us home. Marcus was flabbergasted by the gesture.

"This would *never* happen in the States, man," he kept on repeating. "Never happen. Never, ever. Am I dreaming, Charlie? Please, tell me I'm dreaming…"

Poole seminar in the bag, we made the long trek back north. I'd arranged for Marcus to stay at the Squires Hotel in Wombwell. It was only basic accommodation, but he didn't complain. Brought up in a single parent family in Bangor, Maine, he'd obviously experienced worse during a troubled childhood, frequently getting into fights, being stabbed twice and even getting shot at on more than one occasion. While in town, he attended Better Bodies Gym in order to stay in shape, striking up a cracking relationship with owner Martin Coleman and his extremely able assistant, Big Baz. I was doing a spot of work at the gym at the time and Baz suggested a night out with Marcus in Wakefield, where he worked the doors and boasted plenty of connections. Always up for a few shenanigans, I agreed, wholeheartedly, and off we trundled, Baz behind the wheel of his Land Rover Discovery, with Marcus riding shotgun and Nicola and myself in the back. Credit where credit's due, Baz arranged a brilliant evening, commencing with a three-course meal at an Indian restaurant followed by a few drinks at a sports bar and then a couple of unbelievably hectic hours in a local nightclub. I can only imagine he was owed a few favours, because absolutely everything was free, food, drinks, entrance fees, the lot. Even kebab and chips on the way home were paid on. As for Marcus, he lapped it up, posing for photos and signing autographs, promoting the hell out of himself, the UFC and martial arts generally. Darren England, up and coming Premiership referee, also used Better Bodies and made good friends with Marcus, as did staff and customers at Wetherspoon's Horseshoe pub, across and down a bit. On the seminar front, the man form Boston was as good as anyone we'd had over. Prior to the Barnsley event, he insisted upon fulfilling a request to visit Hesley

Wood Scout Activity Centre, mesmerising kids with a talk about his career and then following this up by putting in an appearance at a local Brazilian jiu jitsu class, hosted by a good pal of mine, Gareth Neale. Seminar attendees were mesmerised by The Irish Hand Grenade. Faces were a picture as he entered the hall, shaking hands and communicating and connecting with as many people as possible. He took a big interest in a young martial artist called Tommy Lawton. He watched him training a while then obtained permission to spar with him. Tommy was only sixteen at the time and Marcus said he'd rarely come across someone so young with such incredible hand speed and punching power, a gift which more than a few opponents would stumble upon to their cost in the months and years ahead. A highly successful seminar and Q&A massively overran on account of Marcus's unrivalled enthusiasm, after which we headed back to Wetherspoons for food and drink. There was a group of ten or twelve lads, occupying the table opposite, a rough old bunch, loud and exuberant, pushing and shoving and playfighting, swilling beer like it was going out of fashion. A couple were wearing hoodies, screen-printed with a single word: *Tapout*. MMA supporters to a man, not one of them recognised Marcus, sitting just a few feet away, unbelievable really, considering the gang's psyche. It was something we'd talked about just the other day, how the majority of people wearing *Tapout* shirts were armchair fans at best and understood very little about the sport. As the group headed for the exit, one stopped in mid-stride, about turning and making a beeline for us. He shook Marcus's hand, then mine, calling each of us by name, saying what a pleasure it was to meet us, international martial artists both. It made us feel good, while blowing the lid off our theory at the same time. Not that we cared and it *did* top off the day brilliantly.

Next morning, we were mobile again, headed for a seminar in Newcastle. After that, it was a trio of events in Marcus's beloved Ireland, before it was sadly time to part company. I have to say that Marcus was my favourite out of all our visitors. On a personal level, we clicked from day one, plus which, I have to say he was the consummate professional, ambassadorial in his representation of MMA. It doesn't end there, though. A week or so later, I received an email from Marcus, containing a video attachment, entitled: My English Son, a personal message to Harley, who he really took a shine to. Harley loved it. I loved it. And so did Nicola. It was testament to the man, someone who will remain in our hearts forever: the one and only, incredible Irish Hand Grenade.

19. Ultimate Fighter GB

His name was William Louis Wallace, aka Bill, an American martial artist, actor and former professional kickboxer, renowned for his adept use of high-speed leg kicks, which earned him the nickname: Superfoot. He was also a professional Karate Association world full-contact champion and Elvis Presley's bodyguard and personal trainer. And he was standing right beside me, preparing to enter Barnsley Metrodome to conduct a much-anticipated seminar. I should have been proud as punch. Deep down, I was; more than anyone could ever imagine. It was just that Bill was touching seventy now and was plainly showing his age, making me wonder if we'd made a big mistake in inviting him over. Walking with a limp, I watched with dismay as he leaned on a wall, stretching tired, aching muscles. Even worse, I clearly heard him mutter: I'm getting *way* too old for this shit. Suspicions confirmed, my skipped a beat. I looked at Nicola and she looked at me, thinking the same thoughts, mind going a hundred miles per hour. What should we do? Pull it now, before it was too late? Or risk total embarrassment and permit the seminar to go ahead? Right on cue, Bill provided the answer, throwing himself on the floor, performing the splits in advance of a series of rapid-fire press-ups. Laugh? You bet we did, until our sides hurt, in fact, and tears poured down our faces in torrents. He'd had us good and proper and we loved him for it, an incredibly amusing precursor to a brilliantly engaging seminar. He further proved his fitness the day after in a training session with a more than useful local martial artist called Craig Richardson. I knew Craig well, having coached him through to black belt. He considered himself super fit, but Bill left him floundering like a fish out of water, gasping for breath and struggling to keep up. For my own part, I felt Bill's immense power and experience in the ring, left reeling from a kick to the head during a more than lively sparring session. All I can say is, it's a good job we were only practising, pulling kicks at the final moment, otherwise I would have been in serious trouble. Call that an admission if you like, because that's precisely what it was meant to be. Bill was dynamite and it fried my brain to contemplate how good he must have been in his heyday.

With Bill headed back to the States, we came to the conclusion we'd reached the end of our UFC road. It had been an amazing experience and we'd earned some proper bunce into the bargain. There was no denying the formula was starting to wear thin, though, and the last thing we wanted was to finish up with egg on our face. I racked my brain which direction to take next and soon found the answer, dreaming up a concept which, if it came to fruition, would propel myself and Nicola into the stratosphere. I'd long harboured a desire to launch a GB version of *The Ultimate Fighter* and realised it was now or never. As ever, I got straight down to work and didn't pull any punches in my determination to make things work, contacting Royce Gracie and reaching agreement with him to be a coach. Fellow countryman, Fabrício Werdum, a four-time Brazilian jiu-jitsu world champion and UFC heavyweight champion, agreed to join him, creating a formidable line-up. All I need now was a production company, willing to give the concept a whirl. I immediately contacted the BBC, ITV, Sky Sports, C4 and several other mainstream channels, pitching my concept, seeing if they would be interested. I received a couple of polite refusals, but the majority never even answered. A few weeks later, I got a call from Pedro, inviting me to accompany him to a cricket presentation in Manchester. We got talking over a few beers and I explained what I was looking to do. He gauged the potential in a millisecond. Pound signs in his eyes, he said he knew someone who might be able to pull a few strings, putting me in contact with a friend of his called Daz Morris, who owned a gym in Salford and was Michael Bisping's Thai boxing coach. He was also in close contact with the producers of a televised show entitled: *Rumble at the Reebok*, a series of muay Thai boxing bouts, filmed at Bolton Wanderers football ground. I visited Daz at the gym one Wednesday afternoon. Nicola and I had Tommy Lawton working for us at the time on work experience. He couldn't believe his luck when I told him where we were going, a feeling massively accentuated when Bisping himself appeared, strolling right up to us for a chinwag.

"Bleeding hell fire," he commented afterwards, smiling from ear to ear. "All my mates are painting and decorating, or sweeping up in the Co-op on work experience, and I'm in Manchester with Master Charlie Green, shaking hands with Michael fucking Bisping. What more can a boy ask…?"

Daz was completely sold on the idea. Bisping also liked it, but said it wouldn't be easy to involve UFC fighters due to contractual issues. He said it was worth a try, though, and so Daz fixed up an appointment for me to meet the rumble-producers a couple of weeks later. Meticulously prepared, I travelled up by train the day before and Daz collected me from the station, ferrying me to the Reebok, where I was staying overnight. At the producers' request, I was afforded proper VIP treatment, including a stadium and function rooms tour, before being handed the keys to my room. Collapsing on the bed, my immediate thought was: just my bloody luck. A nauseating, pungent smell of weed was emanating from next door. I complained to reception, explaining I had a business meeting next morning and the last thing I wanted was to turn up with my clothes stinking of marijuana. I should have saved my breath. The bloke behind reception wasn't the slightest bit interested, fobbing me off with a series of garbled excuses. I came within a hair's breadth of dropping the smarmy bastard, but somehow managed to retain control, calling Daz instead, who got straight on the blower and sorted things out. Relocated with a complimentary bottle of wine, I bedded down for the night, mentally practising my script for morning, determined to get things right. I could do it; I knew I could. I just needed to remain focused.

Morning arrived. I enjoyed a hearty full English, followed by another good look round the complex. I was about to blow the cobwebs off with a long walk when, surprise, surprise, who should appear but an old friend of mine, four times world kickboxing champion,

Ronnie Green. He said Daz told him I was in town and he couldn't resist sticking his nose through the door for a good old catch-up. We enjoyed putting the world to rights over a nice cup of tea. Then Ronnie suggested a trip out to Liverpool to a see a pal of his called Alby, who was experimenting with some kind of new-fangled fight concept. It could have been the best idea since sliced bread; but it wouldn't have registered. Mind elsewhere, I instinctively hummed and hawed and nodded my head at all the right moments, hiding the fact everything went straight in one ear and out the other. Back on the road again, we were soon back in deepest, darkest Lancashire. Good old Ronnie; he'd lived in Manchester all his life, but still managed to get lost somehow, circling the inner ring road like some errant, orbiting satellite. Getting me back to the Reebok in the nick of time, I gave him a right bollocking and he had no other choice but to take it on the chin, just like he'd been doing all his career, lol. I'd planned to have a good wash and brush up before the meeting followed by a final read through my notes. Not a chance. Not now, anyway. Tossed straight in the deep-end, I introduced myself to the producers, a pair of snazzily dressed, likeable young Asians with sleeked back hair and Colgate smiles. Straight into it, I pitched my idea, flawlessly, performing with unconcealed enthusiasm, frequently referring to wads of pre-prepared notes. I felt like a finalist in the latest series of *The Apprentice*, constantly picturing Alan Sugar, uttering the immortal words: you're hired! I knew I had it in the bag and I wasn't wrong. The producers disappeared for a private meeting, which lasted all of five minutes. It was the taller of the two who broke the news.

"Mister Charles, we *love* your idea. Our martial arts submissions process receives countless proposals annually. Most don't make it further than a cursory glance. Yours obviously did. It's patently something different. Something refreshingly new. Something unique. And, now we've heard it from the horse's mouth, we're incredibly excited. Gracie and Werdum. How *did* you pull it off, mister Charles…? In short, we'd like to proceed and proceed with haste. Ultimate Fighter GB will be a *huge* hit. All we need to agree upon is the funding…"

The wind sailed straight out of me. In a split second, I went from experiencing the most incredible of highs to an utterly devastating, gut-wrenching low. I can't remember the precise amount quoted; but it was definitely telephone numbers. Don't stop believing, maybe; but I didn't possess a magic book of spells to raise the annual debt of some bankrupt South American republic. I tried, naturally; but to no avail. Ultimate Fighter GB, my very own TV deal, was on the cusp of bursting on to UK screens until, for reasons beyond my control, the concept unfortunately died a slow and painful death. And, with it, I'm sad to say I lost a large part of the insatiable verve which had kept me going throughout the years. I was perilously close to calling it a day and hanging up my gloves for good. I didn't, obviously; but it was a very close call indeed. As a way of keeping my hand in, I taught taekwondo in the concert room of Station Road WMC, Wombwell, a venue which housed a fully functioning gym in a series of converted rooms underneath. Though I didn't know it at the time, it was a location which would play a huge part in my life in years to come. Harley and a few of his friends signed up as students and I soon had a whole room full of kids, eager to progress. I was delighted, because I could feel the batteries gradually recharging and knew the desire to succeed was still burning as bright as ever. Outside of martial arts, I did a bit of odd-jobbing, predominantly working for an agency, commuting wherever I was sent, including a short stint as a waiter. The money was crap, like; but, hey ho, at least I could put food on the table. After that, it was shelf-filling at M&S in Barnsley town centre, working evenings, prepping the store ready for morning. I remember once, there was a big derby match at Oakwell, the Reds versus Sheffield Wednesday. Everybody was going and I didn't want to miss it, so I told the gaffer my grandma was seriously ill and I couldn't make my shift. He swallowed the bait and off I toddled, happy as a pig in muck, enjoying a few pre-match pints, before taking a seat alongside my pals in the famous Ponty End. I'd only just parked my arse when I felt a tap on the shoulder, hearing a familiar voice, chuntering in my ear.

"How's your grandma, Charlie boy? Still at death's door, is she…?"

I ask you: what were the chances? Twenty-five thousand screaming supporters and the gaffer inadvertently dumps himself on my shoulder. Suffice to say, my M&S career ended abruptly as a consequence. Every cloud has a silver lining, though; I landed a lovely little job at Next, working in the warehouse returns department at the company's distribution centre in South Elmsall, a half hour drive away, a wonderful, multi-national hub, employing people from dozens of different countries. I made friends quickly. Mischievous as ever, I needed a partner in crime and the honour fell to a lovely young lady called Cat Holmes, nowadays Pegg. If I needed a laugh, I'd turn to Amanda Harris, while my resident agony aunt was Julie Cadman, assisting me on all manner of contentious issues. Surprisingly enough, I also had male friends, especially Phil and Glyn, who were always there to watch my back and vice versa. As for the management team, Dale, Jed and Chris, well…I had them eating out of my hand. Whatever I wanted, I pretty much got, including dubious holiday requests to look after my seriously ill grandma again, even though it was common knowledge she'd been dead twenty years. My job title was returns assistant, but everyone looked upon me as the factory jester, constantly winding folk up with incessant practical jokes and piss-takes. All in all, it was a happy ship, but there always one, principally a lady called Brenda, who seemingly got off upon making everyone's life a misery. One day, she turned her attentions on me, blaming me about a misplaced pallet, which was absolutely none of her business. On and on she went, until I'd finally heard enough, sending her packing with the most enormous flea in her ear. Rounds of applause rose up from a gaggle of enthralled spectators, promptly earning me the nickname of Dingle, a reference to my

Barnsley heritage, translating as the neighbour no one wants. It was load of rubbish, naturally, because everyone readily accepted Barnsley was the epicentre of the universe; the birthplace of *Kes* author, Barry Hines, world-renowned chat show host, Michael Parkinson, international actor, Brian Glover, cricketer, Darren Gough, and football's Greenhoff brothers, Jimmy and Brian. Oh, and don't forget little old me: Charlie Green, heart of gold, knob of butter, Cloughfields original and principal raggy lad. There was a guy in the warehouse who I christened *Columbo* on account of a distinctly dodgy eye, a reference to the Peter Falk detective of the same name. Columbo was big and he was brash and no one messed with him. He got away with murder and was also instrumental in propagating my Dingle nickname. I always knew he'd get his comeuppance eventually. What I didn't know was I'd be the one responsible for administering the punishment. On my way home one evening, I happened upon him, parked outside a kebab shop, a mile or so down the road. When I tapped on the window, asking what he was doing, he stumbled and stuttered, saying he was getting some supper. I could tell he was lying, a suspicion confirmed when I saw him parked in exactly the same spot a couple of days later. Pulling up nearby, I switched off my lights, watching with amusement as he disappeared into an upstairs flat with Sofia, a pretty Polish girl who worked in packing. As The Sun headline proudly announced after HMS Conqueror sank the cruiser General Belgrano during the Falkland's War, I instinctively mouthed: Gotcha! I had as well: bang to rights. Next morning, I confronted him with my findings and he looked at me like someone had just stepped on his grave. He suddenly began treating me with respect, calling me Charlie again instead of Dingle. Then, one day, and don't ask me how, nudge, nudge, wink, wink, wouldn't say boo to a blind horse, word of his escapades managed to get out. Overnight, Columbo became the butt of everyone's jokes. Kebab pictures were faxed here, there and everywhere, appearing on notice boards and office doors throughout the warehouse. He took it well to be fair. What other choice did he have? Not much was the answer. All he could do was grin and bear it and suck up the consequences. As for Charlie boy, well…I couldn't stop laughing, blissfully unaware that, before much longer, I'd have very little to laugh at.

20. Beccs

One afternoon, Nicola and I had the most enormous argument and split up. It had been coming a while, so I can't say it was a surprise; but it *did* hit me hard. Not so much because the relationship was over. Shit happens and I'd already reconciled myself with the fact it was over. What bothered me most was I'd lose Harley at the same time, meaning he wouldn't be there to greet me when I got home, smiling and throwing his arms around me as I ruffled his tousled mop top. Don't misunderstand me: I wouldn't be prevented from seeing him. Nicola wasn't like that. We'd agreed in advance that, if we broke up, I could have regular and unfettered access. Work, rest and play, I was in a foul mood in the aftermath. I had fire in my belly and would use any available excuse to vent my anger, taking it out on anyone and everyone. The Next crew were amazing, doing everything possible to make me feel better. I lost count of the number of times I was invited out for drinks or food, or asked to go to the footie or a music festival or something. I turned every single offer down. Not because I was ungrateful. I was just so fed up with what had happened, I couldn't be arsed anymore. After all I'd achieved, I suddenly found myself drifting, aimlessly, not knowing which direction to turn. I moved from house to house, bumming a bed wherever I could, before temporarily moving in back home. I was still teaching taekwondo; but that was about it. Inevitably, I took to drink, spending endless hours in Wetherspoons, killing time by regaling staff and customers with my many tales. Then I met Emma, a pretty little thing from Darfield. We started dating. Nothing serious. A few drinks out and the occasional trip to the pictures was as far as it got. One evening, we joined our Bev and husband, Mark, for a trip to Ward Green WMC, a local night scene ubiquitously known as the shed. There was a group on called Prevention and I remember making everyone laugh by saying I hoped they were better than The Cure. We hadn't been there long when a group of seven or eight blokes walked in. Silly with drink, they were loud and aggressive and clearly looking for trouble. They quietened down a bit when the band came on, standing at the edge of the dance floor, watching the entertainment. Unfortunately, it was only a temporary reprieve. As soon as the set was over, they reverted to form, harassing nearby people and generally making a nuisance of themselves. I went to the bar and got another round in before heading for the loo. On the way back, I spotted one of the agitators nicking my pint off our table. He was a good six-inch taller than I was, but I didn't give a shit, grabbing hold of him and making him give it back. He didn't like it, scurrying off to rejoin his mates with his tail between his legs. I asked Bev where Emma was. She pointed outside and I spotted her in the car park, walking round in circles, phone glued to her ear. It was her boss apparently, wanting her to swap shifts. She obviously wasn't happy. And neither was I when caught sight of Mark, being pushed around over by the door. I was across in a flash and we were soon all outside. A big fucker with a face like a chewed-up toffee kept pushing Mark in the chest, trying to start a fight. I realised it was the arsehole I'd just crossed swords with and instantly made ready. A gentle soul, Mark didn't want any trouble and with just cause: he was a nurse and would lose his job if he was prosecuted for fighting. I pushed toffee face in the chest and told him to do one. As anticipated, he came straight back at me, swinging giant haymakers. I ducked one, two, three in a row, then dropped him with a peach of a left hook. His mate jumped in and I dispatched him similarly, Chuck Liddell style, a devastating overhand right, leaving him spark out on the tarmac alongside his pal. The others thought about it, but wisely stood their ground. The fire in my belly was more like a raging volcano now and I can't deny I was disappointed no one else fancied a go. We made our exit, departing for the bus stop, Bev and Mark leading the way, with myself and Emma bringing up the rear. A large crowd had gathered by this stage, trying to get to the bottom of what had happened. Someone called out to us, a nasty, threatening tone, which left little to the imagination. Moments later came the sound of pounding feet. I looked round and a geezer with a big, black beard was charging hell for leather down the street. We clashed head on and exchanged punches. In a flash, I gripped his head in both hands, bringing my knee up, several times in rapid succession. His nose broke and a yawning cut above his eye began spewing claret. All over, I let him go and he collapsed to the floor like a rag doll. Then the police arrived, a patrol car and a jam sandwich, with a couple of ambulances, bringing up the rear, blue flashing lights, reflecting vividly against a leaden sky. A worried looking copper exited the front vehicle and headed straight for me, sticking his face in mine.

"Where is it?"

"Where's what?" I asked, raising my hands like a surrendering soldier, attempting to take the heat out of the situation. "What are you talking about?"

"You know what I'm talking about. We've had a report you've been assaulting people with an iron bar. Now, where is it...? Own up, do you hear? Own up and things won't be nearly as bad for you."

I laughed, "Iron bar my arse. My fists do *my* talking."

"Fists? Do you think I've just fallen off a Christmas tree, or what? Do you *seriously* expect me to believe you've laid out three blokes using just your fists? Each of whom is bigger than you? Don't make me laugh, because I'll tell you now...I don't believe a word of it."

"Well, you'd better. I'm a kickboxer, aren't I? British taekwondo champion and undefeated international athlete."

He peered deep into my eyes, clearly assimilating what he'd been told. He must have believed it because, all of a sudden, his expression mellowed and he even backed off a yard.

"Kickboxer, you say? Picked on the wrong man then, eh?"

"Just a bit..."

By a stroke of luck, Emma's uncle was one of the attending coppers and she pleaded with him to let me go. He agreed; but only after each of the injured stated they wouldn't be pressing charges. I didn't suspect for one moment they would. It was embarrassing enough to be spending the night in hospital without having to relive the experience in court. We went straight home after. We'd no other choice. My clothes were spattered with blood and the others were hardly in the mood to continue. All in all, it wasn't the best night I'd ever had and it was about to get worse. I realised I'd lost my watch, an expensive Tag Heuer acquired from the proceeds of the UFC tours, exemplifying how far things had slipped, a downward spiral which I could only see getting worse. And so it came to pass: I parted company with Next over something and nothing and Emma quickly went the same way. Not long after, I moved into rented accommodation in Wombwell's Squires Hotel, the same digs where Marcus Davis had stayed during his recent trip, a comfortable en-suite, overlooking St Mary's Church and the High Street. With no job or money to fall back upon, I didn't even know how I was going to pay for the room. I'd scraped enough together to cover the first couple of weeks, but that was about it. Desperately in need of cash, I got my coat on and marched straight into Wetherspoons and asked to see the manager, a nice young man called Chris. We didn't exactly need introducing. I'd done enough boozing there of late that he probably saw more of me than he did of the wife. I laid my cards firmly on the table, explaining I needed a job. As luck would have it, there was a vacancy for a barman and he set me straight on, starting first thing in the morning. Legendary barmaid Kelly drew the short straw, showing me the ropes. I absolutely adored Kelly. Still do, in fact. A no-nonsense girl if ever there was one, she didn't take prisoners, as I quickly found out to my cost. Messing about one night, I mischievously pecked her on the side of the face. It was meant to be a laugh, but I don't think she saw it that way, sending me packing with a vicious rabbit punch, leaving staff and customers roaring with laughter. Kelly's oppos behind the bar were Vicky and Joanne, who were forever telling me off for fraternising with clients. And, no, I don't mean you, Pete and Maurice Batty. Give your heads a shake, can't you? On the martial arts front, I was doing everything I could to keep my hand in, predominantly teaching, but also attending a couple of long-standing MMA events I'd organised. The most memorable took place at Barnsley nightclub, Escapade. Gareth Neale was involved as was Victor Estima, a world and European jiu jitsu champion, making it one hell of a line up. Also on the card was Tommy Lawton. When his scheduled opponent pulled out at the last minute, he was pitched against a much heavier fighter, ten years his senior, boasting multiple fights and an undefeated record. Tommy wasn't remotely phased, smashing him to pieces, before tapping him out with a triangular choke. Greatly adding to his growing reputation, he brought the house down with his performance and I know Marcus would have been proud as punch if he'd been present to witness the demolition, totally justifying the praise he'd heaped upon the promising local youngster.

I knew my luck would turn for the better eventually and it did. Spring was in the air. Birds were singing in blossom-filled trees and fluffy white clouds were floating past in an otherwise crystal-clear blue sky. I was feeling good. Barnsley had just beaten Oxford 3-2 at Wembley in the final of the Football League Trophy. Normally, it would have taken wild horses to make me miss the game. As it was, I passed up on match-day tickets and a day on the piss with the lads to spend a fabulous afternoon and evening with Harley, visiting Experience Barnsley, a council sponsored museum devoted to the heritage and culture of the region. Harley was wearing a specially printed Barnsley Five-0 T-shirt. A reference to the town's notoriously rough, tough hooligan firm, it inevitably reminded me of my time in Hawaii, improving my mood even further, if that were possible. We enjoyed some food. Had a lark around in the Alhambra shopping centre. Spent what little bit of cash I had, purchasing a few bits and pieces and having a go on the slots. I shouldn't have skint myself like that; but it didn't matter in the overall scheme of things. I found fifty quid on the way for the bus, a definite signs things were looking up and meaning we could stop off for chips when we got back.

Next day, I attended Scott Camplin's twenty-first birthday party at Wombwell Main Community Sporting Association. I was there at the behest of a couple of good friends of mine, Scott's parents, Gary and Carole. It was a proper shindig, lots of music, dancing and singing, and also frequented by loads of top lads; Taffy; Toddy; Titch; Frosty and Scriv; Jobba and Marcus Bird. Plenty of beer was flowing as well, making it even more up my street. Carole was taking lots of pictures and I made sure I photobombed as many as possible, sending a very clear message I was young, free and single. I noticed a lady called Rebecca Harvey, aka Beccs, was all over the posts, adding comments and liking photos. I checked out her profile and immediately thought: *phwoar*! I'll spare the detail, other than to say she was young and she was pretty and I fancied her instantly. She had a child from a previous relationship, who I could tell she absolutely adored. Some may have seen it as baggage. Not me. A boy of nine, he was also called Charlie and I took it as a sign. Never backward at coming forward, I sent her a message, introducing myself, saying I'd noticed she'd liked a few of my pictures. When she responded positively, I asked her straight out on a date. The lady from Thurnscoe, she said yes, and we met the following evening, a few beers in Barnsley followed by a spot of Turkish cuisine at the fabulous Lemon Tree restaurant. We got on great from the start and couldn't stop talking. I think it's fair to say we both knew we'd found someone special. I didn't know it at the time, obviously; but the influential and positive impact Beccs would have upon the forthcoming years was nothing short of immense. How I'd have got through the callous shit-storm fate had in store without her was open to conjecture. All I know is she was there for me every single inch of the way and I will love her forever for the strength and fortitude she displayed on my behalf. I may as well mention that Beccs hotly disputes the circumstances surrounding us getting together. Put another way, she's adamant I'm talking absolute shite. She reckons she wasn't all over my posts, I was all over *hers*. Additionally, she says she can't remember anything about a meal out and that I randomly turned up at hers with a bunch of wilted flowers and a bottle of cheap plonk. Later the same evening, she claims she asked me to show her a few kickboxing moves and I walloped her straight on the shin, reducing her to tears. Alright, Beccs, I'll give you that one; but you did ask for it, didn't you? I just got a bit carried away, that's all, lol.

On a whim, I decided to hang my gloves up, pending a retirement fight, which I arranged with the help of a local promoter called Fahad. Taking place at Sheffield's Silver Blades Ice Skating Rink, I was pitted against a top-class opponent with an impeccable record. Much heavier than I was, I knew I couldn't take anything for granted and so worked my bollocks off in the run-up, getting super fit to ensure I went out with a bang. Typically, he pulled out with just ten days to go. With experience of how things like this worked, I fully expected him to be replaced by a last-minute bum and consequently hit the booze from that moment onwards, undoing all my hard work with frequent pub-crawling nights out with Beccs. The day of the fight eventually arrived and I discovered I'd been lined up to fight a geezer called Ryan Hurst, a brawny Sheffielder in his mid-twenties, who would eventually become a close friend of mine. Six-foot-two and eyes of blue, I watched a couple of videos of Ryan in action and was taken aback with how good he was, making me wish I'd kept my guard up and continued my strict training regime. In a fit of panic, I examined myself in the mirror. I'd endured another lengthy session the night before and looked ghastly; pale and completely out of sorts with a pot belly of such prominence it looked like I had a bowling ball hidden up my top. It would have been easy to feign an injury and pull out. And I can't deny it crossed my mind. It wasn't my style, though; I'd never shirked anything during my career and wasn't about to start now. And, so, I turned up as planned, resigning myself to my fate, whatever that might be. Fortunately, Beccs wasn't in attendance; she was at home, looking after Charlie. The rest of the family were there, though, alongside every other man and his dog, including big Phil and a busload of pals from Hoyland; John Stopforth; his dad, Bob, and brother, Tony; Lee Steeples; Roy Kilner's son, Paul; David Dickinson; Mick Siddall and his dad, Malc. In my corner was a couple of experienced martial arts acquaintances, Simon and Ebbr. Both were patently aware of everything I'd achieved and what I was capable of. They also knew how faultlessly I'd prepared for all the other big events in my fighting career and couldn't believe the shape I was in; or should that read *wasn't* in. They didn't judge, though, realising it wasn't a rocket up the arse I needed, more a good old back slap and kind words of encouragement. As such, I entered the ring with renewed confidence, staring my opponent down, a Dolph Lundgren lookalike if ever there was one, pacing the canvas like imposing Soviet boxer, Ivan Drago, on the set of *Rocky IV*. We touched gloves and the bout commenced. Determined to strike first, I swung a vicious leg kick but miscalculated, misconnecting so badly I thought I'd smashed my shinbone. From the corner of my eye, I caught sight of Harley, shouting me on. I was in so much pain from the mistimed connection, I really should have sought time out or even capitulated. But I couldn't; not with Harley watching my every move alongside screaming support from everyone else. Straight on the back foot, it came as no surprise when I lost the first round easily. And the second didn't exactly get off to a good start, either. Ryan caught me with a powerful jumping knee, cracking my ribcage. The sound travelled through my body, assailing my eardrums like rapid rifle fire. I nearly went down, but somehow managed to retain my balance. Tumbling into the ropes, I used the surround as a springboard, fighting back, catching my opponent with a smart one-two, dancing a circle before repeating the move. The crowd noise was deafening as we continued to trade blows, gradually eating up the round. At the close, Ebbr frantically waved me over. Mopping my brow with a John Smith's Bitter towel, he had a stern word in my ear.

"That's it, Greenie lad. Well done, son. I'd call that even. Win the final round and you'll earn yourself a draw. Now focus like you've never focused before. Think what you've achieved. Think how far you've come. Tell yourself how good you've been. How good you *are*. You're a former British champion. A GB team member. Dig deep, Greenie lad. Show this fella what you're about. Don't hold anything back. Just do it. Same as you've always done. Wipe the bloody floor with him…"

Fully charged, I finally got it together, rediscovering not only my fitness but also my speed, strength and power, outpointing my opponent from start to finish, earning an honourable draw. With a very gracious Ryan, holding my arm aloft, I saluted the roaring crowd, who clapped and cheered repeated laps of the ring, celebrating a competitive career which had spanned more than fifty fights, a record so eloquently articulated in a pre-fight Paul Oxtoby live You Tube presentation.

Driven home, I was dropped off at Wombwell Main for a couple of celebratory jars. Eager to be on my way, I'd neglected to cut the bandages off my hands, an honour I bequeathed to Harley, who had travelled back with me. My fighting career was over. Now I had to decide what I wanted to do next. All I knew was one thing: the martial arts candle continued to burn bright as ever and I was determined to stay connected with the sport one way or another. The only question was: to what degree…?

21. Retro Fitness

The euphoria of my retirement fight gradually began to fade. Days became weeks, then weeks became months. November turned. Christmas was just round the corner and my increasingly tenuous grip upon martial arts engagement continued to slip. The candle was still burning; but there was a noticeable lack of oxygen in the air. The flame was fading fast and I genuinely feared the light was about to go out forevermore, finally extinguishing the smouldering embers of a rip-roaring career. I was still teaching at Station Road WMC; but that was about it. I knew I needed to do something. But what? Completely devoid of ideas, I didn't know which way to turn. Then fate stepped in, tossing up an old martial arts acquaintance, Master Kevin Summers, who recommended me to the Bulldog Gym in Gold del Sur, Tenerife, as a temporary taekwondo tutor. Owned and run by Kate Harper and Ian Edwards, it was proposed I pop over for a few days, taking a few classes in between soaking up a few much-needed rays. I was hardly flush at the time but immediately agreed, booking return flights only to have to rearrange for a week later after receiving an out-of-the-blue invite to big Phil's surprise wedding. Marrying a lovely, bubbly, effervescent Elsecar lass called Lisa, I wouldn't have missed it for the world. As the old saying goes: old friends are the best. That was certainly the case where *Jack* was concerned. We went back such a long way. Growing up on Cloughfields, we'd entered adult life together and even fitted in a trip to Australia alongside countless adventures on the martial arts circuit. Like myself, Phil also went on to become British champion, a terrific achievement in what was an overcrowded heavyweight division. A real bruiser, I was always glad he was on my side whenever we got into any kind of scrape. That said, I still took the piss out of him at every opportunity, losing count of the number of times I goaded him to the point where he inevitably lost his temper with me.

"One of these days, Greenie," he'd growl, brandishing a fist as big and hard as a bowling ball, "I'm going to knock you spark out. Just you see if I don't…"

The wedding came and went, a rumbustious, booze laden affair, as you'd expect, leaving me free to finally head off on my travels. Ian met me at the airport and took me straight to the gym. I must admit, I liked him instantly. He was a good man, a brilliant conversationalist and so easy to get on with. Kate was equally agreeable, making me feel welcome the moment I put my foot across the threshold. I couldn't have been more impressed with the facilities and overall ambience of the place. It was a thoroughly happy ship, well supported by a keen, energetic and enthusiastic multi-national client base. Still going strong today, I can highly recommend if anyone is heading down that way and looking for somewhere to do a spot of training or burn off a few calories. As for the classes, I loved every minute, fully engaging with and assisting students at various stages of development, all of whom shared the same goal: to be the best martial artist they could possibly be. The rest of the time I'd spend round the pool, or having a few drinks and a spot of food in the town. I *loved* Tenerife and could have stayed on indefinitely if I'd had the time and the money. Unfortunately, all good things must come to an end. Before I knew it, I was bidding farewell to Ian and Kate and the fabulous Bulldog Gym and winging my way back to the UK, to what was a very uncertain future indeed.

Back teaching, I'd just finished for the night when I was accosted by the WMC steward, Ellen, who informed me the owner of the gym downstairs had called it a day and handed in his keys. I knew what was coming next: was I interested in taking over? In the blink of any eye, a million and one thoughts whizzed through my head, frantically weighing up the pros and cons. There was no doubt in my mind: the potential was immense. It was Locky's old gym, where half of Wombwell had trained at one time or another, keeping fit and learning the ropes. A superb catchment area, it was located right on the edge of town, adjacent the bypass, with loads of nearby parking. On the downside, I'd never run a business before, plus which, I didn't have two halfpennies to rub together by way of investment. It was a big decision. Monumental, in fact. But I couldn't deny I was interested. Normally, I would have said yes in a breath. As it was, I prudently asked if I could view the premises first, buying a bit of time. Ellen led me downstairs, unlocking the door and flicking on the light. I was shocked to the core at the sight which met my eyes. When Locky was the keyholder, the gym was in tip-top condition, clean, tidy and fully kitted out with boxing and exercise equipment. Now it wasn't much more than an empty shell, a shadow of its former self, with perishing, whitewashed walls and the pungent smell of damp. There was a couple of old settees in the corner. A rickety table and chairs. A sink full of dirty pots and a stinky, smelly old fridge. Various other pieces of accumulated junk were piled high at the back of the fitness suite, enough to fill a couple of skips minimum. As for the showers, well…they resembled something out of *The Shawshank Redemption* and weren't somewhere where you'd risk dropping your soap let me tell you. The only salvageable items were a series of heavy bags, suspended from the ceiling. I had to be honest with myself: I badly wanted it, but *didn't* at the same time. If I was to give it a go, it would mean starting from scratch, involving lots of stress, heartache, hard graft and expense. I asked Ellen if I could have twenty-four hours, while I conferred with the family: Beccs, mum, Bev, Mark and my niece, Chelsea. She agreed, but on the strict condition there could be no extension. She already had two or three firm enquiries and was under orders from the committee to secure a new lease at the earliest opportunity.

The ensuing discussion was as long as it was painful. One minute the gym was the best thing since sliced bread, the next we wouldn't have touched it with a barge pole. A close-run thing, it could have gone either way. In the end, though, we decided to go for it, agreeing to invest what meagre funds we could put together. We must have been mad. But at least we weren't going in totally blind, having cobbled together a makeshift plan of sorts. First and foremost, we agreed six months free rent, persuading the committee to get rid of all the junk in the process. Additionally, we demanded a plumbing and electrics upgrade, which was also sanctioned, as was a new external door and lighting. Straight after, we went to work with paint brushes and rollers, systematically moving from room to room, smartening the place up as best we could. Daz Kilner had recently acquired a job lot of mats and allowed us to purchase a complete set at cost. A couple of Jack-of-all-trade mates, Wayne Dyer and Simon Davis, helped out when and wherever possible, and Kev Shipp chipped in with a bit of building work. Beccs had a new carpet fitted in lieu of my Christmas present, while her brother, Rob, knocked a few walls out. And, no, Phil, before you ask, I don't mean *knocked out* as in the boxing ring; I'm talking a few whacks with a sledgehammer, you great pillock! With the interior complete, we needed a name and logo. We dreamed up all kinds of weird names, but eventually settled on *Retro*. The name was Beccs idea, spawned from the fact everything connected with the fledgling business looked so old; bare brickwork; old-school lockers; oddments of leftover equipment and overall atmosphere and aura. She passed the name straight on to her brother's best mate, a talented graphic designer called Neil Garrett, who created us a cracking logo in red, blue and white livery, purposely mod-like in design. On January 2nd, 2018, *Retro* was finally born and we were good to go. We'd kept the heavy bags and had various pieces of exercise equipment we'd bought on the cheap alongside a selection of weights. I was proud as punch, unlocking the door, retreating back inside before the rush started. We'd done what we thought was a pretty decent job, advertising our presence locally; but it obviously wasn't good enough. All I did for days was sit around, doing nothing, waiting for something to happen, a bit like the scene in *Ghostbusters*, where the boys were totally devoid of work. In the first week of trading, we had one customer, tripling attendance in week two, then a few more the week after that, gradually building numbers as word spread. After a dodgy start, we were firmly up and running. It wasn't all good news, though. I fell down drunk one night and smashed my shoulder, necessitating a mad dash to A&E to get it sorted. When the doctor asked how I'd done it, I told him a big gust of wind appeared, just as the world tilted on its axis, causing me to lose my balance. He roared with laughter, making a noise like the famous mechanical clown at the entrance to Blackpool Pleasure Beach. It was ever so funny; or at least for all of five minutes. It's fair to say I wasn't laughing for the next few weeks, though, battling through a seemingly endless string of training sessions with my arm in a flipping sling.

With the boxing side of the business growing exponentially, I enrolled for a two-day intensive training course at multiple world championship winning welterweight Ricky Hatton's gym in Hyde, Greater Manchester. A prestigious establishment, it was frequented by numerous well-known boxers, including the one and only Tyson Fury. I was hoping to bump into the man lovingly referred to as the gypsy king. Unfortunately, I was out of luck; otherwise, I would have been adding another famous name to the growing tick-box of world-renowned boxers and martial artists I'd encountered. The purpose of the course was to gain accredited qualifications, enabling us to expand the boxing side of the business, introducing a ream of new training initiatives. I must admit, I thought it would be a doddle; the reality was I'd never been so unprepared for anything in my entire life. I'd imagined it would be mainly classroom stuff, with a bit of light training thrown in for good measure. I couldn't have been more wrong. The course was seven or eight hours per day of full-on ring-work, learning every aspect of the fight game; jabs; crosses; hooks; uppercuts; ducking and weaving, slips, blocks and footwork. By the end of it all, I was thoroughly exhausted and likely half a stone lighter. Not that it mattered. I had my accreditation and was so buoyed by the experience, I even enrolled for an elite course a few months later. I passed that as well, a physical and written exam at the end of two of the longest and most punishing days imaginable.

It was around this time I decided to re-launch *Musa*. All the old stock had gone and so I needed to start afresh, contacting a promising Pakistani supplier who promptly supplied a range of samples of such excellent quality I unhesitatingly placed a sizeable order. With stock on its way, I realised I needed brand exposure and so contacted an associate called Amir Subsasic, a professional MMA fighter and ex-Bosnian special forces soldier, based in Luton, Bedfordshire. Interestingly, he was also Andrew Tate's kickboxing coach, a man seemingly permanently in the news nowadays for all manner of reasons. I arranged a meeting and took Beccs along for the experience. A seriously tough cookie and genuine all-round good guy, we got along famously and quickly reached agreement on the back of umpteen cups of coffee and colossal amounts of bonding. Big in the game, Amir was sponsoring an MMA super fight series at Wembley Arena, which was being shown live on Sky Sports, and promised to kit-out all fighters and TV crew in freebie *Musa* hoodies and T-shirts. He also insisted I attend as his guest, a VIP spectator with overnight hotel accommodation. I was on the verge of accepting when he leaned across the desk, stating we'd go out for a drink afterwards and have a bit of fun with the ring girls. It goes without saying that Beccs quickly kiboshed that idea, robotically informing Amir I was unavailable on the dates provided. Good old Beccs: you've got to love her. For what it's worth, I wouldn't have gone anyway; but it was nice to see she cared all the same. A couple of months later, the fight went ahead as planned and I made a point of propping up the bar at Wombwell Main, ensuring steward, Harvey Askham, had the correct channel on. With the entire event looking like it had been sponsored by *Musa*, I fielded a barrage of incoming queries with glee, principally based around how much it cost.

"Trust me," I replied, a big, beaming smile, spreading inexorably across my face, "you *don't* want to know…"

Everything we did seemed to turn to gold. Try as we might, we couldn't put a foot wrong. *Retro* continued to go from strength to strength with all profits going into new equipment and décor. As a sideline, I did personal training sessions with a string of professional footballers; Scotland U-19 winger, Fraser Preston; Barnsley midfielder, Louis Wardle; Jim O'Brien, a midfielder who played for the best two clubs in the world in my opinion: Celtic and Barnsley; local lad and Manchester United starlet, Callum Whelan. Attendance continued to grow and we had a production line of promising fighters under our wing. Buzzing like a second-hand fridge, I couldn't sleep at night for plotting the next big thing. The world was our oyster; mine and Beccs. What could possibly go wrong? Nothing. Or so I thought. Then I started seeing TV news reports about a dangerous new virus, a highly contagious disease which was killing large numbers of people wherever it hit. Mimicking Jack Dawson's reaction after the iceberg collision in *Titanic*, I vividly recall saying to Beccs: *this is bad.* As it turned out, I didn't know half of it…

22. Pandemic

In anticipation of what was coming, I moved in with Beccs. A couple of months previous, we'd bought a dog, a beautiful Sprocker Spaniel, one of a litter of pups belonging to Wombwell Mainers, Charlie and Joanne Johnson. Christened Buddy, we had him trained in no time and he was soon my best friend; no offence, Beccs, lol. He was there with us that fateful night, begging as we ate our tea, snuggled up on the settee in preparation for the big announcement. It came as no surprise when Boris uttered those dreaded and much prophesised words: From this evening, I must give the British people a very simple instruction: you *must* stay at home…

Shit bricks. For all the talk, we couldn't believe he'd actually gone and done it. The country was officially in lockdown in order to stop Covid-19 spreading between households. The nitty-gritty of what it all meant was mind-blowing. People were only be allowed to leave home for limited purposes such as shopping for basic necessities, albeit as infrequently as possible, and should use food delivery services whenever possible. One form of exercise a day was permitted, a run, walk, or bike ride, either alone or with members of the same household. People could leave home for medical needs, or to provide care, or to help a vulnerable person. Travelling to and from work was allowed, but only where absolutely necessary and when work couldn't be done from home. People were told they shouldn't be meeting friends or family members who didn't live in the same house. If asked, they should very firmly say no. Gatherings of more than two people in public were prohibited and all social events, including weddings, baptisms and other ceremonies, but excluding funerals, were to be cancelled and curtailed forthwith. As if all that wasn't bad enough, the police would possess powers to enforce the rules, including issuing fines and dispersing illicit gatherings. All shops selling non-essential goods were closed, including clothing and electronic stores. Other premises were also impacted. Libraries. Playgrounds. Places of worship. And, yes, you've guessed it: gyms, exactly what we didn't want to hear.

We'd closed the business a day early, mothballing equipment and facilities until we were told we could open again. In another body blow, we had to cancel a repeat UK and Ireland tour we'd recently arranged with Wanderlei Silva. We had gym seminars signed up left, right and centre and Wand had done several promotional videos, advertising the initiative. Unfortunately, it wasn't to be. Circumstances had intervened and all we could do was take it on the chin. Gutted beyond belief, we did the same as everyone else, staying home, endlessly watching Netflix alongside depressing, doom-laden news reports, escaping to peer out of the window at every opportunity, watching the birds singing in the trees, while praying for dark and another chance to bay at the moon like the deranged inmates of some cruel, despicable lunatic asylum. When we did venture out, it was nothing less than soul-destroying. Seeing long lines of people, queuing outside supermarkets, essential shops and doctors' surgeries only added to the paranoia we were experiencing. Little wonder we felt like we did. It was on the news every waking moment: people were dying in huge numbers throughout the world and the situation was continuing to deteriorate. Like everyone else on the planet, the last thing we wanted was to become just another statistic. It made us feel terribly sad. That didn't mean we didn't feel the pain of adverse personal circumstances, though; our livelihood had been literally snatched away overnight and we had no idea how we were going to survive long term. Then, eureka! The government stepped in with the financial assistance businesses like ours were crying out for. Individuals were already in receipt of furlough pay and now it was our turn. In a massive shock to the system, we were suddenly bequeathed a ten grand grant to help tide us over. It didn't solve anything, but certainly made us feel a lot better. Realising we had to evolve or risk sinking, I decided to take advantage of the beautiful spell of clement weather we were experiencing, performing a series of garden-based keep-fit zoom classes, with Beccs doing her Steven Spielberg bit behind the lens. Soon, we had upwards of fifty attendees, enjoying thrice-weekly bouts of exercise as a means of breaking the monotony. On the news, there was talk of a vaccine being available soon. I'd been monitoring the science closely. Study after study indicated the threat to life of fit, strong, energetic people in my age group was absolutely miniscule, fuelling doubts about whether or not the vaccine would be right for me. In other developments, I utilised the spare time to try out the *Wimm Hof* method of taking daily cold showers to impact positively on physical and mental health, principally with the aim of reducing Covid induced stress levels. I have to say it worked a treat and in ways I hadn't imagined. I became infinitely more alert and lost a few excess pounds I'd gained through months of government enforced house arrest. I'd always possessed irrepressible willpower; don't stop believing and all that. Suddenly, though, I felt like Superman, powering my way through whatever task was laid before me. I found the cold also stimulated my breathing, aiding concentration and assisting me in holding my breath for as much as three minutes. My good friend, Ben Poppleton, sent me books on yoga, which I read cover to cover, specifically sections on pranayama, advanced breathing exercises, promoting physical and mental wellness. When outside fitness classes were sanctioned, we held kickboxing and keep fit classes at Wombwell Stadium and go-kart circuit, utilising the extensive running track to further enhance attendee experiences.

In June, the lockdown finished and we were permitted a bounce back loan, investing the sum in new bags, cardio equipment, replacement mats and another lick of paint. When we were finally allowed to open our doors, the reaction of punters was something else. We weren't surprised. Not only had we survived, but we'd come out the other end even stronger. We weren't under any illusions, though. The government was having its strings pulled by opposition parties, determined to use crisis to its own advantage. Government briefings continually insisted they were following the science. Maybe they were; but *which* science? An increasing number of experts were saying forecasts were based upon apocalyptic, worst-case scenarios and that restrictions were way too harsh. I didn't disagree. Neither did I disagree that the MSM were fuelling the flames, constantly apportioning blame while baying for blood, demanding this and that and the other, principally tougher and longer lasting curbs. The entire situation made my flesh crawl; Beccs, too, a state of affairs made worse by the fact we were continually receiving snippets of contradictory information from around the world, data, statistics and evidence which never saw the light of day on the illustrious MSM. Most information was supplied by a long-standing friend called Lindsey Desage, who nowadays resides in France but was located in Phuket at the time. On occasions, I'd receive a handful of daily messages, but sometimes this could be as many as fifty or sixty. It was a gift, but also a curse, knowing what was really happening; how we were being manipulated and controlled by decision makers, continually ramping up the rhetoric and fear, ensuring the population stringently adhered to unrelenting propaganda. All we could do was shut off our minds and get on with things. A second lockdown provided another swift kick to the bollocks. At my wits end, I sought advice and was informed that, if I could prove I was catering for pro-fighters, people who earned money from combat sports, I would be allowed to keep the doors open, a loophole gratefully unearthed by a Wigan gym owner called Kevin Harper. As a result, the council granted permission to stay open, allowing indoor zoom classes to operate alongside pre-authorised fighter visits. The second lockdown eventually petered out, though rule-based restrictions continued throughout Christmas, lots of petty do's and don'ts which didn't make the slightest bit of sense. Much to everyone's dismay, a third lockdown kick started the new year. It was getting really stupid now, though the government, MSM and general population were clearly distracted by news the much-vaunted vaccine was ready to go. I'd decided by this time it wasn't for me and so had Beccs, alongside millions of others, who were roundly turned upon for expressing heartfelt and legitimate opinions on social media, views which ultimately proved fully justified. Isn't that right, Chris John Dannatt? I hope you received lots of apologies from people willing to eat humble pie; somehow, though, I doubt it. For my own part, I didn't like the way people were being coerced into accepting an experimental vaccine which hadn't undergone thorough safety and effectiveness trials. I also reviled how dissenters were actively being discriminated against; how anyone who refused the vaccine was treated like a leper and labelled selfish, thoughtless and uneducated. I don't suppose I would have minded if the vaccine prevented spread; but it very clearly didn't. People could be vaccinated to the eyeballs and still transmit the disease; so why weren't individuals allowed to make an intelligent and considered choice upon whether to accept it or not? And then there was my long-standing blood disorder to consider, Von Willebrand disease, which I'd carried since junior school. What would be the effect upon that? The simple answer was no one could say. As such, I wasn't willing to take a chance: not in a million years I wasn't.

By the time spring arrived, the third lockdown had stuttered to its inevitable conclusion, though some restrictions frustratingly remained in place. But at least the grants kept coming, gratefully received from Sport England on this occasion, a sum of money which was put to use installing a sunbed room, improving the gym beyond all belief from the ramshackle shell we'd inherited. With the government and MSM continuing to obsess about all things Covid, vaccines, vaccine passports, social distancing, face masks, testing and the like, I decided I needed a break, enrolling for a course in reiki, a Japanese healing practice in which I'd long harboured an interest. The course was being held over the Pennines in deepest, darkest Burnley, and a condition of enrolment was that attendees hadn't been vaccinated. As you can imagine, it was like a breath of fresh air, walking into a room of twenty or so like-minded people, bodies free from contamination by witch's brews concocted by AstraZeneca, Pfizer and Moderna. The overwhelming majority were women, each of whom was a beautiful soul, at peace with mother earth, at one with the universe and literally oozing spiritualty. The course was run by a cool, calm, comforting, softly spoken man called Paul Boys, who spent quality time with every single student, placing lost city of Atlantis marbles in the palms of hands; first one, then two, three, four in a row. The marbles connected with the pineal gland, a walnut-sized endocrine gland in the middle of the brain, stimulating and charging long forgotten links to some distant plane. Eyes firmly closed, I soon became fully engaged with the process, entering a meditative state to the point where I was able to sense people, walking around the room. I also detected a vertical column of pure energy, travelling at high speed and accompanied by the unmistakable sound of deep space static. It was a beautiful, totally addictive experience, making me feel more relaxed than I had ever been in my life. Disturbingly, though, I encountered a scarier side to the process, something which I can't deny shook me up. I had a vision. I was buying clothes, expensive clothes. I was constantly changing my mind, unable to decide which I liked best. I eventually spent three thousand pounds; but I couldn't get it out of my head that I would never get to wear the damned things. I couldn't get it out of my head because I was convinced I was going to fall terribly sick, a terrifying sensation which caused me to exit the session abruptly, sitting up bolt straight, mimicking Dracula, rising from the dead. Afterwards, we were each given the opportunity to lay upon bedchairs, allowing Paul's wife, Heather, to gently hover her hand over areas of skin in pursuit of bodily responses. I immediately felt the warmth of her powers, coursing through my body. I liked it, intensely; but there was a problem. Heather told me she could feel heat in my stomach, informing me something wasn't right. She wasn't sure what and I was sure she was mistaken. I should have known better. Several months later, I would have my gall bladder removed in extremely distressing circumstances, totally substantiating her diagnosis. I should have revisited because I gleaned so much from the experience. Unfortunately, I never made it and it's something I've regretted ever since. One day soon, maybe; never say never.

I did make it north of the border, though, Lockerbie to be exact, courtesy of Paul McNicholas, owner of Barnsley's fantastic Annie Murray's Bar, who came up trumps with a couple of tickets to watch Celtic take-on Ross County. I was meeting an American friend of mine, a guy called Charlie Huber, who would be accompanying me to the game. After an arduous journey north, I had a quick shower, then joined Charlie for the seventy-mile onward rail journey to Glasgow's Celtic Park. Upon arrival, we discovered the last train back was 5.30 due to line maintenance, meaning we would have to miss the last half hour if we were to make it. I couldn't believe my luck. My first ever Celtic game and a random act of fate had conspired to wreck the experience. We quick marched to the ground and suddenly found ourselves immersed in the incredible atmosphere of thousands of chanting supporters, wearing Celtic's famous green and white hoops. All was good for now; but then came another body blow: there was still a face mask mandate in operation. The majority of people appeared to be complying, while we were the odd ones out. We spat, cursed and stamped our feet. Neither of us had worn a mask previously, so why would we start now? Masks didn't have the slightest effect upon transmission and were nothing more than a comfort blanket for the masses, scared half to death by a relentless programme of fear. Shuffling forward, we eventually reached the front. Don't ask me how, but we gained entry without question, but *were* asked to fill in a track and trace form. Determined we weren't doing that bullshit, either, a bitter stand-off with the stewards developed. We were on the verge of being thrown out when a group of passing youths intervened. I'd obviously never seen them before and the opposite clearly applied. It didn't matter. In a random act of kindness, they hoodwinked the stewards into believing they had already completed our paperwork, instantly getting us off the hook. The worst thing was we never got to thank them. They disappeared like a fart in the wind and we were back on our own again, heading through the concourse in search of the bar. We soon found it, punching the air in delight, revelling in the fact absolutely nobody was wearing a mask. We celebrated with a couple of swift ones, striking up conversation with a couple of hoops from Dumfries, naturally explaining our predicament with regards to the return journey. Neither myself nor Charlie could believe it when they offered us a lift back, an act of generosity which would necessitate a significant and expensive detour. Total strangers, who introduced themselves as Chris and Martin, it was a fantastic gesture and one for which I remain eternally grateful, enabling us to see the entire game, a comfortable 3-0 win for the Hoops. Fate had mercifully decided to let us off the hook and take care of us, after all. Good. I just hoped it would do the same moving forward, because none of us were under any illusions: there was a long, hard, painful road ahead before things got anything like back to normal…

23. Shit Street

By October, 2021, the curse of Covid was finally starting to subside. It was a good job, because populations worldwide were increasingly rebelling against insufferable, Orwellian levels of control, arbitrarily and unconditionally imposed upon the masses. Not exclusively, I might add. Large numbers remained completely traumatised by the experience, continuing to wear masks and practice social distancing and the like. The overwhelming majority, however, had clearly had enough. People everywhere wanted an end to it all and to see life return to normal, fuelled by a burning scepticism which was intensifying with each passing day. On a cheerier note, my personal life couldn't have been better. Beccs and I were happy as Larry, plus which, the gym was back operating at full throttle and was starting to show a profit again. It was also good to see the pubs back open and doing a roaring trade. Needless to say, I did everything I could to support the cause, downing a few cold ones with the lads at every opportunity.

After a particularly heavy Friday night, I remember waking up feeling absolutely awful, headache, temperature and a bad case of the sniffles. With Beccs, Charlie and Buddy away at her parents' caravan in Skeg-Vegas, I'd naively agreed to accompany Wombwell's finest, Marcus Bird, to the Barnsley Live Music Festival, taking place at multi-locations across the town centre. I could have done without it to be honest, but made the effort, more because I didn't want to let Marcus down than anything else. The pubs were packed, heaving with happy, smiling clientele, enjoying energetic performances from an impressive line-up of live bands and singers. Volumes were turned up to full, making it impossible to hear yourself think. Conversations necessitated screaming into the other person's ear and vice versa, a situation which did nothing to alleviate my pounding head. As we traversed from pub to pub, it seemed like half of Wombwell was in town. Alongside all the usual main lads, we also bumped into the irrepressible, laugh a minute, tricky Ricky

Micklethwaite. Wombwell's indisputable king of comedy, Paul Casper Haywood, was also present alongside a geezer nearly as good looking as I was, though obviously not quite, the biggest poseur to ever walk the planet, Martyn Wyatt. I could see straight away Martyn wasn't well. He wasn't his usual smiley self and explained he'd recently been diagnosed with myocarditis, or inflammation of the heart in layman's terms. A self-employed personal trainer, he'd been forced to give up work, pending eventual recovery. He was blaming his condition on the vaccine and with good cause. Even the establishment acknowledged a link and he wasn't happy about it, wishing he'd followed his instincts and told the wankers where to shove their hastily contrived, experimental vaccine. If he'd asked my opinion, I'd have told him exactly what I thought. He didn't as it turned out. I was glad, really. I liked Martyn a lot and didn't want to upset him. Unfortunately, the damage was already done and I couldn't help but feel sorry for him. By the same token, I couldn't help feeling sorry for myself. It was years since I'd felt so bad and inevitably made an unannounced exit, slipping away and heading home by taxi for a spot of supper before bed.

I wasn't feeling any better come morning. Making matters worse was realisation I had another all-day commitment scheduled. Barnsley were playing Sheffield United at Oakwell and I was meeting Jobba at Wetherspoons for a few jars with a group of Wombwell Blades; Carl and Adam Wallace; Omi; Sam Ward and his grandad, Tuke, legendary landlord of Wombwell's Prince of Wales boozer. Sold out for weeks in advance, Vicky Stevens, who was Barnsley FC physio, assisted us in getting tickets. It was a fantastic gesture for which we were eternally grateful. It was just a pity the match didn't go our way. By half time, we were losing 3-0 and staring down the barrel of a heavy and embarrassing defeat. What did we do by way of response? Waved the white flag and headed straight to the pub, that's what, enjoying a good old town centre session.

Back home again and feeling worse than ever, I disappeared straight to bed, banking on a good night's sleep to turn things round. Ten minutes short of eighteen hours later, I finally managed to flicker my eyes open. The sun was pouring in and traffic was speeding back and forth outside, rattling the window frames, making a noise like rolling thunder. Convinced I'd be feeling much better, I swung my legs off the edge of the bed and forced myself up. Not a prayer. I collapsed straight back on the mattress, burying my head in the pillow, nursing the most horrific of headaches. I knew instantly something wasn't right. Totally incapacitated, I couldn't move, aching all over and without an ounce of energy. I managed to call Beccs, asking her to arrange a stand-in for my classes. Making matters worse was the fact I had an important taekwondo seminar in Manchester on Friday and needed to be fighting fit. As the days ticked by, however, and my physical state continued to deteriorate, I realised I wasn't going to make it and was forced to cancel. I hadn't eaten a thing all week, surviving on dry bread and council pop. Beccs was on the phone constantly, seeing if I was alright, offering to return early to look after me. I told her not to be silly, insisting I was fine, telling her to concentrate on enjoying her remaining time at the coast. How wrong was I? By the time Saturday arrived, I was almost completely out of it. Weak as a kitten, I managed to conjure up sufficient energy for a walk to the shop for a couple of bottles of Lucozade Sport. Then I disappeared back to bed, sleeping for England once more, going right through till morning. When I awoke, the bedsheets were drenched in sweat. Totally dehydrated, I was burning up and my energy levels felt lower than ever. Struggling to put one leg in front of the other, I knew I needed to do something, first packing a bag, then calling 111. It wasn't a long call. I think the adviser realised pretty quickly I needed help. Advised to call an ambulance, I sat back and waited. Talking with Beccs on the phone, I lit a couple of white sage incense candles, attempting to calm the mind to aid rest and relaxation. It would probably have worked as well; except I couldn't smell a thing on account of my condition. Soon after, I heard a tap on the door. Using the back of the settee for support, I struggled over, pushing down on the handle, finding myself eyeball to eyeball with a couple of green-suited, masked ambulance technicians. The first thing they commented upon was the divine smell of incense. When I told them I couldn't smell anything, I was immediately asked if I'd done a Covid test. I replied I didn't do testing and wasn't about to start, either. Not on your bloody nelly, I emphasised, folding arms defensively across my chest. That did it: the lead technician diagnosed Covid, stating I would only be sent home if they took me through, so I may as well stay put and get my head down. Then they were gone. I let Beccs know then struggled back to bed as instructed, falling asleep the instant my head hit the pillow.

Morning was here before I knew it and nothing had changed. If anything, I felt even worse, if that was possible. On a whim, I decided food was the answer. I still wasn't eating and knew I needed something inside me. The only question was: what? There wasn't a crumb in the house, leaving no other option but to go online and schedule an M&S home delivery. A couple of hours later, I was preparing a roast beef dinner with mashed potato, peas, carrots and gravy, a monumental effort under the circumstances. Peeling the spuds was the hardest thing I'd done since winning the British title. I couldn't get my eyes to focus and was burning up inside, made to feel a thousand times worse by the heat of the oven and morning sunlight, pouring in unimpeded through the back window. I ate as much as I could, which wasn't a lot, wasting a full bottle of red wine into the bargain, unable to stomach the taste, proof as if I needed it of just how bad I really was. By early afternoon, I was back in bed once more. I'd let Beccs know in advance so she wasn't worrying, but then did the stupidest of things: I switched my phone off so I couldn't be contacted, meaning I didn't wake until six next morning. When I did, I cried buckets. I cried not only because of how ill I was feeling, but because I'd lost control of my bowels, defecating myself and spoiling the bedsheets. I'd never seen such a mess. I'd known for a while I was in shit street; now I was looking at hard evidence of the fact. The clean-up operation took forever and I seriously don't know how I managed it, because it tore me apart, mentally as well as physically. I binned the sheets then took a shower, praying to the Lord God above to make me better. It didn't work. And neither did I expect it to, either. But I *did* convince myself he would have listened, same as he had all my life, determining to intervene when the time was right. I sincerely hoped so, because I wasn't sure how much longer I could keep going. I would *never* stop believing, but wasn't convinced I'd make it: it really was that bad. My temperature was through the roof. I was red hot but shivering uncontrollably at the same time. I'd developed a continuous cough and still couldn't smell anything; not the mess in the bedroom; not the coffee I'd made, nor the embers of yesterday's incense candles. Worryingly, I was feeling desperately short of breath, a catalyst for a series of terrifying panic attacks. I drew upon my experience with pranayama, employing a series of breathing exercises to alleviate the symptoms. It worked, but didn't assist with accelerating feelings of exhaustion. I was so, so tired, totally lacking in energy and unbelievably sleepy, despite spending endless days in bed. I was aching all over and my head was splitting down the middle, an excruciating headache which instigated severe visual disturbances, zig-zags, flashing lights and blind spots, which I recognised as migraine aura. My throat was sore and my nose was blocked solid, as if someone had poured a barrel of ready-mix concrete up my nostrils while I was sleeping. Then I remembered my phone. I switched it straight back on and the screen lit up like a belisha beacon, scores of inbound messages and notifications, mostly from Beccs, but also other concerned family members and friends. I phoned Beccs and she answered first ring. I babbled into the receiver, doing my best to communicate how ill I was feeling, though struggling to find and enunciate the words.

"You're not making sense, Charlie. What is it? How *bad* are you? I've never heard anyone sound so dreadful. Do *not* move, do you hear? I'm phoning Bev to see if she can pop round. Then I'm going to ring nine-nine-nine…"

What happened next, I'm not altogether sure; whether or not Bev called I couldn't say. All I remember is answering the door to an ambulanceman, who hurriedly checked me over. A couple of minutes later, I was on a wheeled-stretcher and being loaded into the back of the ambulance. They put me straight on a drip and administered oxygen. It didn't make me feel any better. Not physically, anyway. But at least I knew I was in the right hands, managing a situation the seriousness of which was underscored by the fact we sped away with blues-and-twos blasting. It sharpened my thinking, concentrating whatever strength and mental capacity I retained into battling my condition. Admitted, I was moved straight on to a ward. A flurry of doctors and nurses came and went, checking me over, taking blood and carrying out various tests in between making sure I was comfortable. Still on a drip, I was aware that perilously low oxygen levels were being constantly monitored. Worried sick, I did my best to remain conscious, but was fighting a losing battle. I soon slipped into unconsciousness, sleeping through yet another night, waking with a start next morning, shocked to find I'd been moved to a room of my own. Utterly exhausted, I remained on oxygen and had tubes in my arms and up my nose. A PICC line had been inserted in my upper arm and guided into a large vein above the right side of the heart called the superior vena cava, which was being used to administer intravenous fluids and prescription drugs as required. I also had an arterial line inserted, enabling blood pressure monitoring and sample taking. The nose insertion was a nasogastric tube, used to deliver substances such as food or medications to the stomach. Alternatively, it could be employed to remove unwanted substances, or provide an influx of oxygen if needed. I demanded to see a doctor. I was still displaying multiple symptoms and finding it increasingly difficult to breathe. I wanted to know what the diagnosis was and what the plan was to turn things round. I soon had my wish. A nice young fellow appeared from out of nowhere, smiling behind the obligatory mask. Pulling up a chair, he bluntly and succinctly described my predicament. As predicted, I had Covid, a diagnosis made far worse by complications which had unfortunately led to me picking up pneumonia, a bilateral infection, impacting both lungs. The trigger was suspected to be my immune system, attacking the disease, causing the lungs to become damaged and inflamed, filling with fluid, making it hard to breathe. He was aware of my lifelong affliction with Von Willebrand disease and said this could have left me at increased risk of pneumonia. He couldn't prove this was the case, but thought it was a very real possibility, especially considering my background and how physically fit I was. He mapped out my treatment next. Antibiotics would lead the way alongside application of supplemental oxygen and intravenous fluids, helping me stay hydrated. Attempts would also be made to drain fluid from my lungs by insertion of a catheter or possibly even surgery, while 24/7 observations would be conducted, watching for any significant changes in my physical state. It was at this point I was asked to sign a voluntary consent form, giving permission to receive any type of medical treatment, tests or examinations as may be required. I signed it with a flourish. I didn't have any other choice. Not if I harboured any real hopes of survival. Watching the harbinger of doom disappear on his rounds, I started to genuinely fear the worst. A nurse told me not to worry and I managed a smile and even made her laugh with a silly remark about something or other. I'd no idea what, because my mind was already elsewhere, steeling my entire being for the rigours of what looked like being the mother of all battles ahead.

Morning arrived once more. I opened my eyes and found myself staring into a bowl of cornflakes. I tried a spoonful, but that was about it. The milk was warm and the cornflakes tasted like baked cardboard. Unbelievably, it wasn't food my body was demanding, but more sleep. Not feeling well at all, I slammed my eyes shut and was woken several hours later, breathless and perspiring, to a jacket potato with cheese this time. I impulsively sampled a forkful and it wasn't bad, actually. I tried a bit more and even started to enjoy it. Then the harbinger of doom returned. Even hiding behind his mask, I could tell it wasn't good news. Nothing but nothing, however, could have prepared me for what he was about to say. He let loose a torrent of medical jargon, losing me at several junctures; but the overriding message of his diagnosis was unmistakable: my lungs had deteriorated exponentially and my oxygen levels with it, meaning he had no other choice but to recommend putting me into an induced coma in order to assist recovery. I would be placed on a ventilator, a life-support machine, a process which might involve a tracheostomy, an opening created at the front of the neck, enabling a tube to be inserted into the windpipe, aiding breathing. I suppose I could have refused, but no one offered me the choice. I'd signed the consent form and I suppose everyone simply assumed I'd go along with it. They were right: I did, because I knew I wasn't going to survive without some significant form of intervention. While preparations were being made, I was asked if I needed to make any phone calls. I wasn't stupid. I knew the reason why. Induced coma mortality rates were high. There was a high probability I wouldn't survive and so I needed to say my goodbyes, just in case. Top of the list was my beautiful, darling Beccs. Wondering if I'd ever see her again, I vividly recall explaining the state of play and telling her I loved her. She said she loved me back and we cried and cried in the aftermath, not knowing what else to say; what else to do. Harley was next. He called me in actual fact and we enjoyed a typical, laugh a minute father and son exchange, incredible considering the gravity of the circumstances. Who else I called I can only hazard a guess. I was so far out of it by this stage, it could have been a Catholic priest for all I knew, asking him to read me the last rites, because the honest to God truth was I could feel myself deteriorating with each passing second.

On 6th November, I was transferred to ICU Covid hot-side, which operated a strict no-visitors policy. I was immediately assigned one-on-one care, a stark reminder of the increasingly precarious state of my health. There was all manner of tubes and wires strewn around, connecting complicated-looking medical equipment and heart, blood pressure and blood oxygen monitors, flanking beds on both sides of the room. All the other beds were occupied by patients who looked extremely the worse for wear. I couldn't believe what I was seeing; what I was witnessing. Surely, I didn't belong here? Surely, I wasn't *so* bad? *Was* I? The penny quickly dropped and I suddenly came over even weaker. With a cacophony of heartbeat bleeps, emanating from high resolution, multi-coloured displays, it was a scary place indeed, worse than the worst horror film I'd ever seen. I wanted out and out now. Unfortunately, I was going nowhere. I didn't have enough strength to lift a little finger, let alone rip the tubes from my body and make a run for it. As if by magic, I recalled a good friend of mine worked on the unit, a lovely, vivacious lady called Rachel Banks, who I frequently enjoyed a laugh and giggle with during boozy nights out at Wombwell Main. No sooner had the thought entered my mind, there she was, standing beside me, holding my hand, doing her best to calm me down. It was so nice to see her happy, smiling face, albeit aft of the mandatory mask. Florence Nightingale, I thought, eat your heart out, because you're not even at the races, lady. She cheered me up no end with her soothing tones, fetching fresh rivers of tears, racing down my face and dripping off my chin. I could have been wrong, but I'm certain I also saw Rachel filling up. She obviously knew the score, but remained professional throughout, fielding my concerns with consummate, well-practised ease, managing to put a positive spin on even the most difficult of questions. How serious was it? What were my chances? How long would I be in a coma? Days? Weeks? Or worse? Would I ever get back to full fitness? Would I ever partake in martial arts again? Had I been to my last Reds match and supped my last pint? Rachel was due off shift, but stubbornly refused to leave until I was put to sleep; my words, *not* hers. Because being put to sleep is what it felt like; an animal being put out of its misery, never to see the light of day again. I did my best to stay strong; to never stop believing. I might have been entering the departure lounge, but would need to be dragged kicking and screaming on to the flight. About to commence the biggest battle of my life, I had no idea what the outcome would be. The only guarantee was that I wouldn't go down without a fight.

Suddenly, it was time. I was duly informed all medical procedures would take place when I was sleeping. That much was a relief; but it didn't disguise the fact I might never wake up again. I was unbelievably nervous as the sedative was being administered; a fast-working drug with the sole purpose of shutting me down before I was induced into a state of coma, an enforced hibernation with a complimentary ticket to a terrifying secret world so very few have witnessed. I had no idea what to expect, but intuitively anticipated the worst. Luckily, I didn't have too much time to dwell upon the prospect. The sedative did its job. My eyes closed before briefly flickering open again, permitting a final, despairing glimpse of my surroundings. The last thing I saw was the beautiful, kind, caring soul which was Rachel. Loyal to the end, she continued to squeeze tight on my hand, whispering muffled, almost unintelligible words of encouragement, sending me off with at least a glimmer of hope. Bleeping regimentally away in the background was my heart monitor. My final thought before I slipped into unconsciousness was: but for how much longer…?

24. Coma

I don't know if it happened straight away: it could have occurred seconds, minutes, hours or days later. All I know is I was projected full force into the terrifying secret world I had so feared in advance of sedation. Fast moving images zipped back and forth; ocean views, mountain ranges, city streets and vast expanses of remote, sandy desert. I saw people as well, a myriad of faces, past and present, some familiar, some not so, passing by in such an almighty hurry. I encountered a wondrous surge of colours, flashing chameleon-like before my eyes, as if a sky full of rainbows had come tumbling down and rudely gate-crashed my subconscious. A moment later, everything was black. Not night-time black, but an impenetrable, inky black, the type you would find at the bottom of the deepest, darkest ocean. I started to panic. I'd still no concept of time and the darkness refused to go away, tormenting me endlessly, a disconcerting, distressing experience, which left me burning up inside. Then, inexplicably, I heard words: words I instantly recognised from the Bible: Genesis 1:3: *And God said, let there be light, and there was light. And God saw that the light was good. And God separated the light from the darkness.* The room illuminated; a spinning room in a hospital, somewhere, which I quickly identified as being Doncaster, *not* hometown Barnsley. I was sat on the bed in the lotus position, doing my best to meditate, lungs spent, desperately trying to regain my breath while frying my brain, trying to ascertain why I'd moved hospitals. Was it bad news? Or good? Had I been sent there to die? Or to recuperate? Then, music: *God We Need You Now* by Struggle Jennings formed a loop inside my head, playing over and over, emphasising the troubled state of the planet and the need for people to wake up to rampant violence, hate and deception in society, and the use of manipulation, intimidation and fear by the political classes to divide and control the populace; helpless, abandoned masses that should swiftly adopt meditation and prayer to fortify themselves, seeking love in the face of hate, challenging authority until God intervened to save the world. My mind screamed with terror as the music finally stopped and a deafening flutter of wings permeated the corridor, entering the room with the subtlety and finesse of a hurtling express train. I convinced myself it was Angels, arriving to transport me to my place in heaven. A window clattered open and the blinds lifted in storm force winds, vigorously assailing the building. Nurses were laughing at me and I didn't like it. It absolutely terrified me, because I could tell they knew something I didn't. Then the birds appeared, forty, fifty or more, flying circles around the bed, fast moving, grey hummingbirds, cheeping and chirping, sailing right in front of my face, cooling me with flapping winds, injecting oxygen into my tortured lungs, easing my breathing and providing a much-needed confidence boost.

Darkness returned. I could feel myself floating, as if lost in deep space, drifting helplessly across a never-ending universe. It wasn't a good situation, but I felt happier somehow, invigorated by the hummingbirds encounter and the feel of fresh air in my lungs. An eternity passed; or at least it felt like it. Then I was back in Barnsley and my symptoms had returned. I was burning up and on a saline drip on a bed in A&E. Faceless doctors and nurses were a blur, tending everyone but me. I was screaming for help; but no one was listening. I became excited when the hummingbirds reappeared, flitting from bed to bed, before vanishing into thin air when they reached mine. I was suddenly short of breath again and my stomach felt like it was being fed through a mincing machine. A doctor examined me, lots of painful prodding and poking. He had a mouthful of decaying, uneven teeth, which reminded me of a Halloween graveyard. I looked harder and, to my horror, could see my name, chiselled into crumbling, yellowed enamel. He sneered, poring over me with hot, putrid breath, informing me I had dust in my bowels and it needed removing. He gave me an injection, sending me scurrying to the toilet to rid myself of the hindrance. I did as I was told and the toilet was soon overflowing with dust. It was filling up the pan, floating through the air and gathering in the sink. Biblical words resurfaced: Genesis 3:19: *By the sweat of your face, you shall eat bread, till you return to the ground, for out of it you were taken; for you are dust, and to dust you shall return.* So, that was it: I finally had confirmation. I was dying, returning to the dust from whence I came. A second doctor appeared, wagging a finger and screaming obscenities. He stuck a needle in my arm and it hurt like crazy. Unbelievably, it did the trick: the dust was cast from my body and blew away down the corridor, scores of tumbleweeds, following in its wake. I cried unashamedly with relief. All I wanted was to live and that desire was burning bright as ever. I felt my temperature subside and my lungs refill with air. Then I was gone, cast once more into the blackness of deep space, spinning like a top, drifting for what seemed like forevermore.

An indiscernible noise and a thump in the chest brought me round again. It was Christmas Eve and I was still in hospital. It was snowing outside and I desperately wanted to go home. I pleaded with a nurse and she said I could go at three, but only because she was friends with my niece, Chelsea, regularly using her nail salon. Buoyed by the news, I closed my eyes and fell asleep, dreaming dreams within my dreams, terrifying dreams which tormented my soul, tugging and pulling at my heartstrings, confusing me more than ever with endless twists and turns I couldn't begin to understand. I woke on Christmas Day morning. When I realised everyone had gone but me, I tried to get off the bed. I couldn't move. My arms and legs wouldn't work and I couldn't lift my head off the pillow. I thought I was dead. Then I realised I couldn't be because I could still see and hear. A pair of emaciated druggies appeared, a man and woman with scary, sunken eyes and scrawny, needle-scarred arms, fighting off a trio of pursuing security guards. Watching the departing fracas, I felt my strength return. Now or never, I climbed into my dressing gown and made my escape, catching a taxi to Wombwell, stopping off en route for frozen pizza and bottles of beer. I got home and drank my beer on the settee, one, two, three, four bottles in a row.

Only afterwards did I examine the labels, crying like a baby when I realised it was *Corona*. I knew instantly what it meant. Right on cue, a multitude of debilitating symptoms returned, allowing the virus to run amok once more. An ambulance arrived, carting me off, transporting me to a care home for the elderly, linked by a set of double doors to a pub next door. I pleaded for a drink and was told I would need to test negative for Covid first. Someone, somewhere, was baking cookies. *John Wick: Chapter 2* was showing on a big screen. A game of bingo was in progress and raucous laughter filled the air. I didn't know why because there was nothing remotely amusing about the place. How could there be? Everyone was being held prisoner. *I* was a prisoner. Locked in a room, I clawed the walls until my fingers bled, praying for salvation. Next thing, I was in a mobile hospital ward, speeding down a busy four-lane motorway. It was dark outside and I kept watch over a never-ending procession of passing street lights, disappearing off the scene like transient souls, traversing the stairway to heaven. My heart raced. Was I one of them? Was I already dead? Was I being transported to the back of the queue in readiness? In the bed opposite was a man with a carrier bag over his head. A cricket commentator was sitting beside him, reading out scores. Or was he? Was it scores he was reading? Or was he merely reciting the number of deceased? Of which I was now one? Another grim statistic of a ghastly disease leaked from an experimental lab in dirty China? I smacked my lips. I could taste lamb stew. I could smell it as well and hear lambs, bleating, as they went to slaughter. Death was everywhere. I had a vision of Beccs, walking beside Moses, who was turning the Nile blood red with his staff. Convinced it was my blood, I reached out and grabbed Beccs by the arm, checking the gym was alright. When she said it was doing fine, I smiled what I was sure would be my last smile. Fading fast, I didn't know how much longer I had; but it couldn't be long.

Then, blackness, darker than previous occasions; blacker than the scene down an abandoned coal mine at midnight. I was moving at incredible speeds now. Unable to breathe, I felt myself starting to go. Try as I might, I couldn't hack it anymore and knew it was time to let go. It had been a bloody good fight. Best of my career, in fact. But the time to throw in the towel had finally arrived. *Hadn't it?* No! I snapped out of it, giving myself a right old tongue lashing for even thinking such thoughts. Suddenly, I was back in hospital, landing with a thump, squirming around on my hospital bed. I was still alive, but it was very much touch and go and everyone knew it. I could hear my family, babbling away in the background, deciding what to do with me. A nurse eventually gave me the news: that they had decreed I should be put to sleep by lethal injection. Sweat formed on my brow and I began to hyperventilate. What? What did she say? Did I hear her correctly? Lethal injection? That was ridiculous! My beautiful family wouldn't do that to me. *Would they?* Obviously so! A doctor appeared, shooting serum from a hypodermic needle. Cackling maniacally, he grabbed my arm and made ready to carry out instructions. Then, salvation. Daz Kilner appeared, stating he would pay any amount of money to keep me alive. He was too late. The needle punctured the skin and the deadly toxin began coursing through my veins. Two nurses took over, a slip of a girl and a big, burly sister with a spitting, snarling, angry face, who promptly declared I'd be dead in two minutes. When I didn't die, the pair produced rusting machetes and proceeded to cut my throat. Blood seeped from my neck, pouring across the pillow, soaking the sheets a bright shade of crimson. I lost consciousness, then woke straight back up again, deciding I'd now officially died. As if to confirm my assertion, Charlie Huber's wife, Michelle, was standing at the end of the bed, reading a decree, pronouncing me deceased. Her daughter, Ella, was walking circles round the ward, demanding someone sew my eyes shut in case I reawakened. The machete wielding nurses reappeared and attached me to a drip, feeding a tube into my mouth. I bit down hard, making sure nothing made it past the lips. Alien water technology, it would kill me if it did. Slamming my eyes shut, I awoke hundreds of years previous, standing on the deck of a multi-sail Irish boat, an overcrowded, insanitary and unseaworthy coffin ship, en route to the new world with a cargo of migrants, desperate to escape the famine which was ravaging the Emerald Isle. I could feel the wind in my hair and a powerful ocean spray, whipping my face as the ship crested a succession of towering waves. I was wearing a flimsy woollen shirt with baggy sleeves and a green tartan kilt. Irish music was playing down below, fast moving, energetic and vibrant. Free as air, I was looking forward to making a new life on the other side of the Atlantic, wondering what adventures would befall me in the years ahead. Then, disaster: an enormous wave crashed and splashed across the bow, sweeping me off my feet. Submerged in seawater, I felt my lungs start to fill up, restricting my breathing once more. A second wave washed me clean overboard. Underwater now, I battled to reach the surface and an intake of life-giving oxygen. Somehow, I made it, using every remaining ounce of energy to fast crawl ashore, washing up on a secluded beach with a large sinkhole in the middle. Sand was pouring down the hole, disappearing like the sands of time, emptying through the neck of an hourglass. Exhausted from my exertions, all I could do was lie there and await my fate, slowly but surely being sucked towards the vortex. When the time came, I did my best to cling on, clawing at the edges with outstretched hands. It didn't work. The force of gravity was too much and I was helplessly sucked down the hole, disappearing into the most enormous void, plummeting and falling, tumbling head over heels at incredible speeds. I landed outside a crowded Celtic Park, swathed in green and white, where legendary Scottish manager, Jock Stein, was waiting to greet me.

"Welcome to paradise, he exclaimed, offering me his hand. "Follow me, son, and your journey will be complete."

"I'm afraid it's not my time, Jock," I replied, taking a couple of steps backwards. "Not now. Not this day. Not for a long time. I've too much living to do. So much yet to achieve. And I fully intend making the best of every single second. Just you see if I don't…"

25. Road to Recovery

On the outside, I was now in a deep coma, totally unresponsive and unable to be woken. The good news was that I had a fabulous team of Angels, watching over me morning, noon and night, taking care of my every need while making critical, life preserving decisions. The Angels also commenced a patient diary, penning regular, intelligently scripted entries, enabling me to review specifics of my treatment; that is, should I be lucky enough to pull through. The first entry detailed how tubes and needles were inserted into my body for various medical purposes, including the important task of making sure I was properly fed and could expel waste products. With oxygen requirements increasing, I was soon placed on a ventilator together with increased sedation to keep me comfortable. The plan was to persist with the coma for as long as it took medical staff to stabilise my condition. It was discovered I'd developed surgical emphysema, a disorder in which air leaks from the lungs into surrounding muscles. In my case, I also developed pneumothorax, better known as collapsed lung, a condition where air fills space between the lung and chest wall, adversely restricting lung expansion. A chest drain was sanctioned and I was turned on my stomach to further alleviate the problem. It was recorded that members of the rehab team were washing and shaving me on a regular basis, making sure my hair and teeth were brushed and kept clean. Staff were listening to my chest and lungs, using suction to clear excess fluids. I also had my arms and legs stretched every few days to lessen the chance of atrophy, a gradual decline in muscle effectiveness due to under use. It was logged I'd been moved to a single room and that my space was really peaceful and only disturbed by the bleep of monitoring equipment. The contributor remarked the weather was mild and blinds had been raised to permit a welcome burst of sunshine. While I remained extremely unwell, my condition was fortunately stable. After another wash and shave, it was commented this was performed using my own foam and razor, a Godsend, apparently, as NHS shaving supplies were terrible. The same contributor mentioned she'd spoken with Beccs, letting her know I was okay and that a sudden onset of surgical emphysema was improving; however, I still had high oxygen requirement and had undergone several precautionary chest X-rays alongside a heart scan and further blood tests. As the days rolled by, I was said to be slowly improving. It was 20th November now, a fortnight into my treatment. Ventilator support had been gradually reduced and my blood pressure was showing signs of stabilising, a development which meant associated medications could be halted. The diary observed that Beccs face-timed, playing my favourite George Michael songs, while mum rang shortly after, chatting with me even though I was asleep. In time, medications were further reduced and attempts were made to get me to open my eyes. The entry noted I was responding but couldn't quite manage it, a passage which was signed off with the words: hope you get well soon and that *Allah* gives you goodness. I was being weaned off sedation so I could take my own breaths. The physio team continued to work upon my arms and legs and I'd also been fitted with boots to avoid a condition known as drop foot, which could cause the foot to drag when back walking.

While the diary provided an informative outline of developments and treatment, it didn't paint anything like the full picture. It neglected to mention I was placed on strong antibiotics for sepsis and my blood pressure was up and down like a yo-yo. It also failed to record that Beccs rang morning, noon and night to see how I was progressing alongside numerous other incoming calls from family and friends. Neither did it detail shocking levels worry and apprehension at home. No big surprise really as it was a hospitalisation document only. Another big frustration of my time in ICU was news mountains of nail-biting worry and concern could have been alleviated if Beccs had been made aware that an in-depth brochure, describing every aspect of induced coma procedures, had been sent to my home address. Every little development and twist and turn would have made sense instead of causing innumerable tear-filled and sleepless nights. She found the brochure in the end, of course, bursting into tears when she discovered a pair of knitted red love hearts included, one for each of us, a token of everlasting love and affection. On 17th November, a hospital consultant phoned Beccs, explaining how seriously ill I was and stating there was nothing more they could do. He tempered his brutal analysis by emphasising it didn't mean I was going to die, but that the family should be prepared for every eventuality. He also asked how she felt about authorising a do not resuscitate notice, just in case the worst came to the worst. Beccs was on her way out for a meal with Charlie at the time and the call hit her with the force of a hurtling juggernaut. He tried blinding her with science, describing it as common practice, while throwing complex medical jargon around like confetti. He'd bitten off more than he could chew, though; Beccs wasn't having it, giving him it both barrels.

"Do *not* patronise me," she screamed into the handset. "Under *no* circumstances will I authorise a DNR. Charlie's a winner. He's a fit, healthy young man. He's a fighter. A martial artist. He's fought for his country in international competition. And he'd want *you* to fight for him…"

He asked if I'd been vaccinated. She told him no and asked if it would have made any difference if I had. His reply was telling: the virus was random, unpredictable and extremely complex. It affected everyone differently and would indiscriminately take lives, irrespective of age, fitness or vaccination status, a stark admission, if ever there was one, that vaccines made little difference and had been drastically overplayed. My birthday limped round: 22nd November. The diary noted I was given a full pampering session but detail was scant, leaving actual specifics to the imagination. I also had a new arterial line fitted and was given a chest scan. Not my usual birthday gift, I must confess, but something for which I would have been extremely grateful if I'd been capable of communicating appreciation. My main present, however, wasn't being delivered until the day after. Noted I was looking much better, it was decided I would be given a tracheostomy, enabling the ICU team to gradually wean me off ventilation and commence reducing sedation in order to slowly wake me up. An incision was made on the front of the neck, permitting a secondary incision to the trachea, creating a sustainable surgical airway. An X-ray confirmed everything had gone to plan, meaning the road to recovery was now firmly established. A couple of days later, the diary recorded that a storm was forecast and a belt of snow was moving in. That was the day I finally managed to force my eyes open, gazing semi-conscious at my surroundings; numerous monitors and a tangle of wires and tubes; soft lighting in the ceiling. On the side was a laminated birthday card, signed by Beccs, Mum, Bev and the rest of the family. For all the obvious reasons, nothing from the outside world was permitted in Covid hot-side and I couldn't understand how a simple birthday card could possibly have been deemed an exception. A nurse was there to greet me, my first human contact in weeks, calming me down courtesy of the most gentle, soothing, relaxed voice I'd ever heard. A few hours later, I developed terrible stomach ache followed by severe wind upon which I was informed there had been a problem with my bowel; basically, it hadn't emptied for the best part of a fortnight. Not that there was any cause for concern. Gravity came to the rescue, instigating an enormous fart and follow through, which left both myself and the bed caked in the most disgusting, foul-smelling morass imaginable. A male nurse arrived, cleaning up the mess. I didn't envy him. I wouldn't have wanted to do it. Then again, I wasn't a nurse, was I? I was a gym owner and martial artist, albeit not exactly on the top of my game at the moment. I fell to sleep as soon as he'd gone, waking shortly after to discover my oximeter had become detached. I pressed the buzzer and the same nurse reappeared, rectifying the situation. Another cat nap brought fresh problems. The nurse woke *me* this time, explaining I'd been having a fight in my sleep and my tubes had come out, soaking the sheets with blood. He'd just got everything sorted when I let rip again, defecating the bed a second time. God, it stank. So bad. Enough to make a billy goat puke. If I'd had anything in my stomach, I would have fetched it straight back up again. I could see he wasn't happy and didn't blame him. That said, I didn't like how he administered a full-on bollocking over something which was clearly out of my control. I'd been in a coma, for God's sake: I'd nearly fucking well died! I'd have given him a mouthful, but still couldn't talk on account of the tracheostomy. All of a sudden, I saw him as the enemy, watching him shuffle off, returning with another set of sheets, bitching and moaning while he cleaned up once more. He stripped me down, positioning me on all fours while he commenced the unenviable task of wiping my arse. Again, I wouldn't have fancied it, especially with what happened next. I can't begin to imagine what he thought when I let loose again, pebble-dashing his face with a volley of stinking, lousy, putrid diarrhoea. I didn't do it on purpose, but wished I had, an incident which got me wondering why farts smelled. For the benefit of deaf people, I eventually concluded: it was so they would have some way of knowing.

I was soon making good progress. My bloods were excellent and I was slowly being weaned off oxygen alongside removal of various pipes and tubes. It wasn't all good news, though. I developed an infection, which needed antibiotics, and was also being sick on a regular basis. It took days to settle down and left me feeling utterly dejected, convincing myself this was my life now; how it would be forever. I still couldn't walk and had been diagnosed as suffering from PTSD; perfectly natural in the circumstances, I was assured. Experiencing stomach pains, I was sent for a CT scan, which subsequently revealed a problem with my gall bladder. It wasn't so serious that it prevented the ICU team doing anything other than continuing to assist me making progress; but it was a big worry all the same. My reliance upon oxygen was reduced further and I was soon sitting on the edge of the bed. Then, big problems: my gall bladder problem suddenly took a turn for the worse. Another scan revealed it had turned gangrenous and I was rushed to theatre for it removing. It made me think of my reiki class, when I was told there was heat in my stomach and something wasn't right. If you're reading this, Heather, thank you; your diagnosis was spot on. I was warned up front the procedure would require a blood transfusion and immediately began to question whether or not I was willing to accept vaccinated blood. After much deliberation, I decided I didn't have any real choice in the matter: what transpired I would leave in the hands of God. As luck would have it, the operation went well and recovery was swift. A couple of days later, I managed to wash my chest, a huge effort, according to the diary, which left me thoroughly exhausted, but was sufficient a milestone to convince doctors I was now strong enough to be transferred to ICU cold-side, meaning I could finally have visitors.

Gloved-up and wearing masks and aprons, Beccs and mum arrived the same afternoon. I may have been exhausted, but still managed to keep my eyes open for the duration of the visit. How could I do anything else? It was such an emotional reunion for all concerned. Tears were in full flow, lots of sobbing, sniffling and snivelling, though physical contact was still disallowed. Not that it was required. We knew how we all felt without the need for embrace, because love was in the air, indelibly tinged with massive feelings of relief. It was great to hear familiar voices after all this time; it was just a pity I was still unable to respond verbally, relying upon pen and paper to get my points across. Once things had settled down, Beccs finally solved the mystery of the laminated birthday card. As previously described, because the unit was sterile, there was a strict rule, preventing outside items and objects being brought into ICU. Anyone else would have just accepted it and moved on. Not Beccs, though. Determined to get my card delivered, she convinced staff it would be okay on account it was laminated and could be disinfected upon receipt and then whenever required.

She also elaborated upon the mysterious full pampering session, explaining that, in addition to a wash, shave and brush-up, nurses splashed me with aftershave, before gathering round the bed and reading my card out in advance of joining close family and friends, singing happy birthday in a pre-planned facetime session. On the *Retro* front, Beccs worked her magic by rallying the troops, ensuring the business kept running. Everyone mucked in, going the extra mile to ensure the gym fulfilled all its obligations to a stout and loyal following. Fitness instructor, Gail, was at the forefront, filling in anywhere and everywhere. Popular boxing coach, Chunk, was another hero, as was Harris, a customer and experienced kickboxer, who happily threw his hat into the ring, helping out with coaching sessions. Daz Kilner covered classes at short notice, while our receptionist, Ella, and cleaner, Rebecca, suddenly turned Jack of all trades, turning their hands to all manner of totally alien tasks. Good friend and gym member, Anthony Hodgkinson, was also there when it mattered, getting out of bed and opening up every morning. A few days after the first visit, something incredible happened and again it was Beccs I had to thank. By some miracle, she managed to persuade ICU staff to allow Buddy to visit as part of my recovery programme, receiving more than her fair share of looks and stares as she marched the lively Sprocker Spaniel through visitor-filled corridors and up several flights of stairs to the ward. I can only imagine staff fully understood the impact seeing Buddy would have upon my mental health, because it went down a treat, cheering me up no end and greatly assisting the long drive to recovery. Buddy was a big hit with the nurses as well. Nearly as big as me, in fact. Not quite, obviously; but then again, you wouldn't expect him to be, would you? Impossible didn't come into it.

As the days progressed, I started to gain a little more strength. I'd gone from being unable to lift my phone to sitting unaided. Beccs never mentioned it at the time, but revealed afterwards she couldn't believe how bad I looked when she first saw me. I couldn't say I was surprised. I'd lost over five stone and the trusty pins, which had carried me through countless taekwondo bouts and training sessions, were now little more than sparrow legs. She explained how she discussed my weight loss with a doctor. I couldn't keep any food down and she suggested this might be related to problems I'd previously encountered with colitis. It transpired the hospital knew nothing about my prior encounter with the condition and this caused something of a flap, lots of discussions which eventually led to a change in medication. It did the trick and I slowly began to put on weight, a big step towards making it home for Christmas, though I'd need to prove I could walk first. With the ventilator gone, I had my tracheostomy removed, meaning I could talk at last, a big source of amusement for Beccs. While she said it was great to hear my voice at last, I was so gruff I sounded like big Phil with a sore throat. The only thing missing was eternal broadsides of *Jack* this and *Jack* that, plus which, Beccs eventually remarked I was soon talking so much, she actually preferred it when I was on pen and paper. I learned how to swallow again and received a visit from occupational therapy, helping with exercises designed to retrain me how to use my hands. A diary entry commented that Christmas songs were on the radio and it was great to see me with a smile on my face. The next stage was to get me sitting up in a chair. Once I'd mastered that, I was tasked with standing alone, a momentous occasion which left me thoroughly exhausted. Next morning, I was taken outside for some fresh air, walking with the aid of a Zimmer frame. My reward was a big bowl of vanilla ice-cream. After that, it was soup and bread and then protein drinks to further build me up. Before long, I was demanding a full English breakfast and needed it, too; it was bloody hard work being weaned off oxygen, a process which rendered me totally exhausted and overcome with anxiety. An hour without oxygen quickly became two hours. Two became four; then eight, twelve, sixteen and twenty. Eventually, I managed a full twenty-four hours, tricked into believing I was still being fed oxygen, unaware it had been switched off all along, meaning I'd been breathing unassisted day and night.

Hallelujah: I was finally informed I could go home on Christmas Eve! The accompanying diary entry said what a pleasure it had been to be part of my journey, listing an emergency number to call when I got home should I experience problems. Convinced that was it, I proper bulled myself up to the point where I was mentally and physically exhausted. It was the thought of spending a night in my own bed as much as anything else; or should I say Beccs' bed, because that was where I was heading, deemed too weak to look after myself under my own roof. As a result, I was informed I needed to remain a further night for observation. I wasn't happy; not happy at all, in fact. I felt like kicking and screaming and making an almighty scene about the decision and even contemplated going the whole hog and signing myself out. In the end, though, I simply couldn't do it, principally because everyone had been so bloody good, nursing me back to health from what really was the point of no return. And, so, I awoke Christmas Day still in hospital, putting a brave face on it, same as the staff I supposed, spending the biggest and best day of the year on duty as opposed to enjoying it with loved ones. Then another body blow. Straight after Christmas turkey, I was told I wouldn't be going home until tomorrow. Practitioners had conferred and it was considered it would be too much for me. I immediately called Beccs, who was crestfallen. She had everything prepared and now had to put it all on ice. Again, I could have kicked off, but chose not to for all the same reasons. It was a long night, but I managed to get through it, somehow. Boxing Day arrived and a nurse helped me get my stuff together. A ginormous bag of medication was dispensed on time, meaning all I was waiting for was a PICC line removing from my arm. I stayed calm, watching the clock tick slowly round. Midday came and went and still I was waiting. It was then I was told there was no doctor available to perform the procedure. And, this time, I did kick off. Not big time, but certainly in strong enough terms to make known my feelings upon the situation. Thankfully, someone, somewhere, pulled the necessary strings and the PICC line was removed, enabling me to finally escape my Covid-coma prison. I was absolutely ecstatic. And so was the author of the final diary entry, which jovially announced: *Charlie's coming home day, yippee*!

In no particular order, my Angels were: Claire; Cath; Jayne; Sharon; Louise; Shafiq; Georgie; Katie; Amy; Tina; Emma; Rhys; Adam; Rachel and Jo, plus goodness knows who else, principally ICU's talented and dedicated team of doctors. To each of these beautiful people, I owe my life. I *cannot* thank you enough. Health and happiness; *may good karma take care of each and every one of you.*

26. Home Sweet Home

Boxing Day Night was cold and wet. I remember it vividly, because it was the evening I was delivered by ambulance to Beccs' house, freezing my balls off as I was pushed down the path in a wheelchair, wrapped in itchy, NHS woollen blankets. Beccs cried as I was bundled across the threshold, while Charlie tumbled to his knees, throwing arms around my waist, grabbing me in a straitjacket-like grip. As for Buddy, well…he went stark raving bonkers, bouncing around like a performing dog on *Britain's Got Talent*. I don't know what Beccs and Charlie thought to his antics; but was definitely a big yes from me! A district nurse arrived, checking me over and making sure I had all my medication, totalling an incredible twenty-seven tablets per day. It felt so weird being home. It was so colourful compared to the staid, white décor I'd become accustomed to over the past seventy-something days, making it feel like I'd just tripped out on marijuana. There was a bauble laden tree in the corner. Fairy lights decorated the window and mantlepiece and every available nook and cranny was crammed with Christmas ornaments. The telly was playing away to itself, a *Dad's Army* repeat, which was irritatingly loud with frequent bouts of canned laughter. Tired of hearing it, I asked Beccs to turn over and she got straight on it, channel-hopping until she found *Home Alone*. That was more like it, I thought; something Christmassy instead, setting the theme perfectly for the night ahead. I was home alright, albeit not alone, and the music and comedy made me feel fabulous, a mood greatly enhanced by the fact I had Beccs and Charlie, happily waiting on me hand and foot, fetching and carrying all kinds of yuletide offerings in an effort to build up my strength. The intentions were good. Unfortunately, it didn't work. I was soon feeling sick and so Beccs toned it down a bit, pouring Gaviscon down my throat to settle my stomach. Bedtime came round in the blink of an eye. Pre-warned I'd have a problem with the stairs, Beccs had set me a camp-bed up in the living room. I'd spotted it as soon as I got in, avoiding broaching the subject, lest it was for me, even though I knew it definitely was. Needs must, though; I took it on the chin, going with the flow as Beccs got me ready then tucked me in, kissing me goodnight like a newborn baby, even leaving a nightlight on to make me feel better. Realising how nervous I was, she offered to sleep on the settee. Convinced she would anyway, I foolishly refused her offer, saying I'd be fine, insisting she go to bed. Just my luck, she took my insistence literally, disappearing upstairs, telling me to give her a shout if I needed her. My heart was racing fifty to the dozen as I listened her clomping around, running the tap and flushing the loo before turning out the light. Needless to say, I had a terrible night's sleep, tossing and turning, battling a piece of tubular steel, which insisted upon poking me in the ribcage every five minutes. Morning couldn't come quick enough, commencement of another horrendously long day ahead, popping tablets and fighting off recurrent panic attacks in between a fresh visit from the district nurse and trying to force down a bit of decent grub. The next night was even worse, culminating with an early morning wake up call to let me know Charlie had started being sick and Beccs had tested positive for Covid. I couldn't believe it. No one could. Obviously, all attention was focused on me. Was I safe? Would Beccs need to quarantine? Or would I have to move out? We needed answers and fast. A frantic call to the hospital provided the answers. Beccs and I were advised to stay apart as a precaution; but I'd almost certainly be alright as my immunity levels would be sky high on account of recent severe exposure to the disease. A fraught period of around-the-clock worry ensued. Understandably, I was still pretty much out of the game, meaning Beccs had no other option but to battle on regardless. How on earth she did it was beyond me. She was so ill, but still managed to pull out all the stops, taking care of each of us in turn, gradually fighting her way back to fitness in time for the weekend. Things seemed to be looking up. Then I was struck down with the most awful panic attack imaginable, a real humdinger which left me slumped in a chair, heart pounding and gasping for breath. Beccs did her best to soothe me through it, just like she'd done a thousand times previous. Unfortunately, it didn't work. I was in such a state, she had no other choice but to call 999, requesting an ambulance. She was promised it would be with us in forty-five minutes. Ten hours later, a little after three in the morning, it finally turned up, by which time I was so drugged up on medication I was sitting in the kitchen, fully recovered and grinning like the proverbial Cheshire cat.

New Year's Eve arrived. On a whim, I decided I wanted a drink. Beccs still wasn't a hundred per cent and so I said I'd have a walk to the beer-off myself. She protested, of course; but I was having none of it. Only about half a mile away, I insisted I'd be there and back in no time, like the racing snake I so clearly was. What seemed like a good idea at the time, however, didn't quite turn out as expected. It was the first time I'd been outside properly in months and was soon perishing cold. Half way, I stopped in my tracks and thought: *I can't do this*! Then a pantomime voice inside my head said: *oh, yes you can*! Off I trudged once more, mounting the incline towards the shop at the top of the hill. Panting like the Hogwarts Express, I finally made it. Then another problem: the step up may as well have been Mount Everest for all the energy I had left. I'd no idea how I was going to conquer it. But conquer it I did, Sir Edmund Hillary style, buying up half the shop before commencing the long trudge back, juggling bottles of plonk like Baby, carrying a watermelon in *Dirty Dancing*. Not that there was any cause for concern. Young Charlie suddenly appeared, having clandestinely tailed me on my precarious stop-start journey, escorting me home for which he was richly rewarded with a big cuddle and a refreshing glass of foaming beer shandy.

Beccs' kept up the good work, stuffing my gut full of anything that came to hand; protein shakes, mainly, alongside frequent meals of chicken, steak, pork and a never-ending stream of experimental sandwiches. A couple of weeks into January, I asked if she'd mind cutting my finger and toenails. Resembling Wilhelmina W. Witchiepoo from *H.R. Pufnstuf*, I was shocked when she agreed, though I drew the line when she offered to give me a trim as well. Without a proper cut for months, I looked like Ozzy Osbourne, minus the glasses, arranging for big pal and *Retro* key holder, Anthony, to nip me up Hoyland to the barbershop. Back looking like Burt Reynolds, we headed to the pub afterwards, celebrating the makeover with a couple of swift jars. It was here I met Gav, an old martial artist friend of mine, who back-slapped and congratulated me upon pulling through what he'd heard through the grapevine had been a horrendous experience. We talked about the good old days for ages and then he told me all about what he was up to now; job, family and martial arts career. He asked about Retro next, asking when I planned to return. It was at that precise moment I realised I had to go back to work. Harris was taking exams and Chunk was drowning in work. If I didn't get back soon, there was a good chance the gym mightn't survive. I announced my plans to Beccs and once again she came up trumps. As I walked back through the door for the very first time, all the kids were lined up, cheering and clapping me on, reminding me of the scene where Maximus Decimus Meridius, commander of the Armies of the North and the Felix Legions, was applauded by fellow fighters as he prepared to do battle, striding menacingly into the Colosseum in *Gladiator*. In another surprise, Beccs had arranged for the gym to be repainted in a big spring clean. There was no denying it: it looked blooming marvellous. I felt marvellous as well and was soon very much back on my feet.

A few weeks later, I was back at the hospital for a meeting with my consultant, a nice chap called Dr Longshaw. I was so nervous as I strode across the car park towards the main entrance. My heart was racing. I was hyperventilating and my hands were clammier than I when I walked out to contest the British taekwondo title. On my way up in the lift, I encountered a familiar face, one of my ICU nurses, a lovely lady called Jo King. She looked shocked when she saw me, commenting how well I looked, proudly informing me I was the last Covid patient to vacate the unit. I booked in and took a seat in a room full of people. It was like waiting to be hung, waiting my turn to be seen. When my name was finally called, my hands were even clammier, feeling so moist now it felt like they were coated in Swarfega. We shook and Longshaw wiped a soddened palm down his trouser leg, admiringly looking me up and down.

"I'm *so* glad you're still alive," he enthused with a toothy grin.

"Funnily enough," I replied, pulling out a chair, "so am I…"

He quickly read through my notes, reciting key points out loud.

"Admitted by ambulance with Covid pneumonia. Difficulty breathing. Transferred to ICU. Placed in an induced coma. Ventilation required. Developed emphysema. Suffered a collapsed lung and contracted sepsis. Tracheostomy. Gall bladder removed. Hmmm, I'd say you've been a very lucky young man indeed…"

I couldn't believe the prognosis when it came. Full recovery predicted within six to twelve months. Off I went with a spring in my steps, celebrating with Beccs and fully re-immersing myself in *Retro*. A couple of months later, I received a call from rehab, inviting me for sessions to learn how to walk again. I told them I didn't need it: I was already back at work. Asked what I did, I replied I was a boxing and combat coach and ran my own gym. I was walking miles and participating in daily fitness and sparring sessions. The next question was: how did I do it? How did I make such a rapid recovery? What was my driving force…? My response was unequivocal.

"A positive mental attitude," I said, puffing out my chest in pride. "I'm a martial artist. And a bloody good one as well. An undefeated international athlete. Whatever life has thrown at me, I've never given in…and never will. I've always come out fighting. Trust me, it's the only way. Whatever it is you do, never, ever lose faith. Don't stop believing, do you hear? *Don't stop believing...*"

27. What a Wonderful World

Fast forward: June 6th, 2023. Seventy-nine years to the day, our glorious forefathers embarked upon the largest seaborne invasion in history. The mission: to liberate Europe from the curse of Nazi occupation. My D-Day was totally insignificant by comparison, albeit extremely important on a personal level. In everyone's eyes, I'd earned it. With the incredible support of family and friends, I'd beaten Covid pneumonia, fighting back to fitness after spending weeks locked in an induced coma. With Beccs at my side, Retro continued to go from strength to strength, attracting new members galore on the back of a host of new initiatives, including the long-awaited introduction of Brazilian jiu-jitsu classes. There was a fabulous charity fund-raising event in the offing and I'd recently completed a virtual 837-mile John O'Groats to Land's End sponsored walk. Best of all, though, I had a book coming out, this book, Don't Stop Believing, and you're reading it now, expertly ghostwritten and put together by my personal biographer and close friend, all round good guy, Gary Rowley, who I would heartily recommend to anyone seeking similar services. And now I was returning to Dubai and a date with Tam Khan at his world-renowned TKMMA Fitness, training for my forthcoming second retirement fight in September, with a spot of book promotional work thrown in for good measure. The trip had been booked for months and I was really looking forward to it. It had been a long, cold, wet English winter and I couldn't wait to feel some proper sun, while enjoying some decent scran, of course, and downing a few cold ones, soaking up the sights and sounds of my favourite place on the entire planet.

On the morning of the flight, Bev picked me up early, then went to collect mum, ferrying the birthday girl to Chelsea's nail salon for a relaxing manicure. Afterwards, we headed to Wentworth Garden Centre, enjoying a celebration meal in the company of my two lovely aunties, Maureen and Rita, while being permanently entertained by my funny, livewire cousin, Chris. We had a good catch up, laughing constantly over this and that, and the other, all the old stories and more, a highly amusing day, comically topped off when mum lost her bottom teeth in the car, bringing a whole new meaning to the term, *aperitif.* We found them eventually, thank goodness; but that wasn't the end of the fun. No sooner were her choppers safely reinstalled, than she mentioned she had a problem with a skin rash and that Nick, her partner, was going to cream her when she got in.

"Alright, mum," I protested, grinning all over my face, "just tone it down a bit, can't you? What you get up to in the bedroom is of no interest to us..."

After finishing packing, Chicken Legs collected me and we went to the fabulous Hare & Hounds boozer in Hoyland. Run by my very good friends, Gary and Karina, we had a few drinks and a good old chinwag, discussing all things Barnsley and the latest conspiracy theories. All I'll say is, if you know, you know. Time went so fast, as it invariably does in the company of longstanding friends. Before I knew it, it was early evening. I'd traversed the Pennines, checking in at Manchester Airport, and was boarding a monster Emirates A380, settling into a pre-booked, plush little window seat on the upper deck. Take-off was as powerful as it was flawless and food and drink was soon doing the rounds. Just the job, I even managed a decent kip, waking as the flight descended into the imposing, monolithic surroundings of Dubai International Airport. I can't deny it was daunting, fighting my way through customs and then catching a train to the baggage area; but I managed to get through it without too much trouble. A fleeting taxi ride later, I was checking into my luxurious, airconditioned hotel room, awash with all the mod-cons and amazing views out to sea. I got straight changed, heading to the pool bar for a beer. Big mistake. Huge. Monumental, in fact. A pint of lager and a double Chardonnay came in at fifty-something quid, plus a tenner for a bowl of undercooked chips. The moral of the story: always check Dubai hotel price lists before blurting an order. Well and truly stung, I departed for the famous Palms and a pre-arranged meeting with a couple of old friends, Michelle and Ella Huber, who were staying at the Anantara, a magnificent Thai style hotel I'd recommended. I must admit, I came over shaky as we hugged and kissed and greeted one another. Little wonder. The last time we'd met was during a coma nightmare; the one where Michelle pronounced me dead and Ella demanded someone sew my eyes shut in case I reawakened. We had a fabulous meal at the beach bar, enjoying stunning views across the Palms, reminiscing over numerous good times we'd had, while constantly ripping the piss out of common denominator, husband, father and long-term friend, old Charlie boy himself. As you'd expect, the book got a decent airing, including a few pictures taken against the background of a darkened sky and city landscape, now proudly adorning my popular Facebook page.

Next morning, I made the short trip to TKMMA Fitness, signing up for a four-day pass under the guidance of a lovely young lady called Acce. It was boiling hot outside and the sweat was pumping out of me, courtesy of couple of ill-advised hours, sunbathing by the pool. The gym was located on the 9th floor of a prestigious, glass-fronted tower block. Black, iridescent floor tiles welcomed visitors and elevators were so refined, I fully expected a uniformed lift attendant to be on duty, dutifully tipping his cap as he ferried people to and fro. Gym entry was via fingerprint recognition. A quick touch on the pad and the door swished majestically open. When I stepped inside, I couldn't believe how busy it was, especially for Thursday lunchtime, hundreds of hard-working members, enjoying energetic work-outs, or busy practising boxing, kickboxing and martial arts. Facilities were also available outside on the terrace, commanding unrivalled views across the city. I had a leisurely walk round, checking things out, and was left utterly gobsmacked. I'd spent half my life in gyms and had never seen anything like it. Top of the range equipment was positioned here, there and everywhere, gleaming like exuberant props from the latest sci-fi blockbuster. I could only speculate upon the overall value; probably sufficient to buy up half of Hoyland, truth be known, though obviously nothing like enough to keep that great big pillock, Phil Rudd, in ale for much more than a weekend. The martial arts training area was huge and awash with artists of varying degrees of proficiency, energetically practising techniques. Outside, I discovered another expansive training area alongside a UFC style cage and full-size boxing ring. There were loads of heavy bags about with equal numbers of boxers and martial artists, bashing the hell out of them. Not in any hurry, I took a seat in a relaxation area, watching it all go off, contemplating a dip in the freeform pool to the rear, another luxurious facility the overwhelming majority of UK-based gyms could only dream of. Back inside, it wasn't long before I spotted my first familiar face. Popping my head round the corner of an office door, I tapped Rio Altaie gently on the shoulder. The UFC TV commentator about turned and gazed longingly into my eyes, a big, welcoming smile spreading inexorably across his face as he rose to his feet, giving me a huge bear hug, while gesturing frantically over my shoulder.

"Hey, Charlie," came the shout, a voice I recognised instantly; I knew what was coming next and wasn't mistaken: the man mountain which was Tam grabbed me so tightly, I gasped for breath, desperately trying to hold on to my breakfast. "It's been a long time, my good friend. Great to see you again. How are you doing? How's the book? When is it out? Don't forget I want a signed copy. Let's have a photo. We need to celebrate. We need to make a memory…"

Acce appeared from out of nowhere, flashing her camera phone, lots of cheesy photos, including a whole rake with my book. We got on like a house on fire from the word go. It was as if we'd never been apart, in fact, the conversation flowed so freely. All good things must come to an end, though, and it wasn't long before both men had to depart, disappearing to fulfil prearranged business appointments. As he left, Tam instructed Acce to look after me: to give me food and water, a customised TKMMA Fitness T-shirt and a personalised tour of the facility. Acce was the perfect host. Nothing was too trouble and I couldn't praise her highly enough. Half way round, I found a pair gloves and began pounding a heavy bag, making a hell of a racket and subsequently attracting quite an audience. Six or seven minutes later, I was done. The heat was too much and I concluded my visit prematurely, heading back to the hotel for some much-needed rest. Next day, I was back for more of the same and then again, the day after, milking the facilities for maximum impact, honing skills and building fitness levels. The gym was jam-packed as ever, three or four hundred people, hitting the machines or participating in bootcamp, boxing or MMA. Using weights and dumbbells, I worked on my upper body strength, before moving on to practise Muay Thai and then boxing. A slight nervousness came over me as I entered the ring. Thousands of miles from home, I was lathered in sweat from the warm up, despite being pounded by air conditioning every inch of the way. My coach was a lean, mean Filipino called Dante. Pre-warned of my potential, he soon separated me from the crowd, offering one-on-one tuition. I accepted, wholeheartedly; it was what I was there for, the opportunity to fine tune existing skills and hopefully learn a few new ones ahead of my retirement fight. We commenced with three three-minute rounds of shadow boxing followed by an equal amount of time spent on bag work and fitness drills. Dante absolutely oozed confidence and it was obvious he knew his stuff, meticulous in coaching of advanced attacking and defensive techniques and various forms of associated footwork. I was buzzing by the end of it all, having harvested so much from the experience. But there was a problem: my knees were shot in the aftermath, leaving me no other option but to cut the session short and head back to the hotel, grabbing a protein shake and winding down with a relaxing dip in the pool.

Later that evening, I met a couple of other old friends, St Helens' finest, Simon and Em Hopkinson, who were staying overnight at the Westin Hotel, a ten-minute walk from my digs. We ate, drank and made merry in an amazing Italian restaurant called, Bussola. The décor was stunning and the views over Dubai Marina were simply breathtaking, as were my jokes, lol. Still exhausted from my afternoon exertions, a couple of pints of Stella went straight to my head, prompting me to ask a waiter how long my spaghetti would be. Seeing as I hadn't even ordered spaghetti, the waiter met me with a blank look, totally lost for words when I hit him with: I bet you haven't even measured it, have you? As expected, much of the evening was spent reminiscing about old times and discussing plans for the future. No matter which direction the conversation took, it inevitably reverted to the same old topic: what a hit I'd be in the Emirate, coaching fitness and martial arts. Em was deputy head at the most exclusive private English school in Dubai and the fact she was onside with the idea really got the grey matter working overtime. Had I got it in me? And could I make it work? The only person still requiring convincing, it seemed, was yours truly. We arranged to meet up again the following night, before going our separate ways to catch Manchester City versus Inter Milan in the Champions League Final. City won 1-0 and the star player in my eyes was former Reds defender, John Stones, otherwise known as the Barnsley Beckenbauer. Another day rolled round, commencing with a full body work-out to the background of a top local DJ, spinning a few tracks. I met Tam again and we enjoyed another lengthy chat, during which we posed for another round of *Don't Stop Believing* promotional photos. It was evening again before I knew it. Simon and Em picked me up and we headed out for a visit to Dubai Hills Golf Club, where I was treated to a tour of the most beautifully manicured course imaginable, seductively surrounded by a host of multi-million-pound houses. We got on brilliantly again, enjoying another marvellous meal. Unfortunately, though, I was starting to feel off it, forcing me to bail out early, disappearing back to the hotel to catch up on a few much-needed zeds.

Immediately after breakfast, I headed for the pool, pending a Muay Thai class later. As the hours ticked slowly by, I popped back to my room for a snooze. It didn't happen. I'd barely rested my head on the pillow when my phone started buzzing. Grumbling like Muttley off Wacky Races, I reached out and grabbed the handset, developing scowl converting into a big, beaming smile when I realised it was my old friend, Dubai property developer, Ahmed Zakhi, who I'd trained with on my first Dubai trip. Word had spread fast. He'd been told I was back in town and suggested a quick meet up in advance of my class. Absolutely brilliant news, I jumped at the opportunity, getting showered and changed, gathering my things and hot-tailing it down to the lobby. Ahmed was waiting for me as I stepped out of the lift and we embraced, heartily, back slapping and smiling as good friends do. I told him he'd put weight on. He informed me I'd got uglier and we enjoyed a gentle playfight, before disappearing to the bar for coffee. The quick meet up rapidly became a couple of hours. It mattered not. We had so much to talk about, discussing all things martial arts; living in Dubai; his life and mine. We chatted about my book. Then I revealed how seriously ill I'd been. Listening intently from start to finish, his response was inspirational, encouraging and heartening, all rolled into one.

"You're a warrior, Charlie. A true warrior. It would take more than a virus to take you down, my friend. Let's be honest…a heat-seeking missile would probably struggle."

We headed for Tam's next. Everyone knew Ahmed and he promptly introduced me to all and sundry, making me feel like some kind of visiting dignitary. It was a pleasant surprise to discover a fellow Yorkshireman in the house that morning, Franky Spencer, *ooh Michael*, all the way from Pontefract, or Ponte Carlo as the locals preferred to call it. Ahmed introduced me to my Muay Thai coach next, an absolute monster of a man, nearer seven-foot tall than six, and easily weighing-in at twenty stone. Unsurprisingly, he was incredibly polite, decent and respectful, portraying everything you would expect from a dedicated martial artist. Everyone was still warming up when the class began unexpectedly. I knew it was going to be even tougher than the boxing, comprising innumerable high energy kicks. Surprisingly enough, my lungs coped well, which was really pleasing, especially after all I'd been through. It was my right knee that was the problem, causing constant gyp and frequently giving way, doubling in size before I was forced to throw in the towel and limp off the mats. Not that it mattered. Not now, anyway. After four stimulating, action-packed days training at one of the best gyms in the world, it was mission complete. I'd achieved everything I wanted, sharpening up my game in preparation for my retirement fight and even garnering a few fresh skills along the way. Not bad after all I'd been through, particularly bearing in mind I'd now reached the ripe old age of fifty. As I departed for the hotel, I stopped and turned round, treating myself to one final look at the amazing TKMMA Fitness, making a vow to myself to return one day soon.

"Well done, Charlie boy," I said out loud. "You bloody well did it..."

Tomorrow would see me back home again. Back to Beccs. Back to my family. Back to Retro and a date with old friend, Craig Addy, assisting him coaching his son, Kai, an up-and-coming fighter of incredible promise; ask Retro coaches, Jonno and Chunk, they'll tell you how good the boy is. Unbeknown to most, though, the daily struggles would continue. While, on the outside, I'd always come across smiley and jokey, it was all a façade, masking a multitude of problems beneath the surface. Pins and needles in my head, for one, and arthritis in my neck alongside a myriad of other debilitating symptoms, too long to mention. No surprise there, then: no one could undergo what I did and not experience long-term physical and mental hurt. I'd battle on, though, same as I always had. I'd never stop believing, making every second count, giving my absolute all, while going out of my way to remain kind, treating people as I expected to be treated, hopefully reaping what I sowed, continuing to rub shoulders with the good and righteous and steering clear of life's spitting, venom laden snakes. In the background, an instrumental version of one of my dad's all-time favourite songs was playing. Louis Armstrong, I think. I'd heard the song a thousand times over; but, for some reason, I couldn't quite place it. All I had was a procession of words, swirling round in my head. Over and over, I kept thinking to myself: *what a wonderful world*. It was as well. Bloody marvellous, in fact. And it was my oyster…I literally had it at my feet.

End.

In no particular order, my amazing Sponsors: thank you to you all for your unswerving support and assistance in making this book possible:

Carrie Mahoney
Lee Grain
Richard Micklethwaite
Organic Relief
Moonshine Global Ltd
Jackson Jackpot Lottery
DRC Race Leathers
Chelsea Naylor Luxury Aesthetics ltd
F.R.S property renovation-maintenance
The Glow Job
Cutler Gym Equipment
The Full House, Monk Bretton
S.R.K Building Maintenance
The Countess
MD Scaffolding Solutions Limited
Annie Murrays Irish Barnsley @ Rock & Reggae
Barry's Gas Services
Tam Khan
Safe Hands Framing Services
Parkside Farm Shop
Car Seekers
GR Professional Writing Services
Universal Tyre Solutions Barnsley
Matthew's A Friend in Me
A1 Locksmith's Barnsley
Better You

Printed in Great Britain
by Amazon